D0850468

FIFTEEN POETS OF THE AZTEC WORLD

FIFTEEN POETS OF THE AZTEC WORLD

By Miguel León-Portilla

UNIVERSITY OF OKLAHOMA PRESS : NORMAN AND LONDON

Also by Miguel León-Portilla

*The Broken Spears: The Aztec Account of the Conquest of
    Mexico* (Boston, 1962)
*Aztec Thought and Culture: A Study of the Ancient Nahuatl
    Mind* (Norman, 1963)
Trece poetas del mundo azteca (Mexico, 1967; reprinted,
    1972, 1975, 1978, 1984)
Pre-Columbian Literatures of Mexico (Norman, 1969)
Toltecayotl, aspectos de la cultura nahuatl (Mexico, 1980)
Native Mesoamerican Spirituality (ed.) (Ramsey, New York,
    1980)
Time and Reality in the Thought of the Maya (Norman, 1988)
Endangered Cultures (Dallas, 1990)

This book is published with the generous assistance of Edith
    Gaylord Harper.

Library of Congress Cataloging-in-Publication Data

Trece poetas del mundo azteca. English
    Fifteen poets of the Aztec world / by Miguel León-Portilla,
        p. cm.
    Rev. and enl. translation of: Trece poetas del mundo azteca. 1967.
    Includes bibliographical references and index.
    ISBN 0-8061-2441-5
    1. Aztec poetry. 2. Aztec poetry—Translations into English.
I. León Portilla, Miguel. II. Title. III. Title: 15 poets of the
Aztec world.
PM4068.5T7413   1992
897'.45—DC20   CIP

The paper in this book meets the guidelines for permanence and durability of
the Committee on Production Guidelines for Book Longevity of the Council
on Library Resources, Inc. ⊗

CONTENTS

ILLUSTRATIONS

MAP

PREFACE

This book is the result of my rethinking in English what I gathered years ago and have more recently augmented concerning the lives and creations of a group of composers of songs, probably the first poets known to us in America. The present work was preceded by another book I wrote in Spanish, which, published by the National University of Mexico Press, has been continuously in print since its appearance in 1967.

In preparing this English edition I could not ignore two relevant factors. One is the appearance of other contributions on the same theme—few, indeed, but all deserving to be taken into account with an unbiased yet critical eye. The other has to do with the contents of this book. To simply ask a translator, as skillful as he or she might be, to translate from Spanish to English materials some of which were originally in Nahuatl—the language of the Aztecs and their neighbors—would be risky to say the least. This explains why, assisted in some chapters by Grace Lobanov, who has helped me before, I rethought, augmented, and rewrote in English what in many respects resulted in a new book. I have taken particular care

Map of the country of flower and song, heartland of Nahuatl poetry, art, and symbolism

in dealing with the documentary sources. And, certainly, I have thought it important to offer a direct English translation of the compositions in Nahuatl—indeed, beautiful flowers and songs.

Besides acknowledging Grace Lobanov's assistance, I would like to recall the influence of the pioneer in these studies, the distinguished scholar, Angel Ma. Garibay K. (1892–1967). My gratitude goes also to the National University of Mexico Press, which brought out the predecessor to this book and must be acknowledged for the use of illustrations in the present one, as well as to the publishers of this new work, the University of Oklahoma Press, and its friendly and highly qualified staff with whom, for years, I have been in close contact.

MIGUEL LEÓN-PORTILLA

Paris, France
Mexican Delegation to UNESCO

NAHUATL PRONUNCIATION KEY

Early in the sixteenth century the Spanish alphabet was adapted to represent the Nahuatl phonemes. The grammarian friars who did so, assisted by indigenous sages and students, succeeded for the most part in their difficult task. Today their adapted alphabet is still employed with some minor changes.

No orthographic accent is needed in Nahuatl, as practically all words are stressed on the next to last syllable.

Concerning the vowels, the following examples describe their phonetic value:

a	as	in	f*a*ther
e	as	in	m*e*t
i	as	in	f*ee*t
o	as	in	*o*rgan
u	as	in	f*oo*t

Most of the consonants have phonetic values very similar to those they have in Spanish, with the following exceptions:

h   is used to represent three different phonemes: *h,* at the end of a word, is pronounced with a soft aspiration as in the English word *h*at. *h,* at the end of many syllables, represents a glottal stop, with a sound as in the English word *coopt. h,* in combination with the vowels *h-ua, h-ue, h-ui,* represents a semivocalic phoneme, as in the English words *w*ant, *w*ell, *w*e.

tl   functions as a digraph and therefore should not be orthographically divided. Its phonetic value corresponds to that of the *tl* in the word A*tl*antic.

ts and *tz* function also as digraphs. Their value is very close to that of *ts* in the English word ligh*ts.*

x   has a phonetic value that corresponds to that it had in sixteenth-century Spanish and is the same as in the English word *sh*e.

FIFTEEN POETS OF THE AZTEC WORLD

INTRODUCTION

Songs, music, dance, and ritual performances have blossomed in the universe of the feast whenever humankind
has developed a culture, and in this ancient Mexico was
far from being an exception. Conquerors and friars provide vivid descriptions of what they thought of the indigenous feasts they viewed with astonished eyes. Native
chroniclers, who in some cases had participated in them,
depict their ancient splendor.

Colorful images of the celebrations that occurred during
the solar year appear in some of the extant pictoglyphic
books or indigenous codices. There, and also in several
mural paintings, are representations of sound scrolls, or
volutes, coming out from musical instruments and from
the mouths of priests and other personages, including gods
and goddesses. Some sound scrolls are more complex, depicted with flowers affixed along their edges. They symbolize the flowery words, those that were sung or recited
in the feasts.

Flowery sound scrolls emerging from human mouths
in mural paintings and cylindrical tripod vessels of clas-

sic Teotihuacan convey inscribed signs, which are a sort of glyphic sequences. One can identify in some of those sequences the signs of water, shells, flowers, footprints, interlaced bands (the glyph of movement ?), circles, human or animal heads, stylized feathered eyes, hearts, hands, trumpet conchs, and several other signs. Some scholars are inclined to see in these sign sequences (infixed in the flowery sound scrolls) *graphemes* conceived to be "read" following their linear arrangements.[1] If such an interpretation is correct, we would have in those Teotihuacan paintings from around A.D. 400–450 the first extant records of pre-Columbian songs in the Americas, or at least summary glyphic enunciations of them.

To find full renditions of old native chants in Nahuatl (Aztec or Mexican), one has to turn to a few extant sixteenth-century manuscripts. In them, the fruits of native inspiration are in linear alphabetic writing. Those concerned with such transcriptions of the words to be sung or recited in the feasts tell about the origin of these compositions. A striking coincidence is discernible in their testimonies. The ethnographer-friars Andrés de Olmos and Bernardino de Sahagún, as well as natives like Chimalpahin, Alvarado Tezozomoc, and some others, insist they obtained these productions from oral tradition that was closely linked to the contents of the pictoglyphic books. According to Sahagún: "All those things about which we [he and the old native informants] conferred, they gave me by means of their paintings which is the writing they had in their ancient times."[2] Among those paintings, or pictoglyphic books, were the ones they named *cuicamatl* ("papers of songs").[3]

Alvarado Tezozomoc says in his *Crónica mexicayotl* that the texts he transcribes, including a few songs, could be recalled because "the ancient men and women, our fathers, our mothers . . . told them, repeated them, had them painted for us also in their books."[4] Following the contents of those pictoglyphic books, the songs were

learned and entoned in the *calmecac,* or priestly schools.[5]
An indigenous singer beautifully describes it:

> I sing the pictures of the books,
> and see them widely known,
> I am a precious bird
> for I make the books speak,
> there in the house of the painted books.[6]

How, in fact, singers like this could make their books
speak, not to say sing, is a question that deserves attention. It is closely related to a theme frequently discussed,
that of oral tradition, or more generally, of orality vis-à-
vis written textuality. What happened in Mexico when
the ancient discourses and songs—the pictures and glyphs
of the books that were sung—became commited to linear alphabetic writing? Are the resulting texts genuine
testimonies of the pre-Hispanic culture? If it were possible to say "yes" to this question, there still remains the
problem, of particular interest to us here, that of the
authorship of these compositions. Will it be possible to
say that, even if most of them are anonymous, some at
least can be critically related to the personal creativity of
one or another "face and heart," as the ancient Mexicans
would say?

As the title, *Fifteen Poets of the Aztec World,* demonstrates, I believe it is possible to identify testimonies of
the pre-Hispanic culture in some of the extant written
texts in Nahuatl and to assign certain songs to definite
authors. To have reached such a conclusion necessarily
implies a rather long process of critical analysis and evaluation of the available texts, beginning of course with the
questions of how the old pictoglyphic books could be
"read" or "sung."

HOW AN INDIGENOUS BOOK COULD BE "READ"

An example of how the pictures and glyphs of an indigenous book could be, and actually were, sung or recited, is

provided by the Nahuatl text known as the *Legend of the Suns* that speaks of great cosmogonic happenings.[7] The written text encompasses several pieces of narrative—one could say, epic poems. The *Legend* was rendered in alphabetic writing in Nahuatl; an introductory paragraph gives the exact date—May 22, 1558—on which an anonymous native scribe, probably working with a surviving old sage or priest, either completed or began their work.[8] Starting with the account of the successive foundations and destructions of the sun, earth, and humans, the narration depicts the rediscovery of fire, the formation of a new genre of humans preceded by a trip of the god Quetzalcoatl to the Region of the Dead to recover the bones of past generations. Then one learns about the finding of maize at the Mountain of Our Sustenance, the sacrifice of the gods in a primeval Teotihuacan, followed by the several epic stories. Quetzalcoatl, the culture hero, high priest, and god of the Toltecs, is also present in the narrative. The epic account ends by describing the ruin of Tula, the metropolis of Quetzalcoatl, the ball game between Huemac, its last ruler, and the Tlaloque, the gods of rain, with the former's victory resulting in a great famine caused by the offended gods. The entrance of the Mexicas or Aztecs onto the scene to take the place of the Toltecs closes the text that in this manner becomes a sort of epic national history for them.

In analyzing this narrative one can detect its stylistic features, parallel sentences, a certain rhythm in the expression—traits pertaining also to a *Mexicacuicatl*, a song in the Mexican manner. And, what is particularly important, the analysis also permits us to identify a fair number of referential statements such as *in nican ca*, "here is"; *inin*, "this"; *iniqueh in*, "these"; *inezca in nican can*, "of this, his appearance is here"; *izcatqui*, "here is." Such referential statements, accompanied by the frequent use of the adverbial phrases, *niman ic, niman ye, niman ye ic*, meaning "then, next, following on," reveal that the text is being "read," recited, and rendered to linear alphabetic writing, following the pictoglyphic sequences of an indigenous book.

Two other manuscripts have been preserved, one clearly independent of the *Legend of the Suns* and the other possibly related to it, which shed light on what might have been this process of "reading" and transcription. The first, which is entitled *History of the Mexicans Through Their Paintings*, is also a "reading" of pictoglyphic books with cosmogonic and legendary contents.

Probably a fruit of the research in which Friar Andrés de Olmos engaged as early as 1533, it is also a text in which the introductory paragraphs give its origin. Whatever is contained in it was taken from ancient pictoglyphic manuscripts. If such "reading" was done originally in Nahuatl, the only extant text is in Spanish. Thus, it was put in alphabetic writing around 1536, soon after it was sent to Spain.[9] A close comparison of its contents with what is expressed in the *Legend of the Suns* reveals striking coincidences. It is interesting to discover that what the two independent testimonies put in written form more than twenty years apart (both being "readings" of indigenous pictoglyphic manuscripts) coincides in many respects.[10]

The other manuscript is a pictoglyphic book produced around the middle of the sixteenth century. It is known as *Codex Vaticanus A* because it is housed at the Vatican Library.[11] In it, several of the subjects of the narrative in the *Legend of the Suns* and in the *History of the Mexicans Through their Paintings* are pictoglyphically represented. In particular, one can contemplate in the codex the paintings that represent each one of the cosmic ages or Suns as well as many of the divine performances and human achievements that took place later. One could say that, although this codex is not the one "read" by the person or persons who put the *Legend of the Suns* and the *History* in linear alphabetic writing, it is a partial copy of a pre-Hispanic manuscript, perhaps the one actually consulted and "read."

The case of the two previously mentioned texts, "readings" of a codex, put in linear alphabetic writing, illustrates what is said and repeated by such missionary-ethnographers as Olmos, Sahagún, and other friars like Toribio Motolinía, Diego Durán, Juan de Torquemada, and the Jesuit José de Acosta.[12] They, and several native chroniclers—Chimalpahin, Tezozomoc—and the Mestizos Juan Bautista Pomar, Cristóbal del Castillo and Fernando de Alva Ixtlilxochitl, say many times that they are putting the ancient songs in writing as they were transmitted, following the contents of their painted books.[13] Alonso de Zorita, a contemporary of Olmos, concisely describes the friar's intervention in rescuing the ancient indigenous word:

> The principal Indians preserve them [their ancient words in their painted books] and he, Olmos, asked them to commit them to writing. [This happened around 1535 when several natives already knew the alphabet], and they did it so, without his being present, and took the texts from their paintings which is like their own script, and that they understand themselves well by means of them, and that nothing was changed but a division by paragraphs was introduced.[14]

ORALITY AND THE PICTOGLYPHIC BOOKS

For centuries, at least since the days of the earliest uncovered vestiges of their writing in Monte Albán in the state of Oaxaca around 600 B.C., the Mesoamericans were in possession of two principal means to buttress their memory.[15] They had developed a precise calendar and a pictoglyphic script. With the passing of time, their script became transformed and gave birth to several systems of writing. Today it is recognized that the Maya developed the one that is most complex and rich. Although in many respects limited, the writing system of the Nahua and Mixtec peoples permitted them to record, with extreme precision, dates and places, names of persons, and attributes of the gods as well as numerous ideas, including abstract concepts.[16] Such ideographic and partially phonetic script, combined with paintings rich in symbols and colors that were also conveyors of meaning, was the one used by the *tlahcuiloque,* the scribes and painters who produced the books.

Along with the pictoglyphically represented contents of the indigenous books, the skillfully trained memory of the priests, sages, rulers, and young students in the native schools and temples was a living repository of knowledge. "Following the contents of the books, the happenings of the past, the divine wisdom, the sacred hymns and many other songs, the ancient word"[17] could be memorized. Thus they could also be entoned or recited.

The living repository of the individual's memory, particularly that of the priests and sages, was not opposed, when the circumstances required it, to enrichments and adaptations of the "reading" of the book and the recalling of the word. An illustration of this is provided by the speeches pronounced on solemn occasions, as when a new supreme ruler was installed or an important dignitary died. The essence of the ancient word was always preserved. The wisdom and symbols recorded in the books were in the mind and the mouth of the one who spoke. Indeed, that ancient wisdom had been conceived not as a dry precious flower but as one that would blossom once and again under different rays of the Sun, to become enjoyed and treasured by faces and hearts living in a variety of circumstances.

Some of the extant *huehuehtlahtolli,* Nahuatl texts that were expressions of the "ancient word," put in alphabetic writing and in some cases translated into Spanish, and conveying the same basic ideas, include variants that clearly reflect the circumstances in which they were recited.[18] Astonishing though it may sound, it can be added that, in recent times and in different places within Central Mexico, *huehuehtlahtolli* are still recited. Some of them resemble the ancient compositions in many aspects. Commited also to writing by modern researchers or by members of the community interested in their preservation, these texts can be compared with those from the sixteenth century.[19] The similarities are at times so strong that one could be tempted to say that, contrary to what is often thought, Mesoamerican spirituality is far from dead.

ORALITY AND THE WRITTEN TEXT

At this point it will be pertinent to apply to our subject some specific questions raised by several researchers about the differences between orality and the written text and the problems resulting from commiting orality to linear alphabetic script. Apparently, the modern discovery of orality as a theme of research began in the 1960s. Jack Goody, Walter Ong, and Eric A. Havelock have made important contributions in this field. In his work as an anthropologist, Goody has questioned what is obtained through the practice of recording oral accounts of contemporary peoples totally alien to the idea of writing.[20] Ong has elaborated on the concepts of orality and literacy and their complex implications.[21] Havelock, a scholar in the field of classical Greek literature, discusses what actually happened when, within the same culture, oral recitations of poems such as the *Iliad* became converted to a written text.[22]

Goody considers cases that are somehow more complex, in which a person belonging to a different culture tries to record oral testimonies of an aboriginal group. The anthropologists, who ordinarily belong to a dominant society—and the sixteenth-century missionaries can be compared to them—induce their informants to supply oral accounts by asking questions that at times are completely strange to the latters' own culture. The result can be a compromised recitation in which "the respondent commonly seeks to oblige him, the researcher, by supplying, in oral improvisation, the kind of information he thinks, quite correctly, that the researcher expects or wants."[23]

Even where the transition from orality to written texts took place within the same culture, as in the case of Greek literature, Havelock detects a number of risks. Songs, poems, and narrations were conceived and recited following conceptual as well as idiomatic patterns and rhythms. These and other mnemonic devices could result in losses and enrichments in the recitation or singing. Orality was and is always a living performance. Written renditions deprive it of spontaneity, not to say of the possibility of a musical accompaniment or of what might have been its sacred or profane entourage. Textual expression employs a different kind of language. Contamination can proliferate in the transitions of orality to a written textual rendition. And this will happen whether it occurs within the same cultural frame or in situations of intercultural contact.

Similar arguments have been addressed to the texts of the Mesoamerican tradition, and challenging conclusions have sometimes been drawn. One declares that Mesoamerican orality, converted to linear alphabetic texts, was totally altered. The resulting texts may have little or even nothing to do with the original Mesoamerican expression. Although a few scholars consider the written indigenous texts to be contaminated by Euro-Christian influence,[24] others are more radical and reject them as being fictions, attributable to the friars or to their converted Indian followers. As can be easily perceived an ominous conclusion would have to be drawn if these arguments were valid. The texts that have been so fervently studied, translated, and presented as examples of the ancient literature and as testimonies of the old Mesoamerican culture would have to be put aside, if not as fakes, then as uncertain vestiges of the intercultural confrontations that accompanied the Conquest.[25]

In reflecting on these arguments, it appears that one must listen to them. Yes, it is critical to detect possible or probable Euro-Christian influences in the alphabetically written texts. It is also of prime importance to spell out the absence in the texts of elements inherent to orality such as the music and public performances that accompanied the singing or recitations of the chants. And, especially in the Mesoamerican case, one has also to recognize that orality becomes encapsulated, so to speak, once it is fixed in an alphabetic text. These remarks derived from the arguments about orality and the written texts are crucial.

To duly appreciate the conclusion we can derive from such arguments in the case of Mesoamerica, we have to bring into focus two facts of prime importance. One is the previously mentioned existence in Mesoamerica, for more than two thousand years before the Spanish arrival, of a link between orality and the inscriptions in the monuments and in the pictoglyphic books. As we have seen, such a link of complementarity, not to say support, is amply documented. Particularly in the priestly schools and in the temples, orality was manifested, as the quoted Nahuatl poem expresses, by "singing the painted books."

The other fact, which must be mentioned, is the existence in many cases of more than one sixteenth-century rendition in linear alphabetic script of a particular indigenous text. These written renditions, some of which can be documented as being independent, were at times the result of one or more different recitations of the contents of one or several ancient native books. One can argue that the independently written renditions could have originated from just traditional orality. Even when one accepts that in some instances this might have been the case, one has to recall once more the close links existing between orality and the pictoglyphic script in Mesoamerica that in the schools was the tangible support of tradition.

The fact that the same song, or part of it, appears in more than one written rendition—certainly, at times, with some variants—has to be recognized as proof of the basic reliability of the texts passing this kind of critical examination. Examples have been noted in the *huehueh-tlahtolli* ("ancient word"), collected at different times and places. Concerning the songs, several are found reproduced with slight variants in at least three independent alphabetic manuscripts. An illustration is provided by a song described as a *Mexicayotl*, one entoned in the Mexican manner. Such a song is included in the *Cantares mexicanos* (fol. 37 v.), a primary source for the preparation of the present book. The *Cantares* manuscript is a compilation of different kinds of compositions, done by one or several natives working for a friar during the last part of the sixteenth century. As the *Cantares* will be the subject of critical scrutiny, it will suffice for the moment to underline the fact that parts of this Mexicayotl are also included in the *Anales de Tlatelolco* (fol. 20) and the *Anales de Cuauhtitlan* (fol. 16). The first of these annals is probably the earliest extant alphabetic rendition of several genealogical and historical pictoglyphic books. The work of anonymous Tlatelolcans who had learned alphabetic writing, these *Anales*, which encompass a dramatic account of the Spanish invasion, were terminated in 1528.[26] The *Anales de Cuauhtitlan* are an ensemble of texts with several different origins.[27] In many cases one finds clear indications of their being "readings" of what was included in several painted books. In these three independently written texts, parts of the same song are recorded.

Other examples can be cited of different written renditions, with no or slight variants, or the same song. Those renditions can be identified within the same compilation of the *Cantares mexicanos*, that is in different and quite

Page from manuscript of *Cantares mexicanos* (Mexican songs) (fol. 29 v.), in the National Library of Mexico

distant folios, and also in the other extant compilation known as *Romances de los señores de Nueva España*.[28] This manuscript, whose origin has been placed in Tezcoco, is the other principal source for our book. If the variants of one song may indicate different "readings" or recollections of a composition, they also may reflect the noted living nature of the "singing of the books."

It is obvious that the centuries-old Mesoamerican system of pictoglypic recording differed greatly from that of the alphabetically written European books. When the alphabet was introduced by the friars in Mesoamerica, the prevalent cultural situation became altered in this as in many other matters. But, this being a fact, the case of Mesoamerica is very different from that of the primary orally oriented cultures. To transport the ancient expression of the Mesoamericans into alphabetic writing was not merely to convert orality into a fixed text. The pictoglyphic books also included fixed glyphic sequences that were recited or sung. Listening to those recitations or singing what was anchored in the ancient books, the orally expressed phrases corresponding to the pictoglyphic sequences could be placed, in a parallel form, in alphabetic writing.

THE EXISTENCE OF BOOKS IN MESOAMERICA

The Mesoamericans had an idea of something close to that of a book in Western culture. The word *amoxtli* conveys such an idea. Derived from *ama(tl)* and *oxitl*, it literally means "glued sheets of paper." In those glued pieces of paper, made of the mashed bark of the amate tree (a ficus), paintings and glyphs were drawn.

It is significant to find that the *tlamatini*, "the one who knows," that is, the sage, is described as "he who possesses the amoxtli and the black and red inks."[29] A more vivid picture of the relation of sage to book is offered by the words some commoners addressed to the twelve Franciscans who arrived in Mexico in 1524. When the friars began their preachings telling the Nahuas they did not know the true God, the commoners responded, confessing their ignorance, but adding there were others who were their guides and possessors of wisdom. Those were described as both masters of the word and of what was recorded in their books:

> There are those who guide us . . .
> The priests, those who make the offerings . . . ,
> The *tlahtolmatinime*, sages of the word . . . ,
> who contemplate,
> follow the contents of the books,
> noisely turn their pages,
> with the red, the black inks,
> who keep with them the paintings . . . ,
> They carry us, guide us,
> those who keep the order of the years,
> and know how the days and destinies
> follow their own way.[30]

Among these sages and priests who, according to the same account, came to defend their beliefs with the friars, were the ones who, as declared in the *Florentine Codex*, "taught the young people all their songs, their divine songs, *teocuicatl*, following the contents of their books." The word used to express such action is *amoxohtoca*, composed of *toca*, "to follow," *oh-* (from *oh-tli*), "road," and *amox-(tli)*, "book," that is, "to follow the road or sequence registered in the book."

Once more the relation of sage to book is emphasized, as well as that which existed between the books and the songs. To learn the songs, one had to follow what was pictoglyphically expressed in the books.

An old native lady whose words were transcribed in a huehuehtlahtolli, dating from early post-Conquest times, gave a parallel testimony. In the schools, "others were taught the different crafts . . . , and also painting . . . , and song composition, how to select the adequate words . . .

and the divine books, *teoamoxtli*, which tell about Tloqueh Nahuaqueh, The Lord of the Near and By."[31] Many of those songs taught in the ancient schools following the contents of the books became lost after the Spanish Conquest. The friars prohibited the Indians from singing them anymore. Nevertheless several friars tell that, notwithstanding prohibitions and severe reprimands, some of the songs continued to be recited. To better detect them and what had to be erased from the Indian minds, some friars urged their native assistants to collect those songs for them.

In this manner a few collections of songs in Nahuatl were formed. Compositions of various origins and themes were included in them: sacred hymns to the gods, chants to recall the ancient rulers and their deeds, others of profound distress about the fugacity of life on earth, and the immense difficulty of approaching the supreme Dual God, who is Night, Wind. There were also songs to make the people rejoice and even a few we could label *erotic*. The friars' native assistants did not hesitate to also include songs composed by Indians who were already christianized. Such songs had been conceived to praise Jesus, the Virgin Mary, or a saint. Many of the ancient metaphors and other stylistic features are still visible in those Christian songs of native invention.

The friars for whom the songs were collected were surprised at seeing such a variety of compositions. Sahagún and the Dominican Durán declared the songs were at times so obscure that nobody could understand them. But some friars, like Sahagún himself, endowed with the humanistic background acquired at the University of Salamanca, could not refrain from admiring and enjoying the subtle expressions they could discover in several of the assembled songs. There were to their eyes *cuicatl* (songs) and huehuehtlahtolli (the ancient word) as worthy of preservation as had been the compositions of other "pagans" such as the Romans and Greeks.

The extant collections, that is, what survived of the ancient word, recited or sung, constitute our available sources. A description of them with a critical eye is indispensable. In this way only will we discern whether it is possible to link some of these compositions with a few well-known Nahua faces and hearts—their authors.

THE CORPUS OF NAHUATL SONGS

The corpus of extant Nahuatl songs is integrated by several independently formed collections. Such collections are the following:

The twenty sacred hymns collected by Bernardino de Sahagún

The songs scattered in several annals and other Nahuatl manuscripts like the huehuehtlahtolli, testimonies of the "ancient word"

The manuscript known as *Cantares mexicanos* kept at the National Library of Mexico, collected for an anonymous priest

The manuscript entitled *Romances de los señores de Nueva España*, housed at the Nettie Lee Benson Latin American Collection, of the University of Texas Library in Austin, and probably a result of the searches done by the Tezcocan Juan Bautista Pomar

A critical examination of the contents of each one of these collections is a sine qua non condition to establish their antiquity and, what is more difficult, to eventually link some compositions with discernible authors.

THE TWENTY SACRED HYMNS

The first collection to be examined is that of the twenty sacred hyms, or teocuicatl, obtained by Bernardino de Sahagún from his informants in Tepepulco around 1558 to 1560. There are two available transcriptions of the hymns. One is included in "The First Memorials" of *Códices matritenses*, a manuscript preserved at the Library of the Royal Palace in Madrid.[32] The other, a copy of the former, appears as part of an appendix to Book II of the *Florentine*

Codex. In both cases, the Nahuatl songs are rendered without any translation. The main difference is that in "The First Memorials" the hymns are accompanied by some glosses in Nahuatl, a device to explain certain words or expressions. The glosses were added by native assistants of the Franciscan in consultation with the educated elders who had communicated the compositions. All the hymns are addressed to well-known gods. For centuries these chants remained untouched in the Franciscan's manuscripts. In the case of the *Florentine Codex,* they were accompanied by a brief commentary by Sahagún. Among other things he says that the chants are "an obscure forest and contrivance . . . invented by the Demon, to be employed in his service."[33] The sacred hymns were rescued and transcribed by him to facilitate their identification and further their eradication among the evangelized Indians.

The first to make these hymns known was the American Daniel G. Brinton, who published them in 1880 with a deficient English translation under the extravagant title, *Rig Ved Americanus.* Thus he wanted to call the attention of his readers to the importance of such Nahuatl texts that, in his opinion, could be compared, by their antiquity and contents, with the productions of ancient India. The German scholar Eduard Seler and later the Mexican Angel Maria Garibay prepared the only two available and reliable translations of these hymns into German and Spanish, respectively, accompanied by ample commentaries.[34] They both corroborated Brinton's original statement: In the twenty sacred hymns no trace of any Euro-Christian influence existed. The hymns, in which archaic Nahuatl forms are employed, could be safely taken as alphabetic renditions of the words entoned in the ceremonies dedicated to the various gods. Repeated examinations of the statements of Seler and Garibay—and of the hymns themselves—are critically convincing. If we give credit to Sahagún, who says that these and other testimonies were given to him by means of the painted manuscripts, we will have to accept as true that the hymns had been originally put in alphabetic writing through a process similar to the one already described. This would reinforce the idea of the ultimate pre-Hispanic origin of these compositions. As no mention is made concerning any person in particular as their author, they can be taken as anonymous productions attributable to the ancient priests and sages.

SONGS INCLUDED IN NAHUATL ANNALS AND OTHER MANUSCRIPTS

An important part of the extant corpus is composed of songs scattered in various annals and in other manuscripts, among them the huehuehtlahtolli, testimonies of the "ancient word." In several of the books of the *Códices matritenses* and *Florentine Codex*, in addition to the twenty sacred hymns, there are other epic and lyric chants. In some instances a song is attributed to a legendary or historically known person. The story of Quetzalcoatl, in Book III of both codices, includes songs attributed to the legendary times of the Toltecs. Another chant, particularly worthy of mention, is found in the account that deals with the metropolis of Teotihuacan at the end of Book X of the *Florentine*.

At first sight it will seem foolish to imagine the possibility of having a song in Nahuatl that has come down from the days of classic Teotihuacan (the first through the seventh centuries A.D.). Nevertheless, a critical examination of the assertion made in the codices (as it appears in the *Florentine* and in the *Matritense*), may shed some light on this. The assertion has to be placed in its historical context.

"In a time nobody can reckon . . . ," says the text, there were some very ancient people who lived along the coast of Anahuac toward the east (the shores of the Gulf of Mexico). Those people were ruled by sages and priests, described as already being in possession of the books of paintings, the annals, the books of songs (cuicamatl), the book of the dreams, the calendar, and the music of the flutes. One day it happened that the sages, obeying a command of their god, left their people and marched toward the east. Those who remained, abandoned and destitute—so the text says—succeeded in rediscovering the ancient wisdom, the calendar and the art and science of the books. Sometime later they began to migrate to several regions in Mesoamerica. Some of them arrived and settled in Teotihuacan. The Nahuatl text goes on to describe the main achievements of those ancient men, "real giants" who, among other things, built the two great pyramids.[35]

The account, which seems to be traditional material in which myth and history mingle, adds that those Teotihuacanos were sages, well acquainted with divine things. To those sages the text ascribes a brief song that was addressed to those who died. This song, included in a testimony that accurately places the Teotihuacan Classic period after the development of the ancient culture of the Gulf Coast and before the age of the Toltecs, would be the oldest extant example of poetry in Nahuatl. Without daring to affirm, in the absence of other evidence, that this is the case, I will transcribe the song here, trying to render in English the beauty of its original expression. In any case, it is a composition that a reliable indigenous tradition asserts was entoned in the days of Teotihuacan. Contemplating the corpse, those performing the funeral rites sang the following:

> Awake, the sky is reddening,
> the dawn has broken.
> The flame-colored pheasants are singing,
> the butterflies are flying.[36]

As a commentary to the songs, the *Matritense* adds: "Hence the old men said that he who had died, had become a god. They said he has awakened, he has become a god."

Archaeological evidence from various sites within the Teotihuacan metropolis leads one to affirm beyond any doubt that sacred chants were often entoned by the priests. The previously mentioned glyphic signs known as "sound scrolls" emerging from the mouths of religious dignitaries that are visible in several Teotihuacan mural paintings and in tripod vessels confirm it. Those priests wer indeed entoning their hymns to propitiate the Rain God or some other deity.

A different kind of example, to which a considerable antiquity is also ascribed, forms part of the text of the *Toltec-Chichimec History*, also known as *Anales de Cuauhtinchan*. In this valuable Nahuatl source (paintings accompanied by glyphs and alphabetized Nahuatl text, the work of native scribes) the fall of the Toltec metropolis and the dispersal of the Toltecs are recalled at length. Several songs are included therein. Particularly meaningful is the chant transcribed with the statement that it was entoned by two Toltec chiefs who thus tried to invite a group of Chichimecs to join them. The ideas expressed in the chant were an essential part of the Toltec religious beliefs. The two chiefs act as the composers of the song. Key references are made in it to the supreme Dual God, about whom other Nahua and in general Mesoamerican sources express similar concepts. What is relevant is the form in which, after proclaiming the presence and action of the Dual God, he is also invoked as Tezcatlanextia, "Mirror Which Illuminates Things," a complementary title to that of Tezcatlipoca, "Smoking Mirror":

> In the Place of Sovereignty,
> In the Place of Sovereignty, we rule;
> my supreme Lord so commands,
> Mirror which Illuminates Things.

Now they will join us,
now they are prepared.
Drink, drink!
The God of Duality is at work,
creator of men.
Mirror which Illuminates Things.[37]

If the chant was indeed composed by the Toltecs Quetzaltehueyac and Icxicohuatl, we would have in it one of the earliest productions in Nahuatl to which a determined author can be ascribed. To accept this would imply recognizing the existence of a historical consciousness that permitted the Nahua people to know about happenings that occurred several centuries in the past. Archaeological evidence from another Mesoamerican culture that give support to this are found in the relatively abundant inscriptions of historical content in the Maya stelae of the Classic period. There, the births, deeds, and deaths of rulers are recorded. Parallel evidence is also provided by the contents of the few extant pre-Hispanic Mixtec codices. There, as Alfonso Caso has demonstrated, one can follow the life stories of men and women of noble lineage, some of whom lived in the eighth century A.D.[38]

The *Toltec-Chichimec History*, where this song is transcribed, is in part a linear alphabetical rendition of a Nahuatl "reading" of a more ancient manuscript. We know this by the presence of the glyphs and paintings that accompany its text. Mesoamerican historiography, because of the Conquest's impact, followed sinuous paths, but in the cases of productions due to native scribes it remained as close as possible to the ancient tradition. After all, in the pre-Hispanic priestly schools, one had to learn the art of following the path of the glyphs, "reading," and at times singing, what was pictoglyphically represented.

The *Anales de la nación Mexicana* and the *Anales de Cuauhtitlan* stand out among several other texts in which songs in Nahuatl are transcribed with a mention of the circumstances that led to their production and/or entonation. In the first of these sources, a Nahuatl text put in linear alphabetic writing in 1528, some chants of particular interest are found. There is a song of sadness recalling the Mexica defeat in Chapultepec in a year 1-Rabbit (1246); there is another that is said to have been composed to celebrate the defeat of Moquihuix, ruler of Tlatelolco, and still another, an *icnocuicatl*, or song of orphanhood, depicting the drama of the Spanish Conquest.[39] All of these songs are introduced as anonymous compositions. If we accept the historical validity of these *Anales*, and critically there is no reason to doubt it, we can take these songs as compositions related indeed to the circumstances in which, it is said, they were entoned.

The *Anales de Cuauhtitlan* and the accompanying *Legend of the Suns* are also rich in anonymous epic and lyric compositions. In both manuscripts—as already noted— one finds references indicative of their origins. Phrases such as "this can be seen in another paper," "it has been painted elsewhere," "here is," and "here it can be seen" permit one to assert that the contents put into alphabetical writing derive from the pictoglyphic books.

Besides epic compositions like the one at the beginning of the *Anales de Cuauhtitlan*, in which the goddess Itzpapalotl (Flint-Butterfly) appears in a divine performance shooting arrows to the four quadrants of the world, or that which recalls the cosmic creations and successive destructions of the earth, there are others closely related to legendary or historical situations. This is true of some chants accompanying the accounts about the deeds of the high priest Quetzalcoatl and those about the celebrated Tezcocan ruler and poet, Nezahualcoyotl.[40] A field of research is open in this area to those interested in tracing the vestiges of epic and lyric cycles in Nahuatl literature. One can indeed speak of the cycles of Quetzalcoatl and of Nezahualcoyotl and of happenings such as the Mexica defeat in Chapultepec.

Other manuscripts exist in which several songs are scattered that also belong to the corpus of poetical compositions in Nahuatl. Far from trying to give an exhaustive list of them, I prefer to concentrate on the two sources more directly related to our theme.

THE *CANTARES MEXICANOS:* MEXICAN SONGS

This is the largest collection within the corpus of Nahuatl songs. Preserved at the National Library of Mexico, it constitutes the first part of a volume in which other texts in Nahuatl are also included. The collection of *Cantares mexicanos* encompasses eighty-five folios written on both sides, with the exception of the last, which does not contain any text on its back, or verso.[41]

The *Cantares mexicanos* were collected by one or several anonymous persons of native extraction who worked for a missionary. A clear indication of this is provided by a note in Spanish appearing on fol. 6 recto. There the compiler, addressing himself to a Christian priest, "Your Reverence," declares that some of the songs have an Otomi origin, that is, that they were originally in the language of the Otomis, who for centuries were neighbors of the Nahuatl-speaking people:

> Old songs of the native Otomis which they used to sing in their feasts and marriages, converted into the Mexican language [Nahuatl], keeping always the juice and the soul of the chant, metaphorical images they pronounced, as Your Reverence will understand, and better than I do because of my little capacity. And they go with their proper style and elegance so that Your Reverence will take profit from them and insert them where it will be convenient, being Your Reverence such a learned person.

We know there was a friar who, during the last third of the sixteenth century, was preparing a book of songs to be chanted by the Indians in substitution of their "pagan compositions." To prepare his book better, the friar looked for inspiration in the native songs, metaphorical forms, and other stylistic features of the native songs. Friar Bernardino de Sahagún did, in this manner, proceed in his *Psalmodia christiana*, published in 1583. In his "Prologue to the Reader" he expressly insists upon the fact that the Indians "want very much to sing again their old chants in their homes and communal houses . . . , which makes the sincerity of their Christian faith suspicious because in their old songs, for the most part, they evoke idolatrous things in a style so obscure that nobody can understand."[42]

And he adds that he has prepared his *Psalmodia* to stop the ancient songs being entoned and instead to facilitate their praising God and his saints with Christian expressions. The fact that Sahagún adopted, in his *Psalmodia*, many of the stylistic features of the indigenous songs assembled in *Cantares mexicanos* makes it highly probable that he was the one referred to by the Indian who wrote, addressing himself to a Christian priest, that "the songs, or cantares, go with their proper style and elegance so that Your Reverence will take profit from them and insert them where it will be convenient." The native could have been one of the well-known assistants of Friar Bernardino. In any event, whoever was the compiler, it is apparent from the manuscript itself that it is a transcription of songs collected at different times and places. The songs assembled had been previously commited to writing on separate pieces of paper. The extant manuscript, written in two different hands, includes the same songs more than once in some instances, as happens in fols. 3 v. and 25 r.; 26 r. and 29 v.; and 3 v. and 25 v.

Folios 1 r. to 79 v. are written in a clear and, I will say, elegant script. The last part, from fol. 80 r. to the end in fol. 85 r., is in a different and less trained hand. The songs are not distributed in verses as in modern poetry but in paragraphs, which sometimes run to several lines. The modern transcription and translation of the songs in short lines or verses, as it has been done by Angel María Garibay and many others, is based on some of the stylistic traits of the songs. For instance, the parallel phrases easily permit one to introduce divisions so that each phrase will correspond to a distinct line. Repeated sentences, which in many cases open and close parts of the songs, are another element taken into account to convert a long paragraph into several "line verses."

Many glosses accompany the transcription of the songs. They convey a good number of dates, names of the places of origin of the songs, indications as to their genres, and notes as to how the songs have to be entoned and with which musical accompaniment. In some cases one finds expressions indicative of the particular composer of a given song. In some compositions one finds various interpolated Spanish words, like Santa María and Dios, introduced to "christianize" the respective song.

As to the recorded places of origin, one finds Mexico-Tenochtitlan, Acolhuacan-Tezcoco, Tlacopan-Tepanecapan, Chalco, Huexotzinco, Cuauhtinchan, Ayapanco, Cuauhchinanco, and Tlaxcala. The dates registered in the longer part (fol. 1 r.–79 v.) are mainly if not totally related to the substantial number of songs of clearly Euro-Christian inspiration included in the collection. In most of these cases, the names of the Christian composers are provided. There is a song about which it is stated that it was entoned in 1536 (fol. 42 v.), and another (fol. 43 r.) that, according to the gloss, "was composed when we were conquered," that is, 1520 to 1521. The other recorded dates—all of them related to songs of Christian inspiration—run from 1550 to 1565. This means the collection was formed in time for Sahagún's preparation of his *Psalmodia*, which was not published until 1583.

Contrasting with that longer "first part" of the manuscript, the second, in a different hand, appears as the result of a different compilation. In its first and last folios (which correspond to fols. 80 r.–85 r. of the *Cantares* as they are bound today), one reads the date D 97, most probably a misrendering of 1597, seven years after Sahagún's death. Besides these time references, there are many glosses that attribute a song to individuals who lived in the pre-Hispanic period. But in such cases, no specific date is registered.

The introductory glosses and the separations in the text permit one to distinguish ninety-one different compositions in all the *Cantares*, some of which are closely interrelated. The genres of the songs are specifically indicated. It is worth remarking that Sahagún employs the same terminology appearing in the *Cantares* when he describes the genres of songs that the Nahuas sang in their feasts.[43] This fact perhaps is indicative of his having consulted the *Cantares* collection. Another hypothesis would imply a different source of information. We know that the Nahuatl text of the *Códice matritense* in which Sahagún, based on his informants, included a list describing the song genres, was copied around 1568, a date perhaps too close to that of the completion of the first part of the *Cantares*, which cannot be placed before 1565.

These are the genres that both the *Cantares* and the *Matritense* register: *xopancuicatl* (songs of springtime), *xochicuicatl* (flowery songs), *totocuicatl* (songs of birds), *michcuicatl* (songs of fish), *icnocuicatl* (songs of orphanhood), *cozcacuicatl* (necklace songs), *teuccuicatl* (songs of the lords), *tlaocolcuicatl* (songs of suffering), *cuauhcuicatl* (songs of eagles), *yaocuicatl* (songs of war), *atequilizcuicatl* (songs of pouring water), *cihuacuicatl* (songs of women), *cococuicatl* (songs of doves), *cuecuechcuicatl* (provocative songs), and *huehuehcuicatl* (old songs, or songs of old people). In addition to these genres, other indications tell about the manner in which the songs were entoned and accompanied: *Otomicayotl* (in the Otomi manner), *Chalcayotl* (as those of Chalco), *Huaxtecayotl* (in the manner of the Huaxtecs), and so forth in these moods: *Mexicayotl, Tlaxcaltecayotl, Matlatzincayotl, Huexotzincayotl,* and *Chichimecayotl.*

Two kinds of notations accompanying the songs deserve special attention, as they are indicative of the various manners in which these compositions were chanted. One is the inclusion of several nonlexical syllables such as *aya, iya, huiya, ohuaya,* and others. Such syllables often appear at the end of the paragraphs in which the songs are originally placed. The same syllables are also sometimes inserted within the text of one paragraph. In both cases, their function seems to be exclamatory and perhaps also complementary to the rhythm and cadence of the expression.

The other genre of notation is more directly related to the tone and musical accompaniment of the songs. There is actually a gloss in fol. 7 r. of the *Cantares* that sheds some light on this: "Here the songs named true *Huexotzincayotl* begin. . . . And in this manner the drum will have to resound: one word is being left and the others fall with three *ti,* but one begins well with only one *ti.* And the same is repeated until the drum will resound again."

According to Garibay, "it is evident that such syllables are indications related to the rhythm of the music."[44] And he adds, as a plausible hypothesis, the idea of a correspondence of each syllable with a musical note. A different interpretation was proposed by Karl A. Novotny, who takes the various syllables as markers of different tones, ascending or descending.[45]

Besides the described glosses and notations, others exist that are even more directly related to our interest. Parallel to the references attributing a song to a Christianized native, others indicate that such songs not only had an origin antedating the Conquest but were also the fruit of a particular person's inventions. The reliability of these references obviously depends on the possibility of making two crucial assertions. One is the existence of songs with a genuine pre-Hispanic origin that may have been brought down to us. The other is the possibility of linking one or more of those songs with the name of a composer about whom something can be said.

The meaning and validity of the present book depends on the possibility of making these two assertions. Our critical evaluation of the references to the origins and authors of the songs presented as pre-Hispanic will take into account the internal evidence provided by the manuscripts of the *Cantares mexicanos* and the *Romances*, which will be described, and also the external evidence that can be found in other independent sources.

THE ROMANCES DE LOS SEÑORES DE NUEVA ESPAÑA

This rather bizarre title is attached to the other extant compilation of Nahuatl songs. The manuscript is today preserved at the Nettie Lee Benson Latin American Collection of the University of Texas in Austin. Bound in a small volume, it accompanies the *Geographical Relation of Tezcoco*, prepared by the Mestizo Juan Bautista Pomar in 1582. The whole book, as is noted on its last page, contains 114 folios written on both sides.

The *Romances* manuscript, placed after the *Relation* and written with the same hand, has been attributed by Garibay, its sole editor until now, to the compilations of Pomar. In fact, in his text of the *Geographical Relation*, he declares that "inquiries were made, searching with old Indians . . . looking for very old songs."[46]

As in the case of *Cantares mexicanos*, parts or divisions can be distinguished in the *Romances*. The compiler clearly marks the existence of four parts. This may be taken as an indication of four successive stages in the compilation, as the divisions are not related to the subjects or origins of the songs. No dates are provided, as in the *Cantares*. The only inference that can be made is that the compilation of the *Romances* was finished before 1582, the date of the accompanying *Relation*.

Another difference that can be noted vis-à-vis the *Can-

tares is that very few indications are provided in the *Romances* as to the genres of the various compositions. Only the following are registered: *Chalcayotl tlatocacuicatl,* "in the Chalcan manner or related to Chalco, song of lords" (fol. 9 r); *Huexotzincayotl tlatocacuicatl,* "in the Huexotzincan manner . . . , song of lords" (fol. 10 r.); and *Xopan cuicatl,* "song of green time" (fol. 38 r.). Concerning the places of origin, those that are registered are less abundant than in *Cantares.* The larger part of the compositions is said to be from Tezcoco. Other places of origin are Mexico-Tenochtitlan, Chalco, and Huexotzinco.

Other elements found in both the *Cantares* and *Romances* are the two kinds of notations already described, that is, the nonlexical exclamatory syllables and the employment of *ti, to, co,* and *qui* in various combinations, surely with the same purpose. It appears difficult to establish how many different songs are contained in the four parts of the manuscript. Garibay distinguishes sixty different songs, though he accepts that in determining the precise number doubts may arise as there is not always a clear indication of the end and beginning of the songs. It is remarkable that several songs included in *Romances* are also found with slight variants in *Cantares,* as, for instance, in *Romances* fol. 3 r.–v. and *Cantares* fol. 16 v; and respectively, in fols. 7 r.–8r. and 30 r.; fols 11 r. and 61 r. These and several other cases of inclusion of the same song in the two manuscripts comprise an element to be taken into account in dealing with the origin and eventual authors of at least a few of these compositions.

It is important to note that no compositions of a clear Euro-Christian inspiration are detectable in the manuscript, with perhaps the exception of a few glosses or obvious interpolations of single words such as the recurrent *dios* (God) in Spanish. As to the themes, it can be stated that, as in the *Cantares,* one finds remembrances of the deeds of well-known lords or supreme rulers, eulogies of friendship, and worried expressions of orphanhood on the earth. Several compositions, expressly attributed to the wise ruler of Tezcoco, Nezahualcoyotl, have a unique tone of deep reflection—one could say, of philosophical thinking. This brings us back to two crucial questions: the possibilities of identifying some songs of genuine pre-Hispanic origin in the *Romances* and the *Cantares,* and of linking at least a few of them to the faces and hearts of composers who had lived in the times that preceded the Spanish invasion.

ORIGIN AND AUTHORSHIP OF THE SONGS

The *Cantares* and *Romances* include glosses and other introductory texts, often in the same hand of the scribe who copied the songs, that refer to the circumstances in which the composition was produced and, in a few instances, to its author. In the previously considered cases of compositions whose themes and authors denote a clear Euro-Christian influence, it would be gratuitous to deny validity to the glosses that describe it precisely. The problem arises when it is declared that a song was composed in a specific pre-Hispanic moment and is the work of a person whose name is provided.

To accept or reject such references, one has obviously to submit them to critical scrutiny. A first point is to establish how songs of pre-Hispanic provenance may have been rescued during the third part of the sixteenth century. In the case of the *Romances,* Juan Bautista Pomar states that "inquiries were made searching with old Indians . . . looking for these very old songs." As to the *Cantares,* several glosses declare, as in the case of those described as "Otomi songs," that they are "old songs which they used to sing at feasts and marriages." One can say that the compilers of the two manuscripts agree upon the idea that they had collected at least compositions that antedated the Spanish Conquest. In this they coincide with the testimonies of a large number of previously quoted chroniclers, Spanish and Indian, who spoke about the ancient songs they had heard and knew. One more example of this is offered by the Dominican Durán:

> They, all the lords, had their singers who composed songs about the achievements of their ancestors and of themselves . . . , They, Motecuhzoma and Nezahualpilli, had songs which were composed in their days dealing with their achievements, victories, conquests, genealogies, and great riches. I have heard those songs many times in dances at the open air, which . . . gave me much contentment.[47]

We have seen that by means of the pictoglyphic books one could "read" and "sing the paintings." This was part of the teaching at the calmecac (center of higher learning), where "one learned the divine songs following the contents of the books." When the Conquest occurred, books and old traditions were concealed although they were also detected by the inquisitive eyes of some friars. This proves they survived for at least several decades. No wonder that, during the 1560s and 1570s, one could still compile some ancient songs. In some cases those who provided the compositions also made reference to what they knew about the origin of them.

There is another form of scrutiny to which such information ought to be submitted. Besides the internal evidence provided by the manuscripts, there is, in some instances, the possibility of comparing or correlating the contents of a song with other transcriptions and with closely related historical accounts found in other sources. We can recall the particularly significant case of a song of sadness about the Mexica defeat in Chapultepec in a year 1-Rabbit. The song is included in the *Cantares* (fol. 37 r.), and parts of it also appear in the totally independent *Anales de la Nación Mexicana* (or of Tlatelolco, written in 1528), as well as in the *Anales de Cuauhtitlan*.[48] Such coincidences confirm that the song in question belongs to the ancient indigenous tradition. Similar conclusions can be drawn in the case of compositions included with variants in the two compilations, the *Cantares* and *Romances*. The variants are in themselves indicative of different provenances and independent transmissions.

The same kind of scrutiny has to be applied to the glosses and other references that not only speak of the origin and circumstances in which a song was produced but add information about its composer. The external evidence that other sources can afford in support of what the glosses declare will be a decisive element in our critical scrutiny.

It would be misleading to believe that explicit forms of attribution of a song to a given individual are frequent in the *Cantares* and *Romances*. In fact, at least four-fifths of the compositions therein transcribed have to be considered anonymous. A triple procedure will be followed to discern the reliability of the attributions made in the glosses and other referential statements. The first has to do with the person to whom the song is attributed. One has to find in other independent testimonies reliable information about his or her existence. Related to this is the possiblity of adducing testimonies asserting the fame of the same individual as a composer of songs. The third procedure is a search for eventual independent renditions of one or more of the songs attributed to the same person.

THE FIFTEEN CHOSEN POETS

Although in each chapter of this book, in dealing with a given song composer, the results of this triple form of search are specified, I will apply it in summary form to the list of poets or song composers who are in the selected group to which this book is devoted. At first, let us concentrate upon the five from the ancient domains of Tezcoco-Acolhuacan: Tlaltecatzin, Nezahualcoyotl, Cuacuauhtzin, Nezahualpilli, and Cacamatzin.

Tlaltecatzin, of Cuauhchinanco, as he is introduced when a song is attributed to him in *Cantares* (fol. 30 r.), was ruler of that chiefdom. This we know from Fernando de Alva Ixtlilxochitl, who in his *Historia chichimeca* makes him a contemporary of Techotlalatzin, ruler of Tezcoco during the second half of the fourteenth century. In those days, Cuauhchinanco was part of the Tezcocan dominions. Tlaltecatzin is also mentioned in a song in which Nezahualcoyotl expresses his deep appreciation of him (*Cantares*, fol. 37 r.). The only song that is attributed to him in *Cantares* (fol. 30 r.) is also included with slight variatns in the independently compiled collection of *Romances* (fol. 7 r.–8 v.). There he is introduced as "you have been left in your home you, Tlaltecatzin; you suspire, there, you speak." His fame as a poet is recalled in this manner.

Nezahualcoyotl is a well-known figure, born in 1-Rabbit (1402), in Tezcoco, where he also died in 6-Flint (1472). Several sources exist that provide ample information about his life and deeds: *Códice Xolotl, Tepechpan, Mexicanus*, the *Tovar Manuscript*, The *Anales de Cuauhtitlan*, the *Relación de Tezcoco* by Pomar, and the works of Fernando de Alva Ixtlilxochitl and Juan de Torquemada. In most of these testimonies he is presented as a great sage and sometimes expressly as a song composer. In a dramatic context, this was also declared by his grandson Carlos Ometochtzin, Lord of Tezcoco, who on November 30, 1539, was burnt as a result of an inquisitorial process, having been accused of relapsing into idolatry.[49] Several of the songs attributed to him appear, with minor variants, in *Cantares* and *Romances*. It is remarkable that a few of them were copied twice in *Cantares*. His fame as a great song composer is also proclaimed in several other chants included in the two compilations, as in *Cantares*, fols. 3 v., 17 r., 19 r., 32 v., and 34 r., and *Romances*, fols. 18 v.–19 r.

Cuacuauhtzin, of Tepechpan, as he is presented in the *Romances* (fol. 26 r.) in a succinct attribution of a song to him, was actually the ruler of that chiefdom in the days of Nezahualcoyotl. This we know through the information provided by *Códice de Tepechpan* and by Alva Ixtlilxochitl. In the first of these sources, the year 13-Flint (1440) is registered as that of his death. Nezahualcoyotl himself refers to him in a song (*Cantares*, fol. 25 r.). The song attributed to him appears in the two compilations, also with minor variants, in *Cantares*, fols. 26 r.–27 v., and, by a curious coincidence, also in fols. 4 r. and 26 r.–27 r. of *Romances*. His prestige as a song composer is reported by Ixtlilxochitl, who describes the circumstances in which Cuacuauhtzin composed the song that has come down to us.

Nezahualpilli, son of Nezahualcoyotl, who was born in Tezcoco in 11-Flint (1464) and died in 10-Reed (1515), is a well-known figure about whom several pictoglyphic books and chronicles in Nahuatl and Spanish provide information: *Códice en cruz, Códice Ixtlilxochitl, Atlas of Durán, Anales de Cuauhtitlan, Códice matritense, Relación* of Pomar, and the works of Alva Ixtlilxochitl and of Torquemada. One song is attributed to him in *Cantares* (fols. 55 v.–56 r.). Its theme, the war of Huexotzianco, is also amply documented in the sources. In the *Cantares* (fols. 17 v. and 23 r.) as well as in the *Historia* of Alva Ixtlilxochitl, his renown as a poet is recalled.

Cacamatzin of Tezcoco, was the son of Nezahualpilli. Born around 1494, he was murdered by the Spaniards in 1520. In *Romances* (fols. 5 v.–6 r.) a song of sorrow is attributed to him, with the following caption written in Spanish: "By Cacamatzin, last king of Tezcoco, when he found himself in great difficulties, recollecting the power of his elders, his father and grandfather." The tone of the song corresponds indeed to the dramatic moments he experienced because of the rivalries of his brother, Prince Ixtlilxochitl, and as a consequence of the Spanish arrival. *Códice matritense* and the chroniclers Bernal Díaz del Castillo, Alva Ixtlilxochitl, and Torquemada refer to his short and tragic existence. Although no express mention is made of him as a poet, the fact that he was son of Nezahualpilli provides evidence that he was raised in the spirit of the ancient tradition. Nevertheless, one has to recognize that in this case no other external evidence has been found supporting the attribution of the song to Cacamatzin.

Four more poets from the area of Mexico-Tenochtitlan join this chosen group of ancient composers of songs: Tochihuitzin Coyolchiuhqui, Lord Axayacatl, Macuilxochitzin, and Temilotzin. Following the same procedure, I will briefly refer to existing evidences that corroborate the validity of the glosses in which songs are attributed to them. In the corresponding chapters of this book, a more ample presentation of the sources is provided.

Tochihuitzin Coyolchiuhqui was son of Itzcoatl, according to the *Anales de Cuauhtitlan*. He was probably born around the end of the fourteenth century. The *Crónica mexicayotl*, written in Nahuatl by Tezozomoc, tells that Tochihuitzin rescued Nezahualcoyotl from the hands of his Tepanec enemies. The same *Crónica* adds that he was appointed governor of Teotlaltzinco on the eastern slopes of the Iztaccihuatl volcano. The *Cantares* (fols. 14 v. and 15 r.) attribute two short songs to him that are examples of deep philosophical reflection. Insistently, the text itself—not a gloss—repeats four times: "Thus spoke Tochihuitzin, thus spoke Coyolchiuhqui." Although in this case no other independent evidence is available, the mere simplicity, patent in the words attributed to Tochihuitzin, adds to the credibility of such an affirmation.

Two songs in *Cantares* (fol. 29 v.–30 r. and 73 v.–74 v.) are attributed to Axayacatl, supreme ruler of Mexico–Tenochtitlan. Needless to say, there are several pictoglyphic books and chronicles in Nahuatl and Spanish that report on his life and deeds. Whereas one of the attributed compositions is an icnocuicatl, song of sorrow for the lords gone to the Region of the Dead, the other a *huehuehcuicatl*, or chant of old people, recalls the Mexica defeat in the war against the Tarascans of the present-day state of Michoacan. In the same *Cantares* (fol. 60 r.) it is proclamed that flowers, the precious creations of Axayacatl, are budding and greening. And in another song from Huexotzinco, it is said that "your fame, O Axayacatl, will never come to an end" (fol. 66).

Macuilxochitzin is introduced here as the only woman in the group. As is demonstrated in the chapter devoted to her, there were other lady composers of songs, such as a famous one from Tezcoco, nicknamed "Lady of Tula," to celebrate her poetic genius. Macuilxochitzin was given the name of the deity of dance, music, and the sacred feast. In a song attributed to her in *Cantares* (fol. 53 v.), she introduces her theme invoking the supreme Giver of Life. She recalls the Mexica victory over the Matlatzincas in the days of Axayacatl (year 10-Flint, 1476). Indicative of her feminine feelings is the express mention she makes of the couragous action of the woman of an Otomi warrior who had hurt Axayacatl in a leg. The woman's supplication to Axayacatl saved the Otomi's life. The Mexican chronicler Alvarado Tezozomoc provides information about Macuilxochitzin, who was daughter of the well-known Tlacaelel.

A brief chant in praise of friendship is attributed to Temilotzin in *Romances* (fol. 2 r.). Several references are made to him as a person well known to other composers of songs in *Cantares* (fols. 23 v., 43 v., and 54 v.). He was born in Tlatelolco, where he met Cuauhtemoc and became his close friend. *Florentine Codex* (Book XII) describes his actions during the siege of Tenochtitlan by Hernán Cortés. The *Anales de Tlatelolco* also provide interesting information about the Temilotzin march, along with Cuauhtemoc, in the disgraceful expedition of Cortés to Honduras. Apparently Temilotzin died in 7-Reed—525.

There are four composers of songs from the region of Puebla-Tlaxcala, whose lives and poems are presented in this book. Two of them, Tecayehuatzin and Ayocuan, lived in important chiefdoms in what today is the state of Puebla; the other two, Xayacamach and Xicohtencatl the Elder, lived in the so-called "Republic of Tlaxcala."

Tecayehuatzin, of Huexotzinco, according to *Cantares,* fol. 12 r. and *Romances* 1 r., is the author of several compositions. Some of them are included with variants in the two manuscripts. The chroniclers Diego Durán and the Tlaxcalan Diego Muñoz Camargo provide ample information about Tecayehuatzin during his reign in Huexotzinco. By the end of the fifteenth century, he appears inviting other composers of songs to a gathering in Huexotzinco. Tecayehuatzin's prestige as a poet is recognized by other composers in *Cantares* (fol. 11 v.).

Ayocuan Cuetzpaltzin, of Tecamachalco, appears as the composer of several songs in *Cantares* (fols. v. 2 r., 12 r., and 14 v.). One in particular, as in the case of Tochihuitzin, is accompanied by a lapidary statement declaring, "Thus spoke Ayocuan Cuetzpaltzim in Tlaxcala, in Huezotzinco." The *Historia Tolteca-Chichimeca* includes some references to him that permit us to follow his life during the second half of the fifteenth century and the beginning of the next. Ayocuan was also praised for his creativity as a composer of songs in *Cantares* (fol. 35 v.).

Xayacamach, of Tizatlan, is praised in *Cantares* (fol. 11 v.) as the "composer of a beautiful song." He was ruler of the chiefdom of Tizatlan during the second half of the fifteenth century, according to the Mestizo chronicler Diego Muñoz Camargo. Two songs are attributed to him in *Cantares* (fols. 11 v. and 12 r.).

Lord of Tizatlan after the death of Xayacamach, his brother, Xicohtencatl the Elder, stands out as a valiant captain, wise ruler, and composer of songs. The chroniclers Muñoz Camargo and Alva Ixtlixocnitl, as well as the *Anales de Tlaxcala,* tell about his life and deeds, in particular when the encounter with the Spaniards took

Page from manuscript of *Cantares mexicanos* (Mexican songs) (fol. 55 v.), in the National Library of Mexico

place. In *Cantares* 57 v.–58 r., there is a chant in which he appears, declaring, "I say this, I Lord Xicohtencatl, do not go forth in vain!"

The last two composers whose songs are included in this book, Chichicuepon and Aquianhtzin, were born in the region of Chalco-Amaquemecan, close to the volcanoes Popocatepetl and Iztaccihuatl. Their lives and prestige as poets are particularly well documented in the sources of the indigenous tradition.

Chichicuepon, of Chalco, is presented in *Cantares* fol. 33 r. in the following manner: "Listen to the word which Lord Chichicuepon, the one who fell in the fight, left pronounced." Such a declaration is followed by the transcription of the composition attributed to Chichicuepon. In a striking coincidence with such a statement, the *Anales de Cuauhtitlan* provide information about the adverse circumstances in which this unfortunate creator of songs lost his life. The information provided by these two independent sources supports the attribution of a sorrowful song, the only one we know him for.

The last of our fifteen composers of songs is Lord Aquiauhtzin, native of a small town near Amaquemacan. The poet and ruler of Huexotzinco, Tecayehuatzin, praises Aquiauhtzin, of Ayapanco, for his songs. The native chronicler Chimalpahin describes in detail how Aquiauhtzin became famous, in particular for one of his compositions entoned before Axayacatl, Lord of Tenochtitlan. This composition has been preserved in *Cantares* 72 r.–73 v. with an express attribution to Aquiauhtzin.

THE GROUNDLESS HYPOTHESIS OF THE "GHOST SONGS"

It is true that, in a large proportion, the songs included in the extant manuscripts have to be taken as anonymous productions from the ancient schools of priests and sages and as creations of some rulers and members of the native nobility. But it is also undeniable that in cases such as those described, it is possible to investigate a theme attractive and at once difficult: the author relationship between some "faces and hearts" and their personal creations, their "flowers and songs."

In contrast to the attitude that takes into account the glosses included in the manuscripts and other textual references about the song composers and submits them to critical analysis, a hypothesis has been presented that simply dismisses the possibility of establishing any author relationship in the ensemble of the Nahuatl songs and poems, which are generally accepted as part of the ancient indigenous tradition. The author of the hypothesis claims that those compositions were done in the Colonial days with the specific purpose of being entoned as "Ghost Songs" in rituals similar to those performed by some contemporary North American Indian groups. It is obvious that such a hypothesis, if valid, would contradict almost everything that is expressed in this book. Although a goodly number of critical commentaries have already been published on the work in which such a hypothesis is introduced, I consider it necessary to briefly discuss it here. I refer to the two volumes published by John Bierhorst: *Cantares mexicanos, Songs of the Aztecs*, and *A Nahuatl-English Dictionary and Concordance to the Cantares mexicanos* (1985).[50]

Bierhorst's contribution is, in many respects, remarkable. For the first time he has made accessible to the English reader a paleographic transcription of the Nahuatl text, accompanied by a translation of all the songs included in the manuscript of *Cantares* housed at the National Library of Mexico. Besides, in the second, or companion volume, he has provided, in a classical manner, a dictionary-concordance of the words appearing in *Cantares*, "at least tentatively defined, with a listing of their appearances throughout the manuscript."[51] An analytical transcription of the text of *Cantares*, grammatical notes, and an index of the nonlexical vocables (exclamatory and others) that appear in the songs are valuable additions also included in the volume.

Such contributions would be extremely welcome, were it not for Bierhorst's unexpected assertion that all these songs are "ghost songs," similar in scope to those belonging to the "Ghost Dance Rituals" of North American Indians such as the Kamaths and Modoc, of Oregon, and the Sioux of the Plains. In support of his point of view, which he declares "is no more than a theory that I believe to be consistent with the data,"[52] Bierhorst postulates the existence of a sort of nativistic movement that he does not document at all. In his opinion, the manuscript of *Cantares* gives testimony to a process of cultural "revitalization" that he correlates with the cult to the Virgin of Guadalupe, again without offering any proof.

Disregarding the evidence, provided by numerous Nahuatl texts in the *Florentine Codex, Cantares, Huehuehtlahtolli,* and others concerning the indigenous persuasion that there is no return from the realm of the dead,[53] Bierhorst claims that precisely the paired terms "flower, song" denote persons in the *Cantares:*

> More correctly deceased persons or spirits . . . revenant kings [returning persons], such as Moctezuma and Axayacatl. They descend from the sky world, moreover, and are brought to life on earth through the joint efforts of the singer and his god. These, in brief, are the essential points. Having grasped them, the reader will find that they are reinforced in varying degrees throughout the manuscript.[54]

The examination of Bierhorst's translation of the *Cantares* demonstrates how often he accommodates it to give support to his "Ghost Dance Ritual" interpretation. In other words, what he himself described as "no more than a theory" guides and permeates all his work as translator. As Karen Dakin noted, reviewing Bierhorst's work:

> After an examination that concentrated on the passages that are central to his thesis, it seemed that there were many in-

stances where he [Bierhorst] misunderstood. For example on pp. 176–177 he translates *oncan tiyocoloc nahuatiloque* as "we're created, we who've been summoned." However the first verb is actually in the second-person singular, and Garibay's 1965 translation "you were created, were ruled," which does not support Bierhorst's interpretation, is closer to the literal meaning. In others, one felt that Bierhorst subtly accommodated the English to support his point of view.

Karen Dakin gives other examples and concludes that "Bierhorst is using his translation as evidence for his hypothesis and thus creates circularity."[55] Bierhorst's "no more than a theory" that led him to reject as false the indigenous testimonies that attribute specific songs to specific indigenous composers from the fourteenth and fifteenth centuries has been the cause of his many deviations, not to say errors, as translator. A long list of them could be easily provided. To simply reject the textual attributions on the basis of his "no more than a theory" and to claim in addition the undocumented (and actually nonexisting) nativistic movement is unacceptable from a historical and critical perspective.

I prefer to adhere to the criterion I have described and followed. Only a careful examination, in each case, of the textual attributions of a song to a composer can lead one to accept or reject as valid an author relationship.

THE CULTURAL UNIVERSE IN WHICH THE COMPOSERS LIVED

Although each of the composers of songs will be placed in his or her own historical context, I will describe at the outset some of the main features of the heritage of culture that all of them shared. Their compositions are indeed the final expression in a long sequence of creations by priests, sages, and masters of the word since at least the days of the Toltecs and with ultimate roots in the centuries of splendor of Teotihuacan.

Until recently it seemed absurd to compare the cultures that flourished in pre-Hispanic Mexico with the classic civilizations of the Old World. From the perspective of universal history it seemed sufficient to attend to the ancient inhabitants of the Americas in a chapter most often entitled, "Discoveries and Conquests at the End of the Fifteenth and the Beginning of the Sixteenth Centuries." The historical being of the American Indian cultures was thus focused as if its whole meaning depended on the fact of its being "discovered" by the Europeans. No wonder that frequently, once the total or partial destruction of these cultures was succinctly described, the matter was considered closed. At most there was an occasional allusion to the bloody rites and strange customs of peoples who seemed to merit the label *primitives*.

Several decades of archaeological research, scarcely 100 years of examination of the codices and other indigenous texts, and a deeper understanding of the contemporary native communities that preserve old traditions amply demonstrate that the cultural development and achievements of the indigenous societies of Mesoamerica deserve to be considered, in their own right, as a distinct experience in the broad context of humankind's history. In Mesoamerica, as in Egypt, Mesopotamia, and the Indus and Yellow river valleys, new and remarkable socioeconomic, political, and religious forms of organization developed. Among other things, since at least the first millennium B.C., a kind of protourbanism, magnificent works of art, and various forms of calendars and writing became tangible realities.

Inscriptions that have been dated *ca.* 600 B.C., in the Stelae of the Dancers in Monte Albán I (Oaxaca) and also the thousands of hieroglyphic texts inscribed in stone monuments and in the ceramics of the Maya area, stand out among the early testimonies of the cultural development and wisdom of the Mesoamerican peoples. It is true that the connotative potentials of the writing system employed in Central Mexico were more limited than those of the Maya hieroglyphs. Nevertheless, uninterruptedly, since the days of Teotihuacan (A.D. 0–700) and during the flourishing of Cholula and Xochicalco (A.D. 700–950) and of Tula (A.D. 850–1070) until the final splendor of the Mexica on the eve of the Spanish arrival, cultural continuity is perceptible in aspects so important as the employment of the two calendric counts, writing, and oral transmission in the schools run by priests.

The fifteen composers of songs who are the subject of this book as well as many other sages, chroniclers, poets, and priests whose names are unknown today belonged to this universe of culture. Besides having inherited a millennary legacy of wisdom and art, they were also creators who expressed their own thoughts and feelings. To better approach their faces and compositions, it is, therefore, important to review the main traits of the world view and social structures that prevailed in their times.

NAHUATL WORLD VIEW

It was believed that the present sun, moon, stars, and earth integrate the fifth universe within a series of ages, known to the Nahua people as "Suns."[56] Four other Suns had emerged and come to an end through the machinations of the gods: the ages of Earth, Air, Water, and Fire. The present is that of Olintonatiuh, "The Sun of Movement," which began to exist and to move thanks to a primeval sacrifice of the gods, who, with their own blood, brought it into being and thus also gave life to a new generation of humans. This fifth age not only may perish but actually carries within itself the very principle of death and destruction.

The Mexicas and other Nahua people always had in their minds the belief that somehow they could collaborate with their gods in doing their best to avoid, or at least to postpone, the cataclysm that was to put an end to this age. To achieve this, it was necessary to strengthen the sun, which was a manifestation of the Giver of Life. If, in the beginnings, the sun and moon had been brought into being and moved in an orderly manner because the gods had performed a bloody self-sacrifice, the mission of humans on earth was to repay the gods with the same vital energy contained in the precious red liquid.[57] In the particular case of the Mexica, as if hypnotized by the mystery of blood, they declared themselves the chosen "People of the Sun." Ceremonial warfare, the principal form of obtaining victims for the sacrifice, became a dominant activity in their social, religious, and national lives. In the songs composed by some of these fifteen poets and by many other anonymous masters of the word, the theme of the flowery wars, their meaning and glory, is often present.

The sacrifices of men were a key element in this ancient world view. They were performed in the temples, where a spatial image of the universe was plastically structured. The universe, as expressed symbolically in the plan and arrangement of the towns, and especially in the most sacred space of the precinct of their temples, is conceived as a flat surface divided horizontally into four quadrants or sections. There are many symbols attached to each quadrant. As it is depicted in several codices, what we call east is the region of light, fertility, and life, symbolized by the color white; north is the black quadrant, where the dead are buried; west is the house of the sun, the land of women, and of red color; and south is the place of cultivated fields, associated with the color blue-green.

The pyramids, such as that of the recently unearthed Main Temple in Mexico City, truncated and with superimposed structures, represent a vertical image of the universe.[58] Above the earth, going upward, are thirteen distinct planes. First are the heavens that join the water surrounding the earth and form a blue arch crisscrossed with paths along which move the sun and the moon, the stars, the morning star, and the comets. The heavens of different colors exist at higher planes culminating with the realm of the gods, the Place of Duality, where dwells the supreme god, Tloque Nahuaque, The Lord of the Close and Near, who is Our Lord and Lady of Duality. Below the earth are the lower levels, the paths that must be traveled by those who die to arrive in the lowest level that is Mictlan, "Region of the Dead," the gloomy place about which the poets and sages ask so many questions.

Duality is present everywhere. The supreme god is also called Ometeotl, "The Dual God," with a masculine and a feminine countenance—Ometeuctli, "The Lord of Duality," and Omecihuatl, "The Lady of Duality."[59] On top of the pyramids two shrines are built, as the supreme Dual God resides on the highest of the celestial levels. The ultimate being of the Dual God mysteriously unfolds, giving origin to the many other gods, perhaps attributes or manifestations of his/her own essence.

On the earth everything constantly changes and, finally, comes to an end. This is the "destiny" (tonalli) of all that exists. Destinies are intrinsically determined in accordance with the various divisions of time. The tonalpohualli, or "Count of the Days' Destinies," is a calendar of 260 days that has to be consulted on every important occasion of life. This count intermeshes with the 365-day solar calendar, and in this way it permeates, with the multiple connotations of its destinies, all the moments of time. Our fifteen poets and Nahuatl poetry in general convey anguished feelings time and again, because one knows that an inescapable destiny leads man to the Region of the Dead.

"What is above us" (Topan), that is, the celestial levels, and its counterpart, the "Region of the Dead," with its inferior planes, constitute the most obvious form of duality in the universe. From a different viewpoint, both are seen as opposed to what exists "on the earth" (Tlalticpac), thus introducing another kind of duality. Humans can say something about "what is on the earth"; but they are utterly unable to know "what is above us" as well as the "Region of the Dead." The poets and sages appear deeply concerned with this, one of their main recurring preoccupations, together with the ephemeral condition of all that exists.

We are all born because the gods, in their primeval sacrifice, made it possible for us to exist. In this respect, all humans are *macehualtin*, "deserved" by the gods' sacrifice. But from another perspective, all humans are not equals. In the social realm, duality is also present. The majority have to conform with their condition of macehualtin as commoners, ready to repay their existential debt as soldiers who take prisoners or to be made captives and thus sacrificed. In any case, the destiny of the macehualtin includes the obligation to work to subsist and also to pay the tributes exacted by the ruling group.

Only a few have a clearly different destiny. These few know something else about their own origin. They are acquainted with their lineage, their *pillotl*; thus they are the *pipiltin*, or "nobles." They claim descent, in one way or another, from the lineage of the sage, priest, and high ruler of the Toltecs, Lord Quetzalcoatl, he who is Topiltzin, "The One of Our Lineage." It is the destiny of the pipiltin to be the guides of the people, of all the macehualtin. Thus all the rulers, great pontiffs, chiefs of the warriors, priests of high rank, the principal among the judges and other dignitaries belong to the select group of the pipiltin.

Most, if not all, of the poets and sages—certainly our fifteen composers of songs—were pipiltin. They had received the best education in pre-Hispanic Mexico. They had been instructed in the calmecac, or priestly schools. There they had mastered the science of the calendar, the divine wisdom, the books of the annals, the ancient songs, and the discourses.

THE POLITICAL STAGE

During the last 150 years before the Spanish arrival—the span of time that embraces the more brief lifetimes of our poets—the political scene in Central Mexico underwent many changes. When in 1325 the Mexicas settled in Mexico-Tenochtitlan, two older chiefdoms tried to attain complete hegemony in the Valley of Mexico. The Tepanec chiefdom of Azcapotzalco rivaled Culhuacan, an older domain, the place of refuge of some descendants of the Toltec nobility. But Azcapotzalco's destiny was to prevail upon Culhuacan, expand, and subjugate other people. The Mexicas were tributaries of Azcapotzalco for about a century.

To the eastern side of the lakes another chiefdom was growing to such an extent that the people of Azcapotzalco came to consider it as a threat. The metropolis of that chiefdom was Tezcoco, a town that since the last part of the fourteenth century was frequently visited by many pipiltin from other places, including some sages and poets, such as one of our fifteen, Lord Tlaltecatzin, of Cuauhchinanco. As could be expected, a final confrontation occurred between Azcapotzalco and Tezcoco. To facilitate their own purposes, those of Azcapotzalco murdered the ruler of Tezcoco, Lord Ixtlilxochitl, the father of the famous sage and poet Nezahualcoyotl, in 1418. In that dramatic episode Nezahualcoyotl, among others, was rescued by Tochihuitzin, also a composer of songs, to whom a chapter is devoted in this book.

But it was the destiny of the Mexicas—announced by their god Huitzilopochtli—to triumph over their oppressors of Azcapotzalco. Allied with Nezahualcoyotl, of Tezcoco, and with the people of Tlaxcala—those who had settled on the other side of the volcanoes—they rebelled in 1426 against Azcapotzalco. Their victory brought their independence and the realization of what their god had announced to them. They initiated the last chapter of the history of Mesoamerica, which represented less than a century of achievements and conquests. The Mexicas, "People of the Sun," became the most powerful chiefdom in Mesoamerica. From the Gulf Coast to the Pacific and in many other regions to the north and south, the Mexicas imposed their rule. Exceptions to this were their allies: Tezcoco on the one hand, and on the other, a puppet chiefdom, Tlacopan, which took the place of the destroyed Azcapotzalco. There were also the chiefdoms of Tlaxcala, Huexotzinco, and Cholula that managed to preserve their independence vis-à-vis their Mexica neighbors.

Several of the fifteen poets were born in the area of Tlaxcala and Huexotzinco: Tecayehuatzin, Ayocuan, Xayacamach, and Xicohtencatl. Obviously, poetry also flourished in the metropolis of Tenochtitlan. Besides the many anonymous compositions that come from the great center of Mexica power, the names of some known poets, such as Tochihuitzin, Macuilxochitzin, Temilotzin, and others are proof of it. The prestige of Tezcoco, as the metropolis of the arts and wisdom, was unsurpassed. Five well-identified poets were prominent people in that chiefdom: Tlaltecatzin, Nezahualcoyotl, Cuacuauhtzin, Nezahualpilli, and Cacamatzin. And two at least, Aquiauhtzin and Chichicuepon, were born in the region of Chalco-Amaquemecan, close to the mighty Iztaccihuatl and Popocatepetl volcanoes, a domain that, after fierce resistance, succumbed at last to the ambitions of Mexico-Tenochtitlan. People living in these chiefdoms, beyond local differences, shared one and the same culture. The Aztecs, or Mexicas, had come to exert an open hegemony there, which explains why our fifteen poets are said to have lived in the "Aztec World."

This was the political stage in which the rise and fall of several chiefdoms took place. Many battles were fought there, and much arrogance came to an end. But it was also there—close to the lakes and the mountains—where the fifteen identified poets of pre-Hispanic Mexico lived and composed their songs.

MAIN STYLISTIC DEVICES IN NAHUATL POETRY

Although, in making our acquaintance with each one of these composers of songs, the specific attributes of their respective productions will be discussed, a preliminary approach to the principal stylistic devices often employed by them all is in order.

One should first note the social or community contribution of the act of composing a song. When a composer of songs—or, as a collegiate body, the priests of a temple or a center of learning—had produced a poetic composition, especially in the cases of the sacred hymns or other songs to be entoned in the public ceremonies, it was the duty of a high dignitary to express his opinion about such a new production. According to the *Códice matritense:*

> It was the duty of the *Epcohua Tepictoton* [the tonsured priest of the mother of the pearl, in the cult of the God of Rain] to be concerned with whatever was related to the songs. When somebody composed a song, he made it known to him in order that singers came to sing it at his house. When somebody had composed a song, he gave judgment on it.[60]

For his part, Ixtlilxochitl refers to the house in Tezcoco where the sages and poets frequently met "to sing the songs in which they conveyed their own stories."[61] An eloquent confirmation of the existence of those gatherings of poets and sages is provided by a text included in the *Cantares mexicanos* in the National Library and described as the "Dialogue of Flower and Song." In it, four of our fifteen poets appear, expressing their own viewpoints concerning the ultimate meaning and value of poetry and the universe of symbols.[62]

There are several stylistic features characteristic of Nahuatl poetry. In the songs as they are transcribed in the extant manuscripts, one can easily perceive different "units of expression," that is, paragraphs with closely interrelated sequences, often arranged by pairs. An identical sentence, appearing at the end of the two paired units, emphasizes this. The identical closing sentences can be understood by modern translators as indicative not only of a correlation between two units of expression but also as supporting elements to distribute the song in stanzas or lines of verses forming one division of the poem. Often, several paired units of expression constitute the patterned arrangement of a song. In them, rather than a "linear development" of a theme, one perceives distinctly synchronic and converging approaches to the same central subject.

Among the elements most often found as stylistic devices within the internal structure of a unit of expression, one also finds parallel sentences that usually have one and same subject. Stylistic parallelism is introduced as a means to strengthen a statement, to amplify an image, or to make an idea more explicit. The following examples illustrate this. In a song by Temilotzin, the poet says:

> Now I have come,
> I am standing,
> I will compose songs,
> make the songs burst forth.

Parallel sentences serve Temilotzin to declare his intentions: He wanted to come, stay, compose songs, and make them known.

The song that Tlaltecatzin, of Cuauhchinanco, addresses to an *ahuiani*, "woman of pleasure," also abounds in parallel sentences. Speaking to her, he emphasizes her charms:

> [S]weet delightful creature,
> precious flower of toasted maize.

At her side, Tlaltecatzin experiences an immense joy:

> [M]y heart has tasted it,
> my heart has been inebriated . . .
> the flowering chocolate drink is foaming,
> the flowery tobacco is passed around.

Nezahualcoyotl's poetry also offers numerous examples of this stylistic procedure. Speaking to the supreme Giver of Life, he exclaims:

> Dismiss Your displeasure!
> extend Your compassion . . . !
> The song resounds,
> little bells are heard.
>
> Precious realities You have poured down,
> from You comes joy.

Another stylistic device that is perhaps even more characteristic, also found within the various units of expression of the songs, is that described at times as "difrasism," or "semantic couplets," in which two metaphors are presented together to symbolically convey one thought. Semantic couplets are introduced not only in the poetic composition but also in the huehuehtlahtolli, or "Discourses of the Elders." And it can be added that this stylistic feature, besides being characteristic of Nahuatl literary productions, is also used in other Mesoamerican languages, mainly in several belonging to the Maya linguistic family. See the following examples:

Chalchihuitl (jades), *xihuitl* (turquoise), convey the idea of something precious.
Tizatl (chalk), *ilhuitl* (feathers), are attributes of the warriors, evoking their presence and the struggles of war.
Xochitl (flower), *cuicatl* (song), "flower, song," are a recurring semantic couplet that means "poetry," "art," "symbolism."
Petlatl (straw mat), *icpalli* (chair). To be on the straw mat, in the chair, conveys the idea of authority and rulership.

Tiquauhtli (you-eagle), *tocelotl* (you-ocelot). This is a form used to address the warriors who are eagle and ocelot knights.

Besides the employment of semantic couplets, the frequent presence of an ensemble of recurring metaphors is one of the most typical stylistic traits of Nahuatl poetry. Beyond the thematic differences that can be perceived in these literary productions, one can easily identify them as belonging to the culture of the Nahuas on the basis of the frequent use of a well-known set of metaphors.

Time and again one encounters the universe of flowers and their attributes, colors, odors, and parts or aspects of them such as their corollas, their blossoming, and withering. This is also true of trees, in particular those described as "flowery trees." There are many birds, often mentioned, with names whose translation poses great problems: multicolored like the *tlauhquechol;* "red bird of the agile neck," or "fire bird," the *xiuhtototl;* and the bird crested and brilliant green above and red below, the *quetzal* bird.

At times, the *teonanacatl* ("the divine flesh," hallucinogenic mushrooms), and the *ololiuhqui* (*datura stramonium*, morning glories), as well as tobacco and the foaming chocolate drink, are introduced to connote a variety of thoughts and feelings. In addition to precious stones and metals, various kinds of colorful feathers and musical instruments, such as the *huehuetl*, "drum," *teponaztli*, "kettledrum," *tlapitzalli*, "flutes," *ayacachtli* and *oyohualli*, "little bells," and *tecciztli*, "shells" are mentioned to symbolize the happiness and spiritual wealth humans can long for on the earth.

Related to the sphere of the limited wisdom one can attain on earth, the *xochicalli*, "flowery houses," *amoxcalli*, "houses of books," *tlahcuilolcalli*, "houses of the paintings," *tlilli, tlapalli*, "the black and red inks," are often mentioned. Colors denoting the cosmic quadrants, the arrays of the gods and rulers, and the flowers and birds are also important elements in the realm of metaphors and symbols so distinctively intertwined in this poetry.

Profiting from these and other more personal stylistic resources, the composers of songs, all those who are anonymous to us and the few whose names and deeds we know, created a poetry that conveys a universe of meanings that are strange to us at times but always intensely human. To enjoy the poetry as best we can, let us approach these fifteen masters of the word. It is time to listen to the words they conceived and pronounced, in some instances more than half a millennium ago.

PART ONE

POETS FROM THE REGION OF TEZCOCO

In Acolhuacan-Tezcoco
are kept the marvellous paintings,
the books of the years;
in the houses of books
there are the precious flowers . . .

(Cantares mexicanos, National Library of Mexico, fol. 18 r.)

Tezcoco was the capital of the kingdom of Aculhuacan. Rising on the banks of the lake that bore the same name, it was some ten miles to the east of the island on which the Aztec metropolis, Mexico-Tenochtitlan, was built. The origins of Tezcoco go back to Chichimec times in the Postclassic period, around the twelfth century. The town won political importance, first around A.D. 1300 as a rival of the kingdom of Azcapotzalco, situated at the west of the lakes, and later in A.D. 1428 as a member of the Triple Alliance that also included Mexico-Tenochtitlan and the puppet kingdom of Tlacopan.

Tezcoco's prestige centered in its cultural achievements. According to the Tezcocan chronicler Juan de Pomar: "The laws, regulations, good costumes, and forms of life which were generally observed in all the land, derived from Tezcoco. Their rulers did their best to promulgate them as they were, and by these laws Mexico-Tenochtitlan, Tlacopan, and all the subject provinces were governed. And it was said that in this city they had the archives of their legislation."[1]

Tezcocans had inherited the Toltec arts and the wisdom attributed to the high priest, Quetzalcoatl. They were religious people, well educated in the community schools, industrious, and properly behaved. Mainly among the nobles, a high reputation was acquired by those who devoted themselves to the composition of songs, "in which they referred, in a historical manner, to the prosperous or adverse happenings of their kings and prominent people. And the one who possessed such talent was very much honored, as he perpetuated with his songs the memory and the fame of those happenings. Because of this, he was rewarded by the supreme ruler and by the rest of the nobles."[2]

Several Tezcocan books from the early Colonial period, copies of others of pre-Hispanic origin, have come down to us. *Códice Xolotl,* for instance, in its eight large "pages" painted on indigenous paper, preserves an account of the history of Tezcoco. Warriors, rulers, priests, artists, sages, and common people are depicted in it. Calendrical glyphs and other glyphs that indicate place-names and the names of persons, accompanied by glosses or brief commentaries in the Nahuatl language, provide an adequate complement to the pictorial representations. Among the other best known Tezcocan codices, *Tlotzin, Quinatzin, Tepechpan,* and *"in Cross"* stand out.

The evidence provided by these and other manuscripts such as the *Anales de Cuauhtitlan* and also the testimonies of the oral tradition collected by such chroniclers as Juan de Pomar and Fernando de Alva Ixtlilxochitl make it possible to know about the political history of Tezcoco and its cultural splendor. Among other things, by consulting the works of these chroniclers one can gain direct information about the Tezcocan composers of songs, most, if not all, members of the ancient nobility.

Great renown as a sage was attributed, for instance, to Coyohua, the preceptor of that other famous high ruler, Nezahualcoyotl. Tlaltecatzin, governor of the Tezcocan province of Cuauhchinanco, is mentioned in various sources as a well-known poet. And the same assertion can be made about Nezahualcoyotl and his son, Nezahualpilli. The list also includes the noble Cuacuauhtzin, of Tepechpan, and Cacamatzin, the unfortunate prince of Tezcoco. In addition, in the two manuscripts containing the Nahuatl songs of the ancient tradition, references are made to these composers, and some of their compositions are also transcribed. Precisely because of the great cultural prestige enjoyed by Tezcoco, the capital of the kingdom of Acolhuacan, we will first approach Nahuatl poetry by discussing the *cuicahuicque,* "composers of songs," born in Tezcoco or its domains.

Glyph of Tezcoco

CHAPTER I

TLALTECATZIN OF CUAUHCHINANCO

Singer of Pleasure, Woman, and Death
(Fourteenth Century)

With Tlaltecatzin we begin our tour of poets, no longer anonymous, but in the words of the Nahua, "faces with flesh and color." Tlaltecatzin, of Chichimec lineage, was lord of Cuauhchinanco—in the present state of Puebla—around the middle of the fourteenth century. Among his contemporaries he enjoyed the reputation of being a joyful man. A poet from the region of Chalco named Chichicuepon—who is also considered in this book—said the following: "Tlaltecatzin, Xoquatzin and Tozmaquetzin lived happily. . . ."[1] According to the Tezcocan chronicler Ixtlilxochitl, this composer of songs was a contemporary of Techotlala, high ruler of Tezcoco from 1357 to 1409.[2] Cuauhchinanco, the hometown of Tlaltecatzin, was part of the Chichimec dominions of Tezcoco. At that time the famous Tezozomoc ruled in the powerful chiefdom of Azcapotzalco, Lord Coxcoxtli ruled in Culhuacan, and Acamapichtli had become the first *huey tlahtoani*, "ruler," of Mexico-Tenochtitlan.

Ixtlilxochitl tells of Tlaltecatzin and of some of his colleagues who governed other provinces. He says that "they always came to the court of Tezcoco to meet for any occasion and to consider matters of good government."[3] By that time Tezcoco was becoming an important political and cultural center. The rulers, people of lineage, and priests and sages who met there were undoubtedly influenced by the religious ideas, the widsom and artistic trends that began to flourish in that city, which reached its maximum splendor in later years under the sage rule of Nezahualcoyotl (1402–1472), the best known of the Nahuatl poets.

The Chichimec princes who had governed Tezcoco had long been concerned to improve the way of life of their people. Indeed, Nopaltzin, son of Xolotl, the renowned Chichimec chief, had married a princess of Toltec lineage and had introduced improved methods for cultivation of the soil during his reign, from 1284 to 1315. His sons, Tlotzin and Quinatzin, following his example and heeding advice of some Toltecs, also devoted themselves to the welfare of their town, "beautifying it, and making it orderly with much rule and law."[4] Among other things, Mixtec sages were brought from Oaxaca to teach their ancient form of writing employed in the painted books as well as astrology and the Toltec arts they had made their own. This process of cultural change culminated in the days of Techotlala (1357–1409) when he adopted the religious cult of Quetzalcoatl and induced his vassals to speak Nahuatl in the Toltec manner, as he himself had learned it from his nurse of noble lineage, Papaloxochitl. The chronicler Ixtlilxochitl also noted that the art of polished diction, the use of painted books and other things of a good and orderly government, were flourishing there "because at that time the Tezcocans were already very integrated with those descendants of the Toltec nation."[5]

Tlaltecatzin, who came to the court of Tezcoco "to meet for any occasion and to consider matters of good government," was likely influenced by this cultural flourishing. It is also quite probable that during his visits to the Tezcocan metropolis he made friends among other

Tlaltecatzin, of Cuauhchinanco, which was a political and cultural tributary of Tezcoco around the end of the fourteenth century, under the control of Techotlala (*Códice Xolotl*, v)

poets, including Tozmaquetzin, who is mentioned together with him by Chichicuepon, the poet of Chalco. There, Tlaltecatzin would have had the opportunity to penetrate into the ancient wisdom of Toltec origin, learn the doctrines concerning Quetzalcoatl, and practice the art of polished speaking inherited from those who were masters in it. It is a known fact that Tlaltecatzin became a celebrated *cuicapicqui*, "composer of songs." As an introduction to his poem, it is said of him that "left to yourself in your house, you have expressed your sentiments and spoken rightly."[6]

THE POETIC WORK OF TLALTECATZIN

It is unfortunate that we know only one song by Tlaltecatzin. It is a composition neither too long nor too short, but it was so famous and so well remembered that it is twice recorded in the pre-Hispanic collections with the precise indication of being *Tlaltecatzin icuic*, "A Song of Tlaltecatzin." Although we are dealing with only one poem, it can probably be asserted that it unveils to us at least an aspect of its author's attitude toward life.

This poem of the lord of Cuauhchinanco could be described as an ode to pleasure, but a kind of composition very different from European or modern American literary creations. As is the case among the songs of several other Nahuatl composers, Tlaltecatzin's words about pleasure are interwoven with an anguished sense of the loss of oneself through death. In a few brief verses, he offers an extraordinarily vivid picture of both the reality he craves and the destiny he most fears. In his poem, he converses with an ahuiani, "rejoicing one," or public woman, in the days of ancient Mexico. The painted books and other indigenous sources not only tell of the presence of these ahuianis in Nahuatl society but also depict their image and describe their behavior. In Tezcoco, the growing town Tlaltecatzin visited frequently, one could find the ahuianis. More references to them can be found in the ancient testimonies than one might imagine. The following text is an example:

> The ahuiani, "rejoicing one,"
> with her body gives pleasure,
> she sells her body . . .
> She stands up and waves,
> knows how to primp,
> in all places seduces . . .
> As a flower she poses . . .
> but she is never still,
> knows no rest.
> Her heart is always in flight,
> her fluttering heart . . .
> With her hands she makes signs,
> With her eyes she beckons.
> She moves her eyes in an arch,
> she smiles, goes about laughing,
> shows her charms.[7]

Probably remembering a particular ahuiani, Tlaltecatzin says of her that she is "a precious flower of toasted maize, a delightful creature lying upon a mat of feathers.

"The *alegradoras* beckon, know how to primp, in all ways seduce, like the flowers they wave . . ." (*Códice florentino*, x)

She is like the foaming cacao drink that brings joy to all." Contrary to the opinion of those who believe that ancient Mexicans did not enjoy speaking about sexual pleasure, Tlaltecatzin proclaims that, along with the precious flowers, even more than the foaming chocolate drink and the tobacco that enliven the meeting of friends, there stands that delightful being, a sweet and beautiful woman. Tlaltecatzin remembers his ahuiani and affirms that thus his heart is lulled. Being at the side of her "precious flower of toasted maize," he finds some solace on earth.

But Tlaltecatzin's song of pleasure, in a strange manner from the viewpoint of Western man, becomes also a song of death. In the words he speaks to his "rejoicing companion," he cannot help but repeat once and again: "You will be abandoned, you will have to go, you will become fleshless." And of himself, he adds: "I am alone, a singer, my life is priceless." He, the precious ahuiani, and everybody on earth must depart one day. Contemplating the flowers and remembering the experience of pleasure, a resigned Tlaltecatzin accepts his own destiny: "I must go, my own self shall become lost . . . I will go alone. . . . Thus let it be, but let it be without violence."

This appears to be the core idea, transmitted in an incisive mode of expression. Tlaltecatzin is the first chronologically among the fifteen poets of ancient Mexico whose faces and extant creations are the theme of this book. He lived in the dawn of a cultural renaissance, when Tezcoco was about to become a center of wisdom and art. The time had arrived, as *Códice matritense* states, when the people who had made the Toltec legacy their own, "already polished songs and set aside a place for the kettle drums, for it is said that, in this manner, did cities commence when already music resounded in them."[8]

YCUIC TLALTECATZIN, QUAUHCHINANCO

Nicpiecon tepetl,
canan itololoyan;
xochintlahcuilo, *aya*
Ipalnemoani, in cohuayotl.
Toncahuililoc ye mochaan,
titlaltecatzi,
tonaya tlatoa *yan ca yiu oo, ohuiyya.*

Zan ye ihuan noncuica,
yehuan, noteouh,
in toayatlatoayan,
y ie xochincacahuatl in pozontimani a
xochioctli.

Nocoyayc, *o, o,*
noyol quimati,
quihuinti ye noyol, *ayioo, hui, yoca, ancaya,*
noyol quimati.

Zan ca tlauhquechol,
celiya pozontimani *a,*
moquipacxochiuh,
tinaan, *o, o*
huelica cihuatl,
cacahuaizquixochitl,
zan tonnetlanehuilo,
ticahualoz,

tiyaz,
O ximaaz nican, *ayio.*

Can tiye'coc ye nican,
imixpan o teteuctin, *aya,*
timahuiztlachihualla,
monequetzca, noxiuhtoz.
Quetzalpetlapan,
tonihcaca, *aya*
Cacahuaizquixochitl,
zan tonnetlanehuilo,
ticahualoz,
tiyaaz,
O ximoaz yuhcan. *Ohuaya, ohuaya.*

Ah zan xochicacahuatl in puzontimani,
yexochitl in tlamaco,
intla noyol quimati,
quihuintia ye noyolia.
Aya yece ye nican,
tlalla icpac,
antetecuita, nopilhuan,
a noyol quimati,
quihuintia ye noyol.

Ah zan ninetlamata, niquitohua, *aya:*
Maca niya, *huiya,*
ompa ximohuayan.

Tlazotli noyol,
In nehua, nehua, zan nicuicanitl,
teocuitlayo noxochihuacayo,
In niquiyacahua,
zan niquitta nochan,
xochimamani.

Mach huey chalchihuitl, *ohuaya,*
quetzalli patlahuac
mach nopatiuh?
In zan ninoquixtiz,
quenmanian,
ca zan niyaz,

nipoliuhtiuh, *ohuaya, ohuaya.*
Aoya, ninocahua, *aya,*
Ah noteu, in Ipalnemoani,
ah niquitohua: ma niyauh,
ma ninoquimilolo,
ni cuicanitli,
ma ya ihui.

Ma aca cacizquia noyol ac? *ayyo*
Zan yuh niyaz,
xochihuiconticac ye noyolio, *ayyo.*
Ye quetzal nenelihui,
chalchiutli in tlazotli,
yectla mochiuhtoca.
Acan machotica
tlalticpac.
Zan ihui ya azo,
ihuan in ihuiyan, *ayyo.*

SONG OF TLALTECATZIN, CUAUHCHINANCO

I come to guard the mountain,
somewhere is its story;
with flowers is painted
The Giver of life, the community.
You have been left in your home,
you, Tlaltecatzin,
you suspire there, you speak.

I alone I sing,
to Him, who is my God,
in our place where the lords command,
the flowering chocolate drink is foaming,
the one which intoxicates men with its flowers.

I yearn,
my heart has tasted it,
my heart has been inebriated,
my heart knows it.

O red songbird of the supple neck!
Fresh and burning,

you show your garland of flowers.
You, mother!

Sweet woman,
precious flower of toasted maize,
you only lend yourself,
you will be abandoned,
you will have to go away,
there will be a defleshing.

Here you have come,
before the lords,
you marvelous being,
in an erect pose.
Upon the mat of yellow and blue feathers,
there you stand proudly.
But, precious flower of toasted maize,
You only lend yourself,
soon you must be abandoned,
you will have to go away,
there will be a defleshing.

The flowering chocolate drink is foaming,
the flower of tobacco is passed round,
if my heart would taste them,
my life would become inebriated.
But here
on the earth,
you, O lords, O princes,
if my heart would taste them,
my life would become inebriated.

I only suffer and say:
may I not go
to the place of the fleshless.

My heart is a precious reality,
I am, I am only a singer
but golden flowers I carry,
I have to abandon them,
I only look at my house,
the flowers remain there.

Perhaps big jades,
broad plumages,
are my price?
Alone I must go,
sometime it will be,
alone I must go,
I will perish.
I abandon myself,
O my God, Giver of life,
I say: let me go,
my body will be a funerary bundle,
I a singer,
let thus it be.

Is anyone there who will become the owner of my heart?
Alone I must go,
my heart covered with flowers.
Quetzal feathers,
precious jades,
so perfectly polished,
will be destroyed.
Nowhere on earth is their model,
thus let it be,
but let it be without violence.

(The text of this poem has been established on the basis of the two extant Nahuatl
transcriptions of it in *Cantares mexicanos*, National Library of Mexico, fols. 30 r. and v.,
and *Romances de los señores de Nueva España*, Benson Latin American Library,
University of Texas, Austin, fols. 7 r.–8 r.)

CHAPTER II

NEZAHUALCOYOTL
OF TEZCOCO

Poet, Architect, Man of Divine Wisdom
(1-Rabbit, 1402−6-Flint, 1472)

Many poets of the Nahuatl world, true masters of the word, were addressed as tlamatini. The meaning of this title is "he who knows something," chiefly meaning he who meditates and tells about the enigmas of man on earth, the beyond, and the gods. The sages of ancient Mexico, like several of the pre-Socratic thinkers, made poetry their ordinary form of expression, finding it the best means for communicating the essence of their thought and intuitions.

Among the poets who were authentic sages, the tlamatinime, one must include Tecayehuatzin, of Huexotzinco, Ayocuan, of Tecamachalco, Nezahualpilli, of Tezcoco, Cuacuauhtzin, of Tepechpan, and Tochihuitzin, of Tenochtitlan. But the poet who achieved greatest fame and towered above them all is the much-quoted Nezahualcoyotl.

One might pose the question whether his extraordinary fame as sage and poet was due mainly to his rank of supreme ruler of Tezcoco and counselor par excellence to the Mexica of Tenochtitlan. In reality, although his rank might have contributed to his fame, it is clear that his re-

nown is justified by what is known of his compositions
and other achievements. Several tlamatinime became supreme rulers with power equal to or even greater than
that of Nezahualcoyotl but never attained the prestige accorded the lord of Tezcoco as master of things both human and divine. Nowhere in the sources are there such
words of praise as those expressed about Nezahualcoyotl.
A poet from the Culhuacan region exclaimed:

> On a mat of flowers
> you paint your songs, your word,
> prince Nezahualcoyotl.
> Your heart is in the painting,
> with flowers of all colors
> you paint your songs, your word,
> prince Nezahualcoyotl.[1]

Even greater praise, and probably the greatest for any
poet, is found in another brief poem conceived to point
out the deep roots of the wisdom conveyed in Nezahualcoyotl's words:

> Within you lives,
> within you is painting,
> inventing, the Giver of Life,
> O Chichimec prince, Nezahualcoyotl![2]

The personality of Nezahualcoyotl, so admired and famous during pre-Hispanic times, has continued to attract
the attention of chroniclers and researchers ever since
the sixteenth century. In addition to the many references
to his life and thought, several biographies of him have
been written during the last decades.[3]

Until recent times, the chief difficulty in understanding the expression of the lord of Tezcoco has been the
general lack of knowledge of many of the indigenous
sources of Nahuatl culture. This explains why fantasies
grew up around Nezahualcoyotl. It has often been said
that he discovered "the One and Only God, the cause of
all things." Also, he has been described as interpreting

theological and philosophical ideas that are obviously European in origin. Some poetic compositions attributed to him cannot be accepted as his work. One example will suffice, that of a famous poem included by José Granados y Galvez in his *Tardes americanas,* a work printed in Mexico in 1778. In that often-quoted poem, Nezahualcoyotl is made to speak of "the vaults which enclose pestilent dust," "the roundness of the earth which is a sepulcher," "the royal purple cloth," and "the transitory pomps of this world."[4] Obviously Nezahualcoyotl would not use such metaphors, which are completely foreign to the thought of ancient Mexico.

Nezahualcoyotl's ideas, as preserved in the collections of pre-Hispanic songs, are very different and much more profound than those common platitudes composed in his honor. I will here present his ideas based on those sources in which his own compositions are preserved. My intention is to try to understand how Nezahualcoyotl, conversant with the intellectual legacy of a thousand years, was able to develop forms of thought that, though similar to the thinking and feelings of other tlamatinime (sages), show the color and slant of his own intuition.

Two distinct streams of tradition converged in Nezahualcoyotl: that of the ancient Chichimecs who came from the north and that of the Toltec culture, which included the teachings and doctrines attributed to Quetzalcoatl. As already mentioned in the chapter on Tlaltecatzin, lord and poet of Cuauhchinanco, Nezahualcoyotl's ancestors had introduced Toltec institutions in Tezcoco, including ancient doctrines and religious rites as well as the art of writing and the calendar. According to Ixtlilxochitl, Nezahualcoyotl was influenced from his childhood onward by this resurgence of Toltec culture, as one of the tutors "who contributed to his upbringing and instruction . . . was Huitzilihuitzin, in his way a great sage at that time."[5]

Nezahualcoyotl with his parents, Ixtlilxochitl and Matlalcihuatl (*Códice Xolotl,* vi)

The myths, traditions, and rites of Chichimec origin had not disappeared entirely. Their remnants are found in the texts, but they were undergoing cultural and religious fusion as both Mexica and Tezcocans were in the process of assimilating and enriching the institutions of Toltec origin. The Mexica later transformed these into instruments for their own ideas and ambitions, converting themselves into the People of the Sun with a new mystic-militaristic world view that was the basis for their conquests throughout ancient Mexico.

The cultural blending of Toltec and Chichimec elements took a different slant in the thought and deeds of Nezahualcoyotl and of some other tlamatinime (sages). For them, the doctrines attributed to Quetzalcoatl were a stimulus to a more profound spiritual reflection on ancient themes such as Tloque Nahuaque, "Lord of the Close and the Near"; the evanescent nature of whatever exists on the earth; the perfectibility of faces and hearts; the mysteries surrounding death and the afterlife; the possibility of saying true words in a world where everything changes and becomes destroyed. Nezahualcoyotl's thought, even more than that of his contemporaries, developed within this frame of reference and, guided by his intuition, evolved into one of the most penetrating expressions of what I have described as "Nahuatl philosophy."[6]

Although some anecdotes about Nezahualcoyotl's life will be recalled, the emphasis in this chapter will be on the course of his thinking as he pondered various themes and problems. Principal sources for the study of his life are the *Anales de Cuauhtitlan* and the works of the Tezcocan chroniclers Ixtlilxochitl and Pomar, together with those of Friar Juan de Torquemada and Chimalpahin Cuauhtlehuanitzin. What is known of his poetic compositions, the conveyors of his thought, is found, together with the works of other poets, in the two principal collections of pre-Hispanic songs.

A SUMMARY BIOGRAPHY OF NEZAHUALCOYOTL

Nezahualcoyotl was born in Tezcoco in the year 1-Rabbit (1402). His parents were Ixtlilxochitl the Elder, and Matlalcihuatzin, daughter of Huitzilihuitl, the second ruler of Tenochtitlan. As already noted, he had an excellent tutor in the home of his parents and later received a careful education in Tezcoco's principal school or calmecac, founded on the doctrines and ancient wisdom inherited from the Toltecs.

According to the chronicler Chimalpahin, in the year 4-Rabbit (1418), when the young prince was sixteen years old, he saw his father assassinated by warriors from Azcapotzalco and witnessed the fall of Tezcoco to the power of the Tepanec nation.[7] The death of his father was the beginning of a long series of misfortunes and dangerous harassments recorded in the indigenous annals. However, Nezahualcoyotl's outstanding shrewdness and bravery in all those difficulties were at last to bring him victory over his enemies. During those difficult days he was probably in contact with poets and sages. Significantly, it was Tochihuitzin Coyolchiuhqui, a composer of songs, who

The Tezcocan prince hidden in
a tree witnesses the death of his
father (*Códice Xolotl,* vii)

helped Nezahualcoyotl escape at the very moment when
the warriors of Azcapotzalco murdered his father.[8]

In exile, Nezahualcoyotl won the favor of the rulers of
various neighboring chiefdoms, including Huexotzinco
and Tlaxcala. With their backing and support from his
Mexica relatives on the maternal side, who at that time
were beginning their own struggle with Azcapotzalco, he
decided to undertake the liberation of his father's domain. According to the *Anales de Cuauhtitlan,* in the
year 3-Rabbit (1430), he conquered the territory of Coatlinchan.[9] In close alliance with the Mexica, the Tezcocan army took part in several encounters with the Tepanecs until, finally, Azcapotzalco surrendered and the last
stronghold of the Tepanecs, the town of Coyoacan, was
captured in 1431. Two years later, under the protection of
the Mexica, Nezahualcoyotl established himself firmly
in Tezcoco.[10]

Unanimously, the sources of the pre-Hispanic tradition
describe the flowering of culture and the arts during his
long reign of over forty years. It was a period of magnifi-
cence during which Nezahualcoyotl planned and inaugurated new palaces, temples, and botanical and zoological

gardens. He advised the Mexica high rulers and supervised remarkable architectural and urban works, including the construction of roads and aqueducts to bring drinking water into Mexico-Tenochtitlan (present-day Mexico City). He also designed and built causeways and a dike to separate fresh- from saltwater in the lakes and relieve the constant threat of floods. One of his descendants, the chronicler Fernando de Alva Ixtlilxochitl, speaks about other projects undertaken by Nezahualcoyotl and describes in detail his palaces and halls devoted to music and poetry. According to him, there was the meeting place for the sages, priests, artists, judges, and anyone interested in the most lofty cultural creations inspired by the Toltec tradition.[11]

As a legislator, Nezahualcoyotl promulgated and enforced a series of laws, many still preserved in ancient transcriptions, which show his profound sense of justice and wisdom.[12] Naturally, because of his alliance with Mexico-Tenochtitlan, he had to take part in countless wars and also at times to compromise his own ideas with some of the practices of the Mexica.

If one gives credit to the indigenous chroniclers, mainly to the testimony of Ixtlilxochitl, it appears that in his personal life Nezahualcoyotl somehow dissociated himself from the official religious cult. An enduring testimony to the trend of Nezahualcoyotl's thinking and inner convictions was a temple he built with a high tower, facing the temple of Huitzilopochtli, which had been erected in Tezcoco in recognition of Mexica supremacy. The tower was composed of various sections symbolizing the different floors or celestial planes, and the temple, in which there was no image whatsoever, was in honor of Tloque Nahuaque, "Lord of the Close and Near, invisible as the night and intangible as the wind," the One repeatedly mentioned in Nezahualcoyotl's poems.[13]

Other anecdotes in the life of Nezahualcoyotl are recalled in various chapters of this book, mainly in those that deal with other composers of songs related in one way or another to Nezahualcoyotl. Thus, while introducing the person and compositions of Cuacuauhtzin, lord of Tepechpan, mention will be made of one Nezahualcoyotl's weakness. Suffice it to note here that Nezahualcoyotl deprived Cuacuauhtzin of his life in order to marry his wife. Acting as counselor and ally of the Mexica nation, Nezahualcoyotl sponsored the election of Axayacatl as tlahtoani, high ruler, of Tenochtitlan. References to this are made in the chapter devoted to Axayacatl as a poet. The figure of Nezahualcoyotl is also present in the biography of his son Nezahualpilli, above all in his making provision for the future in the choice of a successor who would add to the well-established prestige of Tezcoco.

Nezahualcoyotl lived to be seventy-one years old. As he felt death approaching, he made known his decision to be succeeded by his son Nezahualpilli. Among his last orders, in addition to placing Nezahualpilli under the guardianship of the prudent Lord Acapioltzin, Nezahual-

Nezahualcoyotl plays ball with his faithful servant, Coyohua (*Códice Xolotl*, ix)

coyotl requested that his death, about which he had medi-
tated for so many years, should not be the cause of grief
for his people. Ixtlilxochitl has preserved what he claims
were Nezahualcoyotl's last words:

> I find myself very near to death and, once deceased, in place
> of sad lamentations you shall sing happy songs, showing in
> that manner confidence and courage, in order that the na-
> tions we have conquered and hold under our command shall
> see no weakening of determination in yourselves because of
> my death, but rather they must understand that anyone of
> you alone is able to hold them subject.[14]

The death of Nezahualcoyotl occurred in the year 6-
Flint (1472). It was recorded by all the indigenous chroniclers and historians with posthumous eulogies that sum-
marized his attributes and achievements, especially as
poet and sage. The following is an extract from the same
Ixtlilxochitl:

> In this way came to an end the life of Nezahualcoyotl who
> was the most powerful, brave, wise, and fortunate prince and
> captain which this New World has seen . . . for he was very
> wise in moral things, and did the best he could in his search
> for light to know about the true God . . . as shown in the tell-
> ing of his story, and as the songs he composed give testi-
> mony. . . . And although he could not do away entirely with
> human sacrifices according to the Mexican rites, still he per-
> suaded them to sacrifice only those taken in war, slaves, and
> captives, and not the children and common people as had
> been their custom.[15]

In order to give greater authority to his words and
to everything said about Nezahualcoyotl, the Tezcocan
chronicler then enumerates the testimonies and sources
he has used:

> The authors of everything mentioned and all the rest about
> his life and deeds are the noblemen of Mexico, Itzcoatzin and
> Xiuhcozcatzin, and other poets and historians in the annals
> of the three principal nations of this New Spain, and espe-
> cially the annals written by Quauhtlatzacuilotzin, first lord

of the town of Chiauhtla beginning with the year of his [Neza-hualcoyotl's] birth and up to the time of the rule of King Nezahualpiltzintli. And likewise it is found in the accounts written by the noblemen of the city of Tezcoco, D. Pablo, D. Toribio, D. Hernando Pimentel, and Juan de Pomar, sons and grandsons of the king Nezahualpiltzintli of Tezcoco; and likewise D. Alonso Axayacatzin, lord of Iztapalapan, son of king Cuitlahuac and nephew of Moteuczomatzin.[16]

The works of some of those Ixtlilxochitl calls "poets and historians" are now lost but the indigenous sources already mentioned, as well as the few biographies of Ne-zahualcoyotl written more recently, permit a much more detailed study of the adventurous and extraordinarily productive life of this very famous lord of Tezcoco.

Because the intention here is to study his thought and poetry especially, the following pages will present a ten-tative interpretation based on the analysis of some com-positions that, after careful scrutiny, can be accepted as his. In the collections of pre-Hispanic songs there are some thirty poems preserved as the work of Nezahualco-yotl. Although the dates of their composition are not given, there are certain themes that form a natural link and follow what might be called a logical sequence. Among the main themes in Nezahualcoyotl's thought the following stand out: time and the fugacity of all that exists; the inevitability of death; the possibility of saying true words; the beyond and the region of the "fleshless"; the meaning of "flower and song"; the enigma of man as related to the Giver of Life; and the possibility of glimps-ing something about the Inventor of Himself. That is to say, he encompassed the problems of an instinctively metaphysical thinking that includes anguish and doubt as attributes of one's existence.

It is inevitable that this presentation of Nezahualco-yotl's thought, as seen through his poetry, will be colored by the subjective interpretation of the author. But we are not alone in this difficulty. There have been similar attempts to elucidate the fragmentary compositions that have reached us from the pre-Socratic thinkers of Greece and from the ancient wise men of India and China. Thus, without naïve pretensions, but with a critical eye, our main purpose here is to unveil what appears to have been Nezahualcoyotl's own way of thinking.

THE THOUGHT OF NEZAHUALCOYOTL AS REVEALED BY HIS POETRY

The first emphasis of Nezahualcoyotl seems to have been his keen awareness of time and change, *cahuitl*, "that which leaves us." Everything in *tlalticpac*, "on the earth," is transitory. It appears for a while but then withdraws and vanishes forever. Here is the way Nezahualcoyotl expresses it:

> I, Nezahualcoyotl, ask this:
> Is it true one really lives on the earth?
> Not forever on earth,
> only a little while here.
> Though it be jade it falls apart,
> though it be gold it wears away,
> though it be quetzal plumage it is torn asunder.
> Not forever on earth,
> only a little while here.[17]

If jade and gold fall apart and wear away, then faces and hearts, which are more fragile, however noble they may be, will dry up like flowers and be erased like paintings:

> I comprehend the secret, the hidden:
> O my lords!
> Thus we are,
> we are mortal,
> humans through and through,
> we all will have to go away,
> we all will have to die on earth . . .
> Like a painting
> we will be erased.
> Like a flower,

we will dry up
here on earth.
Like plumed vestments of the precious bird,
that precious bird with the agile neck,
we will come to an end . . .
Think on this, o lords,
eagles and tigers,
though you be of jade,
though you be of gold,
you also will go there,
to the place of the fleshless.
We will have to disappear,
no one can remain.[18]

The conviction that faces and hearts meet only for a brief time on earth is the cause of Nezahualcoyotl's sadness, but it is also the beginning of his new way of thinking:

I am intoxicated, I weep, I grieve,
I think, I speak,
within myself I discover this:
indeed, I shall never die,
indeed, I shall never disappear.
There where there is no death,
there where death is overcome,
let me go there,
Indeed I shall never disappear.[19]

Several pre-Hispanic sages expressed their doubts about officially accepted religious doctrines on the afterlife concerning the survival of warriors as companions of the sun, the happy life in Tlaloc's (the Rain God's) paradise, and the trials that had to be confronted in the lower depths of Mictlan, the Region of the Dead. Nezahualcoyotl, recalling ancient beliefs, probably of Toltec origin, expresses his own doubt and wonders where one had to go or what wisdom must be acquired in order to arrive at Quenonamican, "Where-In-Someway-One-Lives," *At can on ayac micohua*, "Where-Death-Does-Not-Exist":

> Where shall we go
> where death does not exist?
> But should I live weeping because of this?
> May your heart find its way:
> here no one will live forever.
> Even the princes die,
> people are reduced to ashes.
> May your heart find its way:
> here no one will live forever.[20]

Nezahualcoyotl finds his own way. He proclaims he has discovered the ultimate meaning of "flower and song," the Nahuatl metaphor for art and symbolism. Taking the path of poetry he will be able to approach the realities of "that which is above us, the region of the gods, and of the dead." He describes his discovery concisely:

> At last my heart knows it:
> I hear a song,
> I contemplate a flower . . .
> May they never fade![21]

When the heart at last has found its way, it seeks out the flowers and songs that never perish; hence Nezahualcoyotl is anxious to find the flowers and songs that will not come to an end:

> My flowers will not come to an end,
> my songs will not come to an end,
> I, the singer, raise them up;
> they are scattered, they are bestowed . . .
> Even though flowers on earth
> may wither and yellow,
> they will be carried there,
> to the interior of the house
> of the bird with the golden feathers.[21]

Nezahualcoyotl believes that he whose heart has discovered the universe of flower and song can indeed approach the mysteries that surround the Giver of Life, he who is Tloqueh Nahuaqueh, "The Lord of the Near and

Nezahualcoyotl with the princess Azcalxochitzin and two artists of Tezcoco (*Códice Tlotzin*)

Close"; Moyocoyani, "He Who Invents Himself"; Teyo-
coyani, "He Who Invents Humans, Who Exist On the
Earth." Like the Toltec painters, He also has His own
book of paintings where He sketches our faces and hearts
with the colors of the flowers and songs, drawing and
shading whatever exists on the earth:

> With flowers You paint,
> O Giver of Life!
> With songs You give color,
> with songs You shade
> those who will live on the earth.
> Later You will destroy eagles and tigers:
> we live only in Your painting
> here, on the earth.
>
> With black ink You will blot out
> all that was friendship,
> brotherhood, nobility.
>
> You give shading
> to those who will live on the earth.
> We live only in Your book of paintings,
> here on the earth.[23]

The faces and hearts of humans on earth are close and
yet far from the Giver of Life. Eagles and tigers, brother-
hood and nobility exist in the book of paintings of the
Lord of the Close and Near. Nonetheless, He is for man as
the night and the wind and remains unattainable. Neza-

hualcoyotl reaches out toward Him but expresses clearly the impossibility of unveiling the mystery:

> There, alone, in the interior of heaven
> You invent Your word,
> Giver of Life!
> What will You decide?
> Do You disdain us here?
> Do you conceal Your fame
> and Your glory on the earth?
> What will You decide?
> No one can be intimate
> with the Giver of Life . . .
> Then, where shall we go . . . ?
> Direct yourselves,
> we all have to go to the region of mystery.[24]

In spite of the statement that "no one can say he is intimate with the Giver of Life," Nezahualcoyotl continues his search. He enunciates a series of questions as to the reality and roots of He Who invents His own word and brings us into being in His mysterious book of paintings:

> Are You real, are You rooted?
> Is it only as to come inebriated?
> The Giver of Life:
> is this true?
> Perhaps, as they say, it is not true?
> May our hearts
> be not tormented!
> All that is real,
> all that is rooted,
> they say that it is not real,
> it is not rooted.
> The Giver of Life
> only appears absolute.
>
> May our hearts
> be not tormented,
> because He is the Giver of Life.[25]

Above and beyond the doubts and the mystery that surround the Giver of Life, it is necessary to accept His reality. This is the only truth that can bring peace to the heart. This appears to be Nezahualcoyotl's conclusion in his effort to comprehend the mystery of divinity. Although Tloqueh Nahuaqueh is absolute and incomprehensible, He is also the Giver of Life in whose book of paintings we exist. Human beings must accept the mystery, invoke and pay homage to Him, for in this way it is possible to live on earth.

Flowers, songs, and art—man's finest creation—are the path to come close to Him. It would seem that the Giver of Life Himself, with his own flowers and songs, has tried to intoxicate us here. The following text appears to be the ultimate synthesis of Nezahualcoyotl's thought:

In no place can be the house of He Who invents Himself.
But in all places He is invoked,
in all places He is venerated,
His glory, His fame are sought on the earth.

It is He Who invents everything.
He is Who invents Himself: God.
In all places He is invoked,
in all places He is venerated,
His glory, His fame are sought on the earth.

No one here is able,
no one is able to be intimate
with the Giver of Life;
only He is invoked,
at His side,
near to Him,
one can live on the earth.

He who finds Him,
knows only one thing: He is invoked,
at His side, near to Him,
one can live on the earth.

In truth no one is intimate with You,
O Giver of Life!

Only as among the flowers,
we might seek someone,
thus we seek You,
we who live on the earth,
while we are at Your side.

Our hearts will be troubled,
only for a short time,
we will be near You and at Your side.

The Giver of Life enrages us,
He intoxicates us here.
No one can be perhaps at His side,
be famous, rule on the earth.

Only You change things,
as our hearts know it:
No one can be perhaps at His side,
be famous, rule on the earth.[26]

Nezahualcoyotl's conclusion may appear pessimistic if it is not understood in its intrinsic relationship to the dialectic of his thought. He declares that no one can be a friend of the Giver of Life; no one can be at His side on the earth; but at the same time he asserts that it is man's destiny to seek Him, as one would search for someone among the flowers. He who invokes Him, who seeks Him, will be able to live on the earth. He might even say that he finds himself at His side, near to Him, precisely because He is the Lord of the Close and Near. Purely rational thought leads probably to doubting: "Are You real, are you rooted?" Because "all that is real, they say that it is not real."

The impossibility of knowing Him—the arbitrary one who is like the night and the wind—troubles the heart. On the other hand, to invoke Him is as to have found Him. This brings tranquility and makes it possible to exist on the earth. Nezahualcoyotl appears at rest with

The court retinue of Tezcoco (*Códice Quinatzin*)

this final conclusion: At times the Giver of Life intoxicates us; we keep searching for Him, "as among the flowers, we might seek someone."

This approach to some of the poems certainly composed by Nezahualcoyotl is a first attempt to understand something of his thought. There should be a much more thorough literary and philosophical study of all compositions and discourses that, after critical examination, can be accepted as his. That study will probably show that, although in Nezahualcoyotl's expressions there are elements, ideas, and metaphors belonging to the common legacy of poetry in pre-Hispanic times, there is also a way of thinking that appears to be his own. Further poems of Nezahualcoyotl, transcribed in the following pages in their original Nahuatl and translated into English, convey the essence of the thought and the beauty of expression of the most celebrated sage lord of Tezcoco.

IN CHOLOLIZTLI ICUIC

O nen notlacat, *ayahue,*
o nen nonquizaco
teotl (dios) ichan in tlalticpac.
Ninotolinia! *ohuaya, ohuaya.*
In ma on nel nonquiz,
in ma on nel nontlacat.
Ah niquitohua yece . . . *yeehuaya,*
tlen naiz?
Anonohuaco tepilhuan!,
At teixco ninemi?,
Quen huel?,
xon mimati! *Aya, ohuaya, ohuaya.*

Ye ya nonehuaz in tlalticpac?
Ye ya tle in nolhuil?,
zan nitoliniya,
tonehua noyollo,
tinocniuh in ayaxcan
in tlalticpac, ye nican, *ohuaya, ohuaya.*

Quen in nemohua in tenahuac?
Mach ilihuiztia,
nemia tehuic, teyaconi?
Nemi zan ihuiyan,
zan icemelia!
In zan nonopechteca,
zan nitolotenemi
in tenahuac, *ohuaya, ohuaya.*
Zan ye ica nichoca, *yeehuaya,*
nicnotlamati!,
no nicnocahualoc
in tenahuac tlalticpac.

Quen quinequi noyollo, *yeehuaya,*
Ipalnemohuani?
Ma oc melel on quiza!
A icnopillotl ma oc timalihui, *huiya,*
monahuac, titeotl (dios)
At ya nechmiquitlani?, *ohuaya, ohuaya.*

Azomo ye nelli tipaqui,
ti ya nemi tlalticpac?
Ah ca za tinemi
ihuan tihualpaqui in tlalticpac.
Ah ca mochi ihui titotolinia.
Ah ca no chichic teopouhqui
tenahuac ye nican? *ohuaya, ohuaya.*

Ma xi icnotlamati noyollo, *yeehuaya.*
Maca oc tle xicyococa, *yehuaya.*
Ye nelli in ayaxcan
nicnopiltihua in tlalticpac.

Ye nelli cococ ye otimalihuico,
in motloc, monahuac, in Ipalnemohua. *Yyao, yyahue.*
Zan niquintemohua, *Aya,*
niquilnamiqui in tocnihuan.
Cuic oc ceppa huitze,
in cuix oc nemiquihui?
Zan cen ti ya polihuia,
zan ce ye nican in tlalticpac.

Maca cocoya inyollo,
itloc, inahuac, in Ipalnemohua.
Yyao, yyahue, ahuayye, oohuiya.

SONG OF THE FLIGHT
(Composed by Nezahualcoyotl while fleeing from the lord of Azcapotzalco)

In vain was I born,
in vain have I come forth
to earth from the house of the Lord,
I am sorely lacking!
Would that I had not come forth,
truly better I had not come to earth.
I cannot express it, but . . .
what must I do?
O princes who have come here!
Must I live in the sight of the people?
How will it be?
Reflect on it!

Must I stand up straight on the earth?
Which is my destiny?
I am sorely lacking,
my heart suffers,
You are now my friend,
here, on earth.

How should one live beside the people?
Works he perhaps carelessly,
He who is the sustainer of man?

Live peacefully,
pass life calmly!
I am bent over,
I live with my head bowed
beside the people.
For this I am weeping,
I am wretched!
I have remained alone
beside the people on earth.

How has Your heart decided,
Giver of Life?
Dismiss Your displeasure!
Extend Your compassion,
I am at Your side, You are God.
Perhaps You would bring death to me?

Is it true that we are happy,
that we live on the earth?
It is not certain that we live
and have come on earth to be happy.
We are all sorely lacking.
Is there any who does not suffer
here, beside the people?

Would that my heart be not afflicted.
Do not reflect any more,
truly, I scarcely
pity myself here on earth.

Sorrow has sprung up
near You and at Your side, Giver of Life.
Only I am searching,
I remember our friends.
Will they come once more,
perhaps they will live again?
Only once we perish,
only once here on the earth.
Let not their hearts suffer,
near, at the side, of the Giver of Life!

(*Romances de los señores de Nueva España,*
Benson Latin American Library, University of Texas, Austin, fols. 21 r.–22 v.)

MA ZAN MOQUETZACAN

Ma zan moquetzacan, nicnihuan! *Ohuaya*
In icnoque on cate in tepilhuan,
non Nezahualcoyotzin,
ni cuicanitl, *huiya*,
tzontecochotzin, *huiya*.
Oayye yyayye ayya yyohuia.

Xoconcui moxochiuh ihuan in mecacehuaz.
Ma ica xi mototi!
Zan tehuan nopiltzin,
zan ye ti Yoyontzin.
Ma xoconcua in cacahuatl,
in cacahuaxochitl,
ma ya on ihua in!
Ma ya netotilo,
ma necuicatilo!
Ah nican tochan,
ah nican tinemizque,
tonyaz ye yuhcan.
Yao ahuayya yyao huiya ya huiya.

MY FRIENDS, STAND UP!

My friends, stand up!
The princes have become destitute,
I am Nezahualcoyotl,
I am a singer,
head of macaw.
Grasp your flowers and your fan.
With them go out to dance!
You are my child,
you are Yoyontzin.
Take your chocolate,
flower of the cacao tree,
may you drink all of it!
Do the dance,
do the song!
Not here is our house,
we do not live here,
you also will have to go away.

(*Romances de los señores de Nueva España,*
Benson Latin American Library, University of Texas, Austin, fols. 3 v.–4 r.)

NITLAYOCOYA

Nitlayocoya, nicnotlamatiya,
zan, nitepiltzin niNezahualcoyotl, *huiya.*

Xochitica ye ihuan cuicatica
niquimilnamiqui tepilhuan,
ayn oyaque,
yehua Tezozomoctzin, o yehuan Quahquauhtzin.
a ohuaya, ohuaya.

Oc nellin nemoan,
quenonamican.
Maya niquintoca in intepilhuan, *huiya,*
maya niquimonitquili toxochiuh! *Aya.*
Ma ic ytech nonaci,
yectli yan cuicatl in Tezozomoctzin.
O ayc ompolihuiz in moteyo,
nopiltzin, tiTezozomoctzin!,
anca za ye in mocuic a yca
nihualchoca,
yn zan nihualicnotlamatico,
nontiya, *ehua, ohuaya, ohuaya.*

Zan nihualayocoya, nicnotlamati.
Ayoquic, ayoc,
quenmanian,
titechyaitaquiuh in tlalticpac,
yca, nontiya, *yehua, ohuaya, ohuaya.*

I AM SAD

I am sad, I grieve
I, lord Nezahualcoyotl.
With flowers and with songs
I remember the princes,
those who went away,
Tezozomoctzin, and that one Cuacuauhtzin.

Truly they live,
there Where-in-Someway-One-Exists?
O, that I might follow the princes,
take them, our flowers!
If I could but make mine
the beautiful songs of Tezozomoctzin!
Never will your name perish,

O my lord, you, Tezozomoctzin!
Thus longing for your songs,
I am grieving,
alone I have come to remain saddened,
I withdraw from myself.

I have become saddened, I grieve.
No longer you are here, no longer,
but in the region Where-in-Some-Way-One-Exists.
You have left us without sustenance on the earth,
for this I withdraw from myself.

(*Cantares mexicanos*, National Library of Mexico, fols. 25 r. and v.)

XOPAN CUICATL

Amoxcalco
pehua cuica,
yeyecohua, *yehuaya,*
quimoyahua xochitl,
on ahuia cuicatl, *hue, hahuayya, ohuaya, ohuaya.*

Icahuaca cuicatl,
oyohualli ehuatihuitz,
zan quinanquiliya
toxochayacach.
Quimoyahua xochitl,
on ahuia cuicatl.

Xochiticpac cuica
in yectli cocoxqui,
ye con ya totoma
aitec.
Ho ilili yaha, ilili yio,
hui, ohui, ohui, ohuaya, ohuaya.
Zan ye connanquilia
in nepapan quechol,
in yectli quechol,
in huel ya cuica.
Ho ilili yaha, ililili,
ohui, ohui, ohui.

Amoxtlacuilol in moyollo,
tocuicaticaco,
in tictzotzona in mohuehueuh,
in ticuicanitl.
Xopan cala itec,
in tonteyahuiltiya.
Yao yli yaha, ilili lili iliya,
ohama hayya, ohuaya, ohuaya.

Zan tic moyahua
in puyuma xochitli,
in cacahua xochitli.
In ticuicanitl.
Xopan cala itec,
in tonteyahuiltiya,
yao, ya, oli, yaha,
ilili, lili, iliya, ohama, ohuaya, ohuaya.

SONG OF SPRINGTIME

In the house of paintings
the singing begins,
song is practiced,
flowers are spread,
the song rejoices.

The song resounds,
little bells are heard,
to these answer
our flowery timbrels.
Flowers are spread,
the song rejoices.

Above the flowers is singing
the radiant pheasant;
his song unfolds
into the midst of the waters.
To him reply
all manner of red birds,
the dazzling red bird
beautifully sings.

Your heart is a book of paintings,
you have come to sing,
to make your drums resound,
you are the singer.
Within the house of springtime,
You make the people happy.

You alone bestow
flowers that intoxicate,
precious flowers.
You are the singer.
Within the house of springtime,
you make the people happy.

(*Romances de los señores de Nueva España*,
Benson Latin American Library, University of Texas, Austin, fols. 38 v.–39 r.)

YE NONNOCUILTONOHUA

Ye nonnocuiltonohua,
on nitepiltzin, niNezahualcoyotl, *huia.*
Nicnechico cozcatl,
in quetzalin patlahuac,
ye nonicyximatin chalchihuitl, *yaoo,*
in tepilhuan! *Ohuaya, ohuaya.*
Yxco nontlatlachia,
nepapan quauhtlin, ocelotl,
ye nonicyximatin chalchihuitl,
ya in maquiztli, *ya, ohuaye.*

I AM WEALTHY

I am wealthy,
I, prince Nezahualcoyotl.
I join together the necklace,
the large quetzal plumage;
from experience I recognize the jade,
they are the princes, O friends!
I look into their faces,
eagles and tigers on all sides;
from experience I recognize the jade
the precious bracelets . . .

(*Cantares mexicanos*, National Library of Mexico, fol. 16 v.)

ZAN YEHUAN

Zan yehuan,
Ipal nemohua.
Ninentlamatia,
Ac azo aic ic? *Ohuaya.*
Ac azo aic?
Nonahuiya in tenahuacan, *ohuaya, ohuaya.*

In zan tictlazotzetzelohua, *ohuaya,*
in motechpa ye huitz in monecuiltonol,
Ipal nemohua!
In izquixochitli, cacahuaxochitli,
zan noconelehuiya,
zan ninentlamatia, *ohuaya, ohuaya.*

HE ALONE

He alone,
the Giver of Life.
Empty wisdom had I.
Perhaps no one?
Perhaps no one?
I was not content at the side of the people.

Precious things you have poured down,
from you comes joy,
Giver of Life!
Sweet-smelling flowers, precious flowers,
with eagerness have I longed for them,
empty wisdom had I.

(*Romances de los señores de Nueva España,*
Benson Latin American Library, University of Texas, Austin, fol. 20 r.)

XON AHUIYACAN

Ica xon ahuiyacan ihuinti xochitli,
tomac mani, *aya.*
Ma on te ya aquiloto
xochicozquitl.
In toquiappancaxochiuh,
tla celia xochitli,
cueponia xochitli.

Oncan nemi tototl,
chachalaca, tlahoa, *hahaya*,
hual on quimati teotl ichan, *ohuaya, ohuaya.*
Zaniyo in toxochiuh
ica tonahuiyacan.
Zaniyo in cuicatl, *aya*,
ica on pupulihui in amotlaocol.
In tepilhuan ica yehua,
amelel on quiza, *ohuaya, ohuaya.*
Quiyocoya in Ipalnemohua, *aya*,
qui ya hualtemohuiya
moyocoyatzin,
in ayahauilo xochitli,
ica yehua amelel on quiza, *ohuaya, ohuaya.*

BE JOYFUL

Be joyful with the intoxicating flowers,
those which are in our hands.
Now put on
the necklaces of flowers.
Our flowers from the season of rain,
fragrant flowers,
now open their corollas.
There flies the bird,
he chatters and sings,
he has known the house of God.
Only with our flowers
we are happy.
Only with our songs
does sadness disappear.
O lords, in this way
your sorrow is put to flight.
The Giver of Life invents them,
he has sent them down,
the Inventor of Himself,
the joyous flowers,
with these your sorrow is put to flight.

(*Romances de los señores de Nueva España*,
Benson Latin American Library, University of Texas, Austin, fol. 19 r.)

CHAPTER III

CUACUAUHTZIN OF TEPECHPAN

Singer of Betrayed Friendship
(Middle Fifteenth Century)

Once Itzcoatl, high ruler of Mexico-Tenochtitlan, and the renowned sage Nezahualcoyotl, of Tezcoco, had subdued the Tepanecs, of Azcapotzalco, around 1431, they turned their attention to reorganizing their respective nations. Among other things, Nezahualcoyotl appointed the noble Tencoyotzin as governor of Tepechpan, a town located southwest of Teotihuacan, the ancient metropolis of the gods. Tepechpan was an important tributary of Tezcoco. The chronicler Ixtlilxochitl records that Tencoyotzin, as well as the local rulers of thirteen other jurisdictions including Acolman, Coatlinchan, Huexotla, and Otumba, attained at that time the rank of counselors in the court of Tezcoco.[1] The indigenous manuscript known as *Mapa Quinatzin*, of Tezcocan provenance, represents this event in a painting of Nezahualcoyotl's palaces with a large reception room in which the counselors each appear with the glyph for his name, including, of course, Tencoyotzin of Tepechpan.[2]

Another codex from the same region registers, year by year, the history of that place with drawings, glyphs, and glosses in Nahuatl.[3] Particularly interesting is the information it provides about Tepechpan at the time of the prosperous reign of Nezahualcoyotl. This codex confirms that Tepechpan was one of the most prosperous domains of Tezcoco.

Although there are discrepancies in the dates given by the *Quinatzin* and the *Tepechpan* codices, it is certain that Tencoyotzin died very young and was succeeded as governor by his son Cuacuauhtzin. According to Ixtlilxochitl, Cuacuauhtzin had taken part as captain in various wars against the enemies of Tezcoco and Mexico. In one of his campaigns he obtained a large quantity of gold and precious stones, mantles, plumage, and slaves as booty.[4] Part of this treasure he used for palace expenses and for adding splendor to his local court in Tepechpan. In addition he made a magnificent present to Temictzin, a Mexica of noble lineage, whose daughter, Azcalxochitzin, he wished to marry. According to the *Tepechpan codex*, Cuacuauhtzin attained his wish in the year 12-Flint (1440), and the young princess, who was "very beautiful and endowed with natural grace and charm," finally arrived at hs palace. Because Azcalxochitzin was still very young, Cuacuauhtzin decided to wait before consummating his marriage with her. He considered this union, so long desired, the principal constituent of his future hap-

Cuacuauhtzin, Lord of Tepechpan about the year 4-Cane (1431) (*Mapa de Tepechpan*)

piness. But instead of happiness, Azcalxochitzin was to bring him misfortune and even death, as happened soon afterwards.

Although the young princess was to be the cause of Cuacuauhtzin's misfortune, it was Nezahualcoyotl's destiny to become the real agent of the Tepechpan ruler's disgrace. In all other respects, Nezahualcoyotl had been wise and just, but Ixtlilxochitl, who tells the story, admits that in this matter he was to blame. However, to exonerate the poet king, he added, "although those who discovered this secret, his son and grandchildren, condemned him for this, being the worst thing Nezahualcoyotl did in his life, they found nothing else that could be considered evil or repugnant, accepting that in that episode love and passion had blinded him."[5] There is proof that Nezahualcoyotl felt guilty and came to repent his action in regard to Cuacuauhtzin, as is shown in one of his songs:

> I am sad, I grieve,
> I, the prince Nezahualcoyotl;
> with flowers and with songs
> I remember the princes,
> those who went away,
> Tezozomotzin and that one, Cuacuauhtzin.[6]

To understand Nezahualcoyotl's sorrow and Ixtlilxochitl's condemnation, one has to remember what happened when the king of Tezcoco, by mere chance, met the princess chosen by Cuacuauhtzin. The *Historia Tolteca-Chichimeca*, minimizing the matter in favor of Nezahualcoyotl, recalls that "having been fortunate in all his affairs . . . the lord of Tezcoco had not yet married according to the custom of his ancestors, which is to have one legal wife of whom were born his successors."[7] And the text adds that this caused him "great sadness and depression."

In this mood, one day Nezahualcoyotl left his palace to take a walk through the woods along the edge of the lake

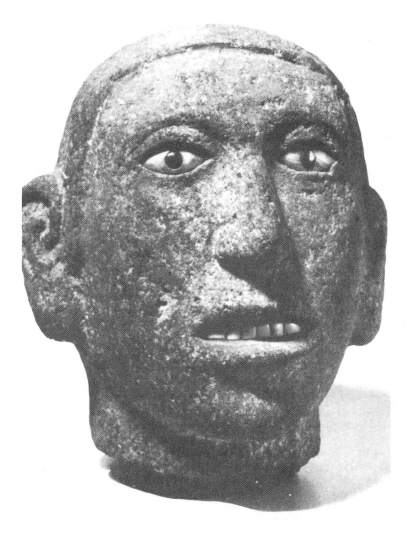

Head of a man. Aztec sculpture in stone, in the National Museum of
Anthropology, Mexico

until he came to Tepechpan. By coincidence Cuacuauhtzin saw him and, with the respect he owed to the high
ruler, invited him to enter his palace to rest and have
some food,

> That he should be better entertained Cuacuauhtzin had
> Azcalxochitzin serve him at the table . . . he was bringing up
> this young woman in order to marry her and make her his
> wife, but up till now he had not enjoyed her because she was
> not yet of an adequate age . . . King Nezahualcoyotl when he
> saw this young woman . . . , so very beautiful and endowed
> with such natural grace and charm, left behind all the de-
> pression and sadness he had brought with him, as she had
> stolen his heart. Concealing his passion as best he could, he
> took leave of this lord and went back to his court, where he
> ordered, with the greatest secrecy in the world, that Cua-
> cuauhtzin should be killed so that his deed would appear
> better.[8]

What happened shortly afterwards is strangely similar
to the story of David and Urias as told in the Old Testa-
ment. Cuacuauhtzin should be sent to take part in the
fighting against Tlaxcala. Two Tezcocan captains were
given instructions to place him in the most dangerous
position to insure his death there. Soon came the order
for the lord of Tepechpan to go out to the field of combat
in the vicinity of Tlaxcala. After some inquiries, Cuacuauhtzin realized Nezahualcoyotl's hidden motive but,
faithful to his lord, he obeyed and set out for the war that
was for him the same as marching to his death.

Cuacuauhtzin, besides being ruler of Tepechpan, was
also a composer of songs. Thus he was able to leave in his
poetry the testimony of his sadness. Ixtlilxochitl, the
principal recorder of this episode, makes this comment:
"Thus, suspecting his adverse fate, he composed some
pitiful songs which he sang at a farewell reunion with his
relatives and friends."[9]

Cuacuauhtzin perished in the war. His death, according to the *Tira de Tepechpan*, occurred in a year 3-Reed,
1443.[10] Nezahualcoyotl could then achieve what he de-

Woman of noble lineage. Aztec sculpture in stone in the National Museum of Anthropology, Mexico

sired. He made the princess Azcalxochitzin his wife. She was to give birth, among others, to the most famous of his sons, Nezahualpilli.

Besides the account of this intrigue offered by Ixtlil-xochitl, the testimony of the Tepechpan manuscript and the commentaries by other chroniclers, including Torquemada, we are fortunate in having transcriptions of the pitiful songs that Cuacuauhtzin composed and sang at the reunion he gave for his relatives and friends. These songs appear three different times in the pre-Hispanic collections, which clearly indicates that they were well known. They appear twice in the manuscript at the Mexican National Library and once more in the collection at the University of Texas.

CUACUAUHTZIN'S SONG OF SADNESS

Cuacuauhtzin, in the company of his friends for the last time, makes clear, in veiled form, the motive for his sadness. He recalls that during all his lifetime he has cultivated flowers and songs: "My heart desires them," but finding that he must go away forever, he now repeats that the very reality that had been the cause of his happiness is now the occasion of his sadness: "Now I only suffer with the songs . . . I crave the flowers, that they be in my hands . . . I am dispossessed."

He knows he is being sent to his death in the war. He would want to avoid it, and for that reason he asks his friends: "Where would we go that we never have to die?" But more than death itself and perhaps, even more than the loss of his princess, Cuacuauhtzin is tormented by the evil intention of Nezahualcoyotl, whom he had considered his friend. He refers to the lord of Tezcoco in his song, saying to him: "You make resound your kettle drum of jade, your blue and red conch shell."

Nezahualcoyotl is a composer of songs, a sage and a poet, but now his purpose is perfidious. Because of this, "the hearts of our friends are sorrowing." Cuacuauhtzin

Cuacuauhtzin with the young Azcalxochitzin, 13-Flint (1440). The text in Nahuatl says: "Cuacuauhtzin made the daughter of Temictzin of Mexico his wife." (*Mapa de Tepechpan*)

makes one further allusion. He addresses the absent and hostile Nezahualcoyotl by his nickname Yoyontzin, "Panting One," beseeching him not to give way to treachery but to let his heart open "to learn to tread the lofty heights." He says to him, "You have hated me, you have marked me for death, now I go to His house." Realizing his destiny is unescapable, he adds, foreseeing what is to happen: "Perhaps because of me you will weep . . . , you, my friend, but now I will go, now I am going."

The end of Cuacuauhtzin's poem is addressed to his friends, whom he has invited to the banquet. It is his legacy, his message: "Only useless effort . . . , enjoy, enjoy here my friends . . . I alone am in need, I, Cuacuauhtzin . . . I will take with me the beautiful flowers, the beautiful songs."

At the moment of his great misfortune, on the eve of his death planned by his poet friend, "flower and song" symbolism and the art of poetry remain the only means of easing his heart. Yet through those sad songs entoned at the reunion with his friends and relatives, Cuacuauhtzin's memory maintains for us its value and meaning, human indeed, as that of the great tragedies of other times and latitudes.

CUACUAHTZIN ICNOCUICATL

Quinenequi xochitli zan noyollo, *yehuaya,*
zan nomac on mani *ya.*
Zan nicuicanentlamati,
zan nicuicayeyecohua in tlalticpaqui,
oye, ni Cuacuauhtzin,
ninonconequi xochitl,
zan nomac on mani,
in ninentlamati,
aya, ayeyo, ohuaya, ohuia.

Can nelpa tonyazque
in aic timiquizque.
Ma zan ni chalchihuitl,
ni teocuitlal,
zan ye on nipitzaloz,
on nimamalihuaz in tlatillan, *oo.*
Zan noyoliyo,
ni Cuacuahtzin, zan ninentlamati
aya, ayeyo, ohuaya, ohuiya.

Mochalchiuhteponaz,
in moxiuhquecholquiquiz,
yuh tocon ya pitza,
zan ye ti Yoyontzin.
In o ya hual acic,
on ya moquetza in cuicanitl, *yohuiya.*
Cuel zan xon ahuiyacan,
ma ya hualmoquetza
a inyollo in cocohua,
in o ya hual acic
on ya moquetza in cuicanitl, *y yohuiya.*

In ma moyollo motoma,
in ma ya moyollo acotinemi.
Tinechcocolia,
tinechmiquitlani.
In nonoya ye ichan,
ninopolihui.
Ac azo yo oc ic noca xi hual choca,
noca xi hual icnotlamati,

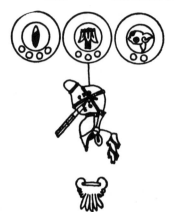

Cuacuauhtzin dies in battle, 3-Cane
(1443) (*Mapa de Tepechpan*)

zan tinocniuh,
zan ye niyauh,
zan ye niyauh ye ichan, *ohuaya, ohuaya.*
Zan quitohua noyollo,
ayoc ceppa ye nihuitz,
ayoc ceppa niquizaquiuh in yece in tlaticpac,
zan ye niyauh, zan ye niyauh ye ichan, *ohuaya, ohuaya.*

Zan nen tequitl,
Xon ahuiyacan *huiya,*
xon ahuiyaca, tocnihuan, *huiya*
Ha tamonahuizque,
ha tahuellamatizque, tocnihuan? *Huiya, ohuaya, ohuaya.*
Ca niccuiz in yectli xochitli,
in yectli yan cuicatl, *hahuayya, ohuaya, ohuaya.*

O aic in xopan niquichihua,
nican zan ninotolinia,
zan ye ni Cuacuahtzin, *huiya.*
Ha tamonahuiyazque,
ha tahuellamatizque, tocnihuan, *ohuaya.*
Ca niccuiz in yectla xochitli,
in yectli yan cuicatl
Hahahuaya, ohuaya, ohuaya.

SAD SONG OF CUACUAUHTZIN

My heart craves the flowers,
that they be in my hands.
With songs I am saddened,
I only try to compose songs on the earth.
I, Cuacuauhtzin,
with anxiety I desire the flowers,
that they be in my hands,
for I am dispossessed.

Where would we go
that we never have to die?
Though I be precious stone,
though I be gold,
I will be dissolved,
there in the crucible melted down,
I have only my life,
I, Cuacuauhtzin, I am dispossessed.

You make resound
your kettle drum of jade,
your red and blue conch shell,
you, Yoyontzin, Panting One,
Now he has come,
now the singer has risen.
For a short time be happy,
come and be present,
those with the sad heart.
Now he has come,
now the singer has risen.

Open the corolla of your heart,
let it tread the lofty heights.
You have hated me,
you have marked me for death.
Now I go to His house,
I will perish.
Perhaps because of me you will weep,
because of me you will be sad,
you, my friend,

Tributaries of Tezcoco, among which appears the lord of Tepechpan (*Códice Xolotl*, viii)

but now I will go,
now I am going to His house.
Only this my heart tells,
I will not return,
never will come back to the earth,
now I will go, I am going to His house.

Only useless effort,
enjoy, enjoy, my friends.
Should we not be happy,
should we not have pleasure, my friends?
I will take with me the beautiful flowers,
the beautiful songs.

Never I do it in springtime,
I alone am in need,
alone am I, Cuacuauhtzin.
Should we not enjoy, my friends?
I will take with me the beautiful flowers,
the beautiful songs.

(*Romances de los señores de Nueva España,*
Benson Latin American Library, University of Texas, Austin, fols. 26 r.–27 v.)

CHAPTER IV

NEZAHUALPILLI

Sage and Poet, Successor to Nezahualcoyotl
(11-Flint, 1464–10-Reed, 1515)

Friar Juan de Torquemada, writing about Nezahualpilli in his *Monarquía indiana,* has this to say:

> Our Tezcocan Nezahualpilli was not one of those who could complain that nature had been sparing in giving him much and very good reasoning and a noble understanding, by means of which he knew how to rule and govern all the years of his reign. And with this understanding he made himself lord, not only of the hearts of his vassals, but also of all the kings and lords who had dealings with him and who benefitted from his opinions and knowledge.[1]

Other testimonies about Nezahualpilli agree entirely with Torquemada's opinion. Among the high rulers of Tezcoco, only Nezahualpilli's father, Nezahualcoyotl, attained greater glory and renown in that metropolis where, in the fifteenth century, the ancient Toltec culture was reborn.

An abundance of information has survived concerning the life of Nezahualpilli. As is the case with other famous personages, in addition to the actual facts, there are many anecdotes about him. Although some of these sound like myths, they give us a view of the image his people came to develop of their learned lord. There were legends about both his birth and his death. Torquemada records that "His people took him to be a sorcerer.... About his childhood they said that his nurses, while caring for him, often saw him in his cradle in the form of different animals; sometimes he appeared to them as a lion, sometimes a tiger, or an eagle flying."[2]

His descendant, the chronicler Ixtlilxochitl, telling of his death in the palace of Tecpilpan, related that "he withdrew to the most remote of his palaces where sad, thoughtful, and filled with anxiety, he finished his life."[3] Afterward, the event was kept secret and for some time his vassals believed "that their king Nezahualpilli had not died, but had gone to reign in the northern regions. And they said that it was the time he foretold that he would go away to govern them."[4]

Thus the memory of the birth and death of Nezahualpilli remain wrapped in myth and legend. But in the more precise field of history his actions as ruler and the principal events in his life as a wise man, poet, orator, architect, and astronomer were set down. Nezahualpilli began to rule over Tezcoco while still a child. Ixtlilxochitl says that

> Nezahualcoyotl being near to death, ordered one morning that [his son] Prince Nezahualpilli be brought, who was seven years of age or a little more, and taking him in his arms, he covered him with the royal vestments he was wearing, and he ordered the ambassadors of the kings of Mexico and Tlacopan to come in.... And then he said to them: You see here our prince, your lord, although a child, wise and prudent, who will keep you in peace and justice, maintaining you in your rank and command, and whom you will obey as loyal vassals.[5]

Nezahualpilli began to govern with the assistance of the noble Acapioltzin, who guided and advised him during his younger years. He had to participate in several wars and conquests together with his Mexica allies. The indigenous annals state that he distinguished himself as a captain in the campaigns against the Totonaca and in the Oaxaca region, as well as in the wars that were carried on at regular intervals against the neighboring chiefdoms of Huexotzinco, Atlixco, and Tlaxcala.

But it was not in wars and conquests that the face and heart of Nezahualpilli won greatest renown. Being scrupulously just, he not only promulgated laws, as his father had done before him, but when necessary he also applied them to those related to him by blood or affection. In his first choice of a wife and queen of Tezcoco, Nezahualpilli had a sad experience. Ixtlilxochitl records the episode, a story of court intrigues with such pungent human interest that it has been retold by more than one modern writer, including the Spaniard Salvador de Madariaga in his novel *Heart of Jade*.

Nezahualpilli, anxious to find a wife and queen, had princesses and daughters of nobles brought from different places. The young Mexica girl Chalchiuhnenetzin, daughter of Axayacatl, high ruler of Mexico, attracted him above all. But although Princess Chalchiuhnenetzin had every grace and charm, in her heart she was prone to sensual delights and prohibited pleasures. Thus she began

> to show a thousand weaknesses, and whatever gallant youth or lord appeared to her pleasant and charming, she secretly ordered him to come to possess her and, having satisfied her lust, she had him killed. Then she would order a statue or a portrait made of him and, having adorned it with rich garments, jewels of gold and precious stones, she put it in her own room. There were so many statutes of those she had killed that they were round about almost the entire room. And when the king [Nezahualpilli] went to visit her and asked about these statues, she replied that they were her gods.[6]

Chalchiuhnenetzin's fickleness, transformed into crimes, was finally discovered. When the facts of the case were known, Nezahualpilli, very distressed, had to dispense justice. Chalchiuhnenetzin, in spite of being the daughter of Axayacatl, the ruler of Mexico, paid with her life for her infidelity and her crimes.

Years later, Nezahualpilli, though married, still did not escape other forms of involvement in which his devotion to justice appears strangely intertwined with his love for women and his interest in poetry. Among the various concubines of this lord of Tezcoco was one, known as the "Lady of Tula," who had stolen his heart. Ixtlilxochitl explains that they called her by that name, "not because of her lineage, for she was the daughter of a merchant, but because she was so learned that she could discuss with the king and the wisest men in his kingdom, and she was very gifted in poetry. With these graces and natural gifts she held the king subject to her will so that whatever she wished, she obtained from him."[7]

About this time Nezahualpilli's eldest son, Huexotzincatzin, who also was said to be a good poet, began to notice his father's concubine, "and he composed a satire to the Lady of Tula. And as she herself was versed in the art of poetry, the two went along giving and receiving their compositions, for which it was suspected that he was making advances to her and the affair became a matter for judgment which, according to the law, was treason against the king, and he who was guilty, was condemned to death."[8]

Thus this was an affair in which all those involved were also lovers of poetry. Nezahualpilli, considering it carefully, and although sick at heart, determined to apply the law and passed the death sentence on his son.

A remarkable testimony has come down to us, included in a huehuehtlahtolli, "Speech of the Elders," the tradition of "The Ancient Word," in which an old man, survivor of the Spanish Conquest, relates this same episode: "And thus I also saw how they hanged lord Huexotzincatzin; he was the eldest son of the Lord, ruler Nezahual-

Birth of Nezahualpilli; above, the day 12-Serpent, and below, in Tezcoco the year 11-Flint (1464) (*Códice en cruz*, plate ii)

pilli. They executed him because he had composed songs to the lady of Tula, his stepmother, who was among the women of the lord [Nezahualpilli]."[9]

To make clear that if the high ruler of Tezcoco was extremely stern in his application of justice, he was also deeply humane, the same witness adds the following: "And he went to keep apart from others in his palace, he, Lord Nezahualpilli, had named "The Palace of Tears," because he wept very much over the death of his beloved son."[10]

Ixtlilxochitl records another case in which justice and poetry also played a key role. Nezahualpilli attended a feast being held in one of his palaces. Among those invited was the wife of a noble named Teanatzin. To her misfortune, Teanatzin's wife, who had developed a strong inclination toward Nezahualpilli, told him of her feelings. Pleased, the lord of Tezcoco decided to have his pleasure with her. Only later did Nezahualpilli learn that this woman was married. Teanatzin's wife had committed adultery and had incited the high ruler to do likewise. The law in this case stated that the woman should die. But there is a sequel to the story in which poetry once more played a part.

Teanatzin, who still loved his wife in spite of this offense, when he learned of the decision, said that "Once the king has enjoyed her, why should she have to die? To allow her to live and thus not lose, as he would lose, a woman whom he loved so much, seemed to him more reasonable."[11]

Nezahualpilli, hearing this argument, was offended because it seemed to him that it showed "little regard for the honor of the king" and had Teanatzin put to prison. At last the story has a happy ending through the medium of poetry:

> Teanatzin, finding himself in his lengthy and dark prison, composed a very elegant song in which he described all his

tragedy and his troubles. And, by an arrangement he made with some friends and acquaintances who were the king's musicians, as a favor they found a way and means of singing that song at one of the king's feasts and balls. Which song had such emotional and persuasive words that it moved the king's heart to compassion and thus he ordered him released from prison immediately.[12]

There are other anecdotes that show Nezahualpilli's respect for justice and his love of the arts and poetry. But, naturally, not everything in his life was related to poetry. There are also episodes in which the lord of Tezcoco appears obliged to take part in the wars and conquests undertaken by his powerful allies, the Mexica. It was his destiny to live a complicated life and, as in the case of his father Nezahualcoyotl, circumstances often required him to take positions that seem contradictory.

For instance, although at the insistence of the Mexica, Nezahualpilli had to dedicate a temple in honor of Huitzilopochtli, he privately held to the religious beliefs he and his father had cultivated as part of their acceptance of the Toltec traditions. In this respect, as Torquemada says, at least in public this wise ruler "had to follow the opinion of those more powerful, especially the kings of Mexico who were his relatives and kinsmen . . . and though he was incited by these same Mexicans, on the whole he did not follow much their opinion nor did he appear much inclined to their religious practices."[13]

His discourses and what is known of his poetry bear witness that in his heart he followed the ancient faith of Tloqueh Nahuaqueh, Lord of the Close and Near, the supreme God of Duality, inventor of humans and of everything that exists on the earth. Whenever Nezahualpilli had the possibility to free himself from his administrative duties and his obligations as the ruler of a chiefdom that was a member of the Triple Alliance, he gave his attention to matters more important to him. Among other interests, he felt inclined to observe the movements of the celestial bodies: "He took pride in his understanding of the movements of the celestial bodies. . . . He made inquiries throughout all parts of his realm for those who knew anything about this . . . and told them all he knew. At night he went up on the roof of his palace and from there observed the stars and discussed with all those who asked about them."[14]

Like his father, he also advised neighboring rulers, especially the Mexica, concerning good government and matters that today would be considered technical. The *Anales*, among other things, recall the advice he gave on the occasion of the flood in Mexico-Tenochtitlan in the days of the high ruler Ahuitzotl, who had brought water to the city from the spring called Acuecuexatl in the vicinity of Coyoacan. Following a design by Nezahualpilli, a large water reservoir was built of stone and mortar that controlled the water supply without further damage to the Mexica capital.

The prestige of Nezahualpilli continued to increase throughout his lifetime. Although respected by the Mexica, he had disagreements with them on more than one occasion. Particularly after Motecuhzoma Xocoyotzin assumed command, the lord of Tezcoco had to adopt a defensive attitude against the intrigues originating in Tenochtitlan. This must have been very painful for Nezahualpilli, who had taken an active part in the election of Motecuhzoma and had given the principal address when the latter was installed, describing the new ruler's merits. Nezahualpilli's words on that circumstance are further testimony to his literary ability. Torquemada notes that "the memory of his speech, certainly very eloquent, was preserved for a long time."[15] Although the original text in Nahuatl is unknown today, the more or less paraphrased version transcribed by the historian shows Nezahualpilli's depth of thought and his own personal religiosity. Speaking before Motecuhzoma and the other leaders of Mexico, he expressed himself as follows:

The great good fortune which has come to this entire kingdom of being worthy to have you as its head, most noble lord, is well recognized in the facility and harmony of your election, as well as in the general happiness which all show in regard to it. And certainly this is entirely right, because the Mexican empire is now so large and so extended that it requires all the strength and courage of your firm and noble heart, all the calmness, wisdom, and prudence you possess to rule such a world and carry such a heavy burden.

I see clearly that the all omnipotent God Tloqueh Nahuaqueh loves this city, for He has given it the light to search for what it needs. Can anyone doubt that a prince who accepts the responsibility of the kingdom after having studied the nine levels of the heavens will accomplish, with his keen insight, the things of this earth which are necessary to assist his people? Can anyone doubt that the great strength which you have so valiantly shown in time of stress will now be more than enough for all that is necessary? Can anyone imagine that in such valor there will be any lack of assistance for orphans and widows? Can anyone fail to realize that the Mexican empire has now arrived at the summit of its authority, for the Lord of creation, Tloqueh Nahuaqueh, has given you [Motecuhzoma] so much that, only looking at you, it is communicated to those who see you?

Rejoice, O fortunate land, that the Creator has given you a prince who will be a firm pillar on which to lean. He will be father and protector to aid you; he will be more than brother in piety and compassion for your own. Most certainly you have a king who will not take advantage of his position to enjoy himself, to lie abed, or be occupied with amusements and vices; before restful sleep, his heart will rouse him and keep him vigilant in the cares he must have for you. The most tasty morsel from his table he will not notice, his imagination occupied with your well-being. Tell me then, O fortunate kingdom, if I am right in saying that you now rejoice and take heart with such a king?

And you, O most magnanimous young man and powerful lord, have confidence and courage for the Lord of all that is created [Tloqueh Nahuaqueh], who has given you this position, also will give His strength to uphold it. And you may be confident that He Who has been so generous with you in times past, will not deny you His greatest gifts once He has placed you in this high office, of which may you remain in possession for many and good years.[16]

Lack of space prevents further mention of other anecdotes and events in the life of Nezahualpilli. Unfortunately, there is no adequate biography about him, notwithstanding the relatively abundant information that can be found in the sources. Suffice it to mention the *Anales de Cuauhtitlan*, the works of the Tezcocan chronicler Juan de Pomar and of Fernando Alvarado Tezozomoc, and those of the historians Diego Durán and Juan de Torquemada, on whose testimonies one can rely to depict the most relevant traits of the face and heart of Prince Nezahualpilli.

NEZAHUALPILLI AS A POET

Ancient Mexican songs mention Nezahualpilli often and exalt his gifts as ciucapicqui, "composer of poetry." Unfortunately, not much of his work survived the general destruction. Although there are some thirty compositions by his father, only one icnocuicatl, "song of sadness," a sort of elegy, can be attributed to Nezahualpilli. In it he recalls a well-known historic event, the death of the princes Macuilmalinatzin and Tlacahuepan in Atlixco during the war with Huexotzinco.

Ixtlilxochitl mentions this song as an example of the eloquence of the learned lord who contemplated the stars and venerated Tloqueh Nahuaqueh. He also provides the title of this elegy, *Nenahualizcuicatl*, which means "Song That Makes Known Disloyalty and Deceit," especially the fraudulent deceit of war that resulted in the death of two Mexica princes, much esteemed friends of Nezahualpilli.[17] Prince Tlacahuepan in particular was so greatly admired that, as we will see, other poets such as Teoxinmac and several anonymous composers of songs have left compositions describing his deeds.

The sadness of the song is set forth along with the dazzling picture of war, as "water, fire," the florid liquor that intoxicates in the region of smoke, there where the eagle screams and the tiger incites to battle. Nezahualpilli drew an extraordinary picture of war but with no idea of making an apology for it nor explaining the causes of the struggle undertaken by his Mexica allies. For him war is an intoxication. The warriors exclaim: "Again and again I drink the flowering liquor. . . . Let them share the precious flowery nectar!"

Throughout the poem those who fight are spoken of repeatedly as *cuextecas,* an ethnic group in ancient Mexico, an allusion to the myth of the almost chronic drunkenness of that people. Drunkenness disfigures faces; war does away with everything. It is the complete destruction of jade and quetzal plumage, the symbols of beauty. The warriors are "intoxicated by death"; they are like cuextecas; blinded by the flowery liquor, their duty is to kill and to die.

Men are covered with glory in war, but their friends also die there. The owners of the flowers have to go away to the region of mystery. Their faces, covered with blood, turn yellow. They have to be bathed with the flowery liquor of war before being carried to the place where the corpses are buried. They were intoxicated, and they are made drunk once more. The eagle screamed and the tiger howled. In the midst of this dance of death, friends are departing for the region of mystery.

The remembrance of this is cause of intense grief. Nezahualpilli insists that it makes him weep. With the vision of war in his heart, he feels as if he were also intoxicated, possessed by the liquor that breeds death. But if, in his recollection of that war that brought the death of his friends, Nezahualpilli touches upon the inescapable destiny of the Mexica, at the same time he condemns those struggles in which jades, quetzal plumages, and human faces are torn down. Perhaps it could be added that Nezahualpilli, the composer of songs and observer of the stars, where peace reigns and the Giver of Life dwells, has brought his message down to our times in his poem. A rejection of violence that arose out of a world where war

Nezahualpilli at eight years of age began his reign, 6-Flint (1472) (*Códice en cruz*, plate ii)

was destiny acquires new meaning for us, still unable to avoid such intoxication invented by man to do away with himself.

The personality and deeds of Nezahualpilli need to be comprehensively studied. These few pages are merely a brief introduction. Although his life was comparatively short, his accomplishments as lord of Tezcoco were far reaching. As Ixtlilxochitl has recorded:

> He ruled forty-four years, at the end of which time, being fifty-one years old, which was very little in comparison with the age of his ancestors, he died from grief over certain disputes he had, especially because of the great pride of Motecuhzoma who had used treason against him. And thus it happened that many of the common people who did not attend his burial and funeral rites, believed him to be alive and bewitched in some cave. And even until today some old people with little understanding hold this opinion.[18]

ICUIC NEZAHUALPILLI
YC TLAMATO HUEXOTZINCO

Nihuintian, *aya,*
yhuintia noyollo:
Tlahuizcalla moquetza ya,

o tlahtohua ya zaquanquechol
chimaltenanticpac,
tlacochtenanticpac.

Ximocuiltono, ti Tlacahuepan,
tinohueyo, quaxomotl,
quaxomocuextecatl, *ayoo.*
Zan teoaxochioctla yc yhuintic,
ye oncan totoatenpan,
aya quaxomotl, *aya.*

Yn chalchiuhtli teteyca,
quetzalli popoztequi,
a nohueyotepilhuanytzin,
miquiztlahuanque,
yc oncan amillan ypano,
atempan, *aya a*
y mexica y mehetla.

Yn quauhtli ya pipitzcan,
ocelotl chocatica,
tinopiltzin, Macuilmalinalli,
zan ye oncan poctlan,
tlapallan,
yecoya [o] chihua
o yn mexica, *a* . . .

In ye o nihuintic, ye nicuextecatl,
y ye nixochiquaxoxo, ya,
nictotoyahua ye xochiaoctli,
ya, ye, oya, ye, oya, ye, aye, ayeo.
In ma temacon quetzalocoxochitl,
nopiltzin,
titlahpaliuhquetl,
yn ye nixoxoya.

In teotl y mancan,
yahue ompozontimani,
teoaxochioctica *ya, a,*
ihuinti in mexicame.
Chichimecatl *aya* noconilnamiquia,
zan nichoca, *y hue.*

Ic aya yyahue onnichoca ya ni Nezahualpilli,
noconilnamiqui.
Zan iya mani,
ompa ye cueponi a yaoxochitl,
y ya noconilnamiqui a can nichoca, *y hue.*

Ciliquipan Chailtzin,
aytzin, mahuia.
Ixtlilcuechahuac yca ye onmahuiztia,
quinamoya in quetzalli,
patzaconxiuhquiyamoya cuextecatl, *ahua,* quen.
Atl ia yxtla,
yhtec tlachinolacueyotl,
y topan yc pozonipilia Ixtlilotoncochotzin,
a ycan ye mahuiztia,
quinamoya y quetzal,
y patzaconxiuhquiyamoya.

Yn quetzalaxomotzin ompapatlantia,
noxochihueyotzin, yn Tlacahuepantzin, *aya,*
zan quitocan tochin teuctlapaliuhquetl,
yn cuexteca meyetla.

A ytec o cuica ya,
a ontlahtoa *oo yaye y.*
Yn zan quitlahuana, chachalaca,
in quecholpohuan in tecpilli,
ya yn cuexteca meetla.
Oyatihuintique notatahuan,
tlapalyhuintitly.
Ma nemaytitotilo ya!
Za can ye ichan huehuexochihuaque,
a za quetzalchimaleque,
ye tlatileque ya,
yolimale ya,
anca quimittotia.
Ini huatzalhuan
huehuexochihuaque,
o za quetzalchimaleque.

Yezo yahqui nopillotzin,
cozahuic cuexteca totec,

tzapocueye,
Tlacahuepan motimalohua,
ya quenonamican,
ayyaye aye oya yayaa.

Yaoxochioctica,
yhuintitiaqui a nopillotzin,
cozahuic cuexteca totec.
Ye onmahpantia yn teoaxochiaoctli yn Matlaccuiatzin.
O cen yahque quenomamican, *yyao yayea.*

Yn teoaticaya tlac yhcuilihuitiquetl,
ya nohueyo nopiltzin Nezahualpilaya,
chimalli xochioctla ica ihuintique,
a ye oncan cuexteca,
netotilo aya in Atlixco, yayyaya.

Zannoconyapitza ya
yn oceloacaquiquiz,
za onquauhtzatziticac
in notemalacac,
ipan tecpilli.
Yahqui ya y huehuehtzin,
y chimalli xochioctla yca
yhuintihua ye oncan cuexteca,
netotilo ya yn Atlixco, *ya.*

Moteoxiuhhuehueuh xictzotzona *ya,*
xochiahacuinta y metl,
y moxochicozqui,
mahci aztatzonyhua
timotlac ya yhicuilo,
Yayocaque, ye onnemi,
y xochiquaxoxome,
Yn tlahpaliuhquetl,
a ocelochimaleque mocuenpan i, *hue.*

Zan ye onnentlamati y noyolio,
nitlahpalihuiquetl ni Nezahualpil, *ya.*
Zan niquintemoa machihua,
o yahquin teuctli,
a xochiquetzal, *ya,*

yahqui tlapaliuhquetl,
ylhuicaxoxohuic ichan.
Tlatohuatzin in Acapipiyol mach,
ocquihualya xochiaoctli *y ya,*
ye nican nichoca ica, *ohuaya.*

SONG OF NEZAHUALPILLI DURING THE WAR WITH HUEXOTZINCO

I am intoxicated,
intoxicated is my heart:
Day is dawning,
already the *zacuan* bird is singing
above the inclosure of shields,
above the inclosure of darts.

Be merry, you, Tlacahuepan,
you, our neighbor, of shaven head,
like a Cuexteca with shaven head.
Drunk with the liquor of flowery waters,
there at the edge of the water of the birds,
shaven head.

The jade and plumes of quetzal
with stones have been torn down,
my great lords, those intoxicated with death,
there on the ground planted in water,
at the edge of the water,
the Mexica in the land of the cactus.

The eagle screams,
the jaguar howls,
and you, o my prince, Macuilmalinalli,
here, in the region of smoke,
in the land of red color.
Bravely the Mexica are fighting.

I am intoxicated, I, Cuexteca,
I of the flowery shaven hair,
again and again I drink the flowering liquor.
Let them pass the precious flowery nectar,
O my son,

you, young man and strong,
I grow pale.

Where the divine waters spread out,
there they are inflamed with passion,
the Mexica intoxicated
with the flowery liquor of the gods.
I remember now the Chichimec,
only for this am I saddened,
For this I moan, I Nezahualpilli,
now I remember him.
Alone he is there,
where the flowers of war open their corollas,
I remember him and for this now I weep.

Above the bells, Chailtzin
within the waters rejoices.
with this Ixtlilcuechahuac achieves renown,
takes possession of the quetzal plumage,
the Cuexteca takes the turquoises.
Before the face of the water, within the battle,
under the spell of water and fire,
Ixtlilotoncochotzin rises up in fury,
with this he achieves renown,
he takes possession of the quetzal plumage,
he takes the turquoises.

The bird of the fine plumage is flying,
Tlacahuepatzin, my possessor of flowers;
like rabbits he pursues them, the strong youth,
the Cuexteca in the land of the cactus.

Within the waters they sing,
the divine flowers call out.
They are intoxicated, they shout,
the princes who look like precious birds,
the Cuextecas in the land of the cactus.
Our fathers are intoxicated,
the intoxication of strength.
Begin the dance!
To his house have gone those with the spoiled flowers,
those who had plumed shields,

those who guarded the heights,
those who took prisoners alive,
now they dance.
Vomiting blood they go
the owners of the spoiled flowers,
those of the flowery shields.

Stained with blood my prince goes,
our yellow lord of the Cuexteca,
the one of the dark-zapote skirt,
Tlacahuepan is exalted
Where-One-Somehow-Exists.

With the flower of the liquor of war
my prince has become intoxicated,
our yellow lord of the Cuexteca.
Matlaccuiatzin is bathed with the liquor of war,
together they go to Where-One-Somehow-Exists.

With divine water, the one of painted torso,
my great, my prince, who as Nezahualpilli behaves,
there the Cuexteca are intoxicated
with the shield's flowery liquor,
a dance is performed in Atlixco.

Make resound
your trumpet of the tigers,
the eagle screams,
upon the circular stone
where the gladiatorial fight takes place.
The old men are leaving,
there the Cuexteca are intoxicated
with the shield's flowery liquor,
a dance is performed in Atlixco.

Make resound your turquoise drum,
inebriated cactus, with flowery water.
your necklace of flowers,
your pendant of heron feathers,
you of the painted body.
Now they hear it,
the birds with flowery heads

accompany the strong youth,
the owner of the shield of the tiger, who came back.

My heart is sad,
I am young Nezahualpilli.
I look for my captains,
the lord has gone,
the flowering quetzal,
the young and strong warrior has gone,
the blue of the sky is his house.
Perhaps Tlatohuetzin and Acapipiyol will come
to drink the flowery liquor,
here where I weep?

(*Cantares mexicanos*, National Library of Mexico, fols. 55 v. and 56 r.)

CHAPTER V

CACAMATZIN OF TEZCOCO

*Ruler and Poet Who Had
a Brief and Tragic Life
(Ca. 2-Rabbit, 1494–2-Flint, 1520)*

Cacamatzin could rightly claim descent from the most illustrious family in Tezcoco, which was well known through several of its members, wise rulers and famous poets. Son of Nezahualpilli and grandson of Nezahual-coyotl, Cacamatzin (as well as his many brothers) was probably guided in his education from childhood by the memory of his grandfather and the teachings of his father.

Apparently Cacamatzin was born around 1494. His father, Nezahualpilli, famous in history for his many accomplishments, was also famous for the number of women he had loved and for the even greater number of children he had brought into the world. Although, according to most chroniclers, Cacamatzin was not a legitimate son of Nezahualpilli, he had the good fortune, which later proved to be a disgrace, of being the offspring of a love affair between the lord of Tezcoco and a sister of Motecuhzoma Xocoyotzin. As a nephew of the great Mexica ruler, Caca-matzin became his protégé and, under his sponsorship but against the wishes of others, succeeded his father as ruler of Tezcoco.

Cacamatzin's life is another example of the double role played by many composers of songs in the Nahuatl world. He passed his brief existence in an environment where not only the arts and the glory of power but also betrayal and tragedy thrived. While still a child, he knew that his elder brother, the prince and poet Huexotzincatzin, had been condemned to death for the illicit relations he had with one of his father's concubines, nicknamed "Lady of Tula" because of her charm and ability in art and poetry. Cacamatzin admired his father's great intellectual gifts. He saw him conversing with wise men, knew the songs he composed, his ability as an architect, and his dedication to observe the stars. But he was deeply distressed over the by-then obvious disagreements between Nezahualpilli and his uncle Motecuhzoma. He was particularly saddened by the death of the Mexica prince Macuilmalinatzin, son of his uncle and husband of one of his own sisters. He knew that Macuilmalinatzin had been the victim of a treachery that, according to Nezahualpilli's version of the story, the Tezcocans attributed to Motecuhzoma.

Like other members of the nobility, Cacamatzin attended the calmecac (center of higher education or priestly school) in Tezcoco and later was trained in the arts of war. With his father and other captains, he took part in various campaigns. Living in the midst of Tezcocan splendor and the extraordinary power of the Mexica but in an atmosphere of hidden hostility, he became aware of the attitude developed by his father that made him withdraw from others. One day in 10-Reed (1515), when he was only twenty-one years old, he was told that his father had retired to be alone in one of his palaces. Shortly afterwards he learned of his death.

The following year, 11-Flint (1516), brought days of great uncertainly for the people and the nobility of Tezcoco, particularly for Cacamatzin and his brothers, Ixtlilxochitl and Coanacochtzin, as to who would succeed

Nezahualpilli as new ruler. Discord broke out, and soon the strong hand of Motecuhzoma was felt in Tezcoco. The *Historia Tolteca-Chichimeca* tells how the Mexica lord, at that moment,

> sent his ambassadors so that, together with the electors and leaders in the kingdom, they should give their votes to his nephew Cacamatzin, since they say that he liked him very much. He was old enough to be able to rule, and in past wars he had proven well his courage and was a very brave captain. And being decided who was to rule, all the elders and lords should come with his nephew to the City of Mexico, where he wanted him to take the oath, as it had been the case with his father and grandfather.[1]

In spite of the open intervention of Motecuhzoma, Cacamatzin's rivals in the Tezcocan court were not discouraged. At first, the name of the prince Tetlahuehuetzquitzin had been mentioned, but it was decided that he was "not competent to reign and govern a kingdom so great as that of Tezcoco."[2]

Thus the contest was finally between Prince Ixtlilxochitl, said to be "an extremely courageous youth," and Cacamatzin, who had the support of his brother Coanacochtzin and, what is more important, the firm decision of Motecuhzoma.

In the midst of such dissension Cacamatzin went to Mexico, where shortly afterwards he was consecrated as ruler. Two different reactions to this accomplished fact developed. On the one hand, Coanacochtzin and other nobles of Tezcoco recognized Cacamatzin as sovereign. But on the other hand, Prince Ixtlilxochitl, who considered his brother's election an act of despotism on the part of Motecuhzoma, left Tezcoco and retired north, toward the Metztitlan Hills. There he won the support of various tributary chiefs and collected a strong army with which to attack Cacamatzin. It was only due to the prompt action of Motecuhzoma, who also resorted to the force of

Cacamatzin, son of Neza-
hualpilli and unfortunate
lord of Tezcoco. His reign
began in the year 1-Cane
(1515). (*Códice florentino*,
viii)

arms, that Cacamatzin could return to Tezcoco and resist
Ixtlilxochitl from there.

The ancient prosperity of Tezcoco went into decline.
The kingdom was sadly divided. Cacamatzin held the
capital and the southern provinces; Ixtlilxochitl, who
considered himself the legitimate ruler, controlled the
northern dominions. The strife continued when messengers from the Gulf Coast brought reports of the arrival
of boats so large that they looked like mountains, with
men aboard of unknown faces and speech. Motecuhzoma
was more disturbed than anyone else on hearing the information brought by his messengers. The texts in which
the *Vision of the Vanquished* is preserved describe in detail the growing concern of the Mexica lord.[3]

By the year 1-Reed (1519), reports about the strange foreigners who brought with them weapons that spit forth
fire and animals so high that they were taller than deer
began to disturb Motecuhzoma far more than the difficulties in the kingdom of Tezcoco. He called many priests and
sages to ask them what the meaning of the presence of
the mysterious beings could be. Opinions differed. Some
thought that it had to do with the announced return of
Quetzalcoatl. Others pointed out the possibility that the
foreigners were enemies capable of crushing the Mexica
power. In this critical situation, probably remembering

that formerly the wise advice of the Tezcocans, especially Nezahualcoyotl and Nezahualpilli, had been asked, Motecuhzoma called Cacamatzin and other counselors, including his own brother Cuitlahuac, to his court.

Although, because of his youth and the prevailing disturbances of his chiefdom, Cacamatzin did not enjoy the prestige of his father or his grandfather, Motecuhzoma nevertheless wanted to hear his opinion. Cacamatzin, Cuitlahuac, and the other counselors assembled with him in Tenochtitlan to hear the reports and descriptions of those who had landed on the eastern coast of Mexico. Consulted by Motecuhzoma as to what should be done, Cuitlahuac was of the opinion that it would be better to confront them from the very beginning and not allow them to approach the Mexica metropolis. Cacamatzin advised differently. Perhaps thinking that it could be the return of Quetzalcoatl, confident in the Mexica power and in the wisdom of his uncle Motecuhzoma, he declared that it would be an act of weakness to shut off all contact with those whose intentions were not even known. It would be better to receive them as possible ambassadors from a great ruler until their true objectives were known, and then, if they were hostile, there would be more than sufficient force of arms to drive them out of the Mexica domain.

Cacamatzin's advice seemed correct to some, but actually Motechuzoma did not follow it, nor did he follow that of Cuitlahuac. He did not send his army to harass the foreigners or to prevent them from advancing, nor did he decide to welcome them and eventually receive them in his court at Tenochtitlan. Uncertain in his own mind, he tried with gifts and messages to persuade the foreigners not to come to Mexico.

The history that describes the consequences of Motecuhzoma's hesitation, in contrast to the positive determination of Hernán Cortés to penetrate to the very heart of the Mexica dominions, is well known. And what Cacamatzin did during these events is also known from the chronicles and other accounts.

Reports came that the foreigners had won the support of Tlaxcala. Their entry into the Valley of Mexico was imminent. Cacamatzin, by order of Motecuhzoma, went out to meet them in the capacity of royal messenger. Near Ayotzinco, almost on the slopes of the volcanoes, he spoke with Cortés for the first time. Bernal Díaz del Castillo, who witnessed this encounter, speculated on the wealth and manner of the person he had been told was "the great lord of Tezcoco, nephew of the great Motecuhzoma."[4]

Cacamatzin's mission apparently was a last attempt to dissuade Cortés from his intention of entering Tenochtitlan. It was unsuccessful, but the Tezcocan prince acted to please his uncle, against his own advice to open the gates to the foreigners.

A few days later, on November 8, 1519, the meeting occurred in which the great Mexica ruler, now unable to do otherwise, received "the men of Castile." Along with other princes, Motecuhzoma was accompanied by Cacamatzin and Tetlepanquetzaltzin, lord of Tlacopan, that is, by the other two heads of the Triple Alliance.

Cortés and his men became guests of Motecuhzoma in Tenochtitlan. Cacamatzin then returned to Tezcoco to attend to the still-unsettled conflict with Ixtlilxochitl. In fact Ixtlilxochitl, very astutely, was about to ally himself with the foreigners for support against his brother and against Motecuhzoma himself. The latter, almost without realizing it, was to become the prisoner of Cortés within a very short time.

Cacamatzin, harassed by his brother and now fearful for Motecuhzoma, went back to Tenochtitlan. Some chroniclers said he went in response to a summons from his uncle; others affirm that he fell prisoner to Cortés's men while preparing his army to free his uncle. The fact

is that in the year 2-Flint (1520) he was captive in Tenochtitlan along with Motecuhzoma and the lord of Tlacopan.

The last days of Cacamatzin were ones of great affliction. Having witnessed the grandeur and power of Motecuhzoma, he now saw him taunted and in a pitiful state.
He knew of the extortions of gold and other precious
objects. It must have been some relief when he saw Cortés leave to confront other foreigners'—Narváez and his
men—said to have come to take over Cortés's command.

But Cacamatzin could not foresee that the departure of
Cortés, far from bettering the situation, was to be the occasion for still greater evils. Pedro de Alvarado remained
in command in Tenochtitlan. It is very sad to recall
crimes, but impossible to avoid them when speaking of
Alvarado. He was later accused and censured for his actions not only by the indigenous chroniclers who wrote
in Nahuatl and later by those of Guatemala who expressed themselves in the Quiche and Cackchiquel languages but also by his own companions, who testified
against him when he had to face a residence judgment.[5]
He was accused, during his first stay in Tenochtitlan, of
having Cacamatzin's hands and feet tied and burning
charcoal thrown on his body. This was followed by his
subjecting Cacamatzin to a bath of hot melted pine resin,
until he gave up the gold and other treasures that he had.
As a result of this treatment, according to witnesses, the
Tezcocan prince was at the point of death.

But the torture Cacamatzin endured was only a pre-
amble to his other misfortunes. It was very painful and
ominous for him to contemplate another treacherous action of Alvarado a short time later. The Spanish and indigenous chronicles coincide at this point. The Mexica
celebrated the feast of Toxcatl in honor of their god Huitzilopochtli, one of the most important religious com-
memorations. The people and the nobles, priests, dignitaries of the government, and unarmed warriors all

participated. As one of the texts describes it: "When one of the religious dances was being performed and one song was entwined with another, and the songs were as the uproar of waves, the Spaniards entered into the temple. . . . They attacked the one who played the drum, cut off his arms, his head, and it rolled across the floor. . . . They attacked all the celebrants, stabbing them, spearing them, striking them with their swords."[6]

Alvarado had decided in this way to become master of the Mexica metropolis while Cortés was absent. This episode, known later as "the slaughter of the Main Temple," took place in May 1520. A few days later Motecuhzoma was murdered. In whatever manner the supreme ruler had perished, Cacamatzin could foresee what was also reserved for him.

It is not certainly known whether Cacamatzin was killed then or a few days later. The Spanish chroniclers insist that he lost his life in the fight that accompanied the escape of the Spaniards from Tenochtitlan. The native writers, including Tezozomoc, Ixtlilxochitl, and Chimalpahin, declare that he was hung or that he was stabbed forty-seven times immediately before the men of Castile abandoned the city. Sad, indeed, was the end of the brief and unfortunate life of Cacamatzin, a sensitive youth who left in the keen perception of his poetry a testimony of what was happening both to him as an individual and to his people as a nation.

It is not merely a supposition to say that Cacamatzin, like his father and grandfather, was also a composer of songs. Although it is not known at what moment in his life he began to take an interest in poetry or when he began to polish his songs, he likely felt attracted to this art early in childhood when he listened to the compositions of Nezahualcoyotl and of his own father. Whatever the songs Cacamatzin may have composed, there remains only a brief series of poems that date from the last days of his life.

THE POEMS OF CACAMATZIN

In fol. 5 v. of the Nahuatl manuscript of *Romances*, in the Nettie Lee Benson Latin American Collection at The University of Texas, Austin, the following notation about the songs transcribed there says: "By Cacamatzin, last king of Tezcoco, when he found himself in great difficulties, recollecting the power of his elders, of his father and grandfather."[7]

It may well be asked, what were the "great difficulties" in which Cacamatzin found himself and to which this notation refers? There would appear to be two possible answers. The reference could be to the conflict with his brother Ixtlilxochitl regarding the succession to the throne, or to the later and even greater difficulty in which Cacamatzin found himself from the moment that Motecuhzoma was made a prisoner of the conquistadors. A brief examination of the Tezcocan's songs will show why the second possibility seems more probable.

Cacamatzin, who had suffered greatly at the time of his election as lord of Tezcoco, begins these songs by expressing a profound disillusionment: "Let no one live deluded by a pretention of royalty; the fury, the clashes, let them be forgotten, disappear in due time from the earth." If, after fighting so violently to reach royal supremacy, it no longer is important to him, a probable explanation could be found in the loss of the kingdom and in his and his uncle Motecuhzoma's being in the hands of the powerful foreigners.

In the days of his struggle against his brother Ixtlilxochitl, Cacamatzin relied on his uncle's support. Now no hope was there. Perhaps because of this, he alluded to what had been said to him earlier on the ball court: "They said, they murmured: 'Is it possible to work mercifully, is it possible to act prudently?'" And the Tezcocan added: "I know only myself. Everyone says this, but no one speaks truly on earth." The poem goes on, describing a

"These darken the color of the flowers, there is thunder in the heavens . . ." (*Códice de Durán*, plate 29, from *Visión de los vencidos*)

feast in the midst of which fighting breaks out. Does this refer to the feast of Toxcatl, during which Alvarado attacked the Mexica, the last thing Cacamatzin contemplated a few days before his death? One can compare this part of his poem to the account of the Toxcatl feast as told by the indigenous chroniclers in the *Vision of the Vanquished:* "When one of the religious dances was being performed and one song was entwined with another, and the songs were as the uproar of waves."[8]

In Cacamatzin's words, "The conch shells resound. . . . Flowers rain down, they interweave, whirl about. . . . In the place where the precious drums play, where are heard the beautiful flutes of the precious God, Lord of the Heavens." The indigenous historians recall what happened next: "The men of Castile came there, all came armed for war. . . . They came up to those who were dancing, they rushed to the place of the drums. . . . They ran their spears through the people, they hacked them, with their swords, they wounded them. . . . The battle began, they struck them with javelins, with arrows."[9] Then came the reaction of the Mexica: "As if it was a yellow mantle, the stems of the darts spread over them."[10]

Cacamatzin, for his part, gives what may well be a picture of the same event: "A mist wraps round the song of the shields, over the earth falls a rain of darts, these darken the color of all the flowers. . . . With shields of gold there they dance."

And perhaps because he already knew of Motecuhzoma's death and felt that his own was near, Cacamatzin recalls for the last time his father and his grandfather, Nezahualpilli and Nezahualcoyotl. With the awareness of one who foresees the end, near and inescapable, Cacamatzin finishes his song sadly: "Am I perchance a shield of turquoise, will I, as a mosaic, be embedded once more in existence? . . . Will I be shrouded in fine mantles? Still on earth, near the place of the drums, I remember them."

If, as seems probable, Cacamatzin's poem was conceived during those great difficulties in which he found himself shortly before his death, it might also be that some of the many companions who remained near him to the end knew and memorized this composition, thus rescuing it from oblivion and making possible its survival to the present day. Be that as it may, the sad songs of Cacamatzin reflect for us something of the face and heart of the poet, as well as the agony of a culture already condemned to death.

Cacamatzin Icuic

In antocnihuane,
tla oc xoconcaquican:
macazo ayac in tecunenemi,
Cualanyotl, cocolotl,
ma zo ilcahui,
ma zo pupulihui,
yeccan tlalticpac, *ohuaya, ohuaya.*

No zan noma ye nehuatl,
nechonitohua in yalhua,
tlachco on catca,
conitohua, conilhuiya:
Ach quen tlatlaca?
Ach quen tlatlamati?
Ac zan ninomatin.
Mochi conitohua,
am in anel nitlatohua tlalticpac, *ohuaya, ohuaya.*

Ayahuiztli moteca, *ohuaya,*
ma quiquiztla in cahuacan,
nopan pani tlaticpac, *huiya.*
Tzetzelihui, mimilihui, yahualihui xochitli,
ahuiyaztihuitz in tlalticpac, *ohuaya, ohuaya.*

O ach, yuhqui nel ye ichan,
totatzin ai (in dios), *yyahue,*
ach in yuhqui xoxopan in quetzalli,
ya xochitica on tlacuilohua,
tlalticpac ye nican ipalnemohuani, *ohuaya, ohyaya.*
Chalchiuhteponaztli mimilintocan, *ah iyahue*

on chalchiuhtlacapitzohuayan,
in itlazo teotl (dios), a in ilhuicahua, *ayahue*,
ihui quecholicozcatl
huihuitolihui in tlalticpac, *ohuaya, ohuaya.*

Cuicachimal ayahui,
ylacochquiyahui tlalticpac,
in nepapan xochitli on yohuala ica,
ya tetecuica in ilhuicatl, *aya.*
Teocuitla chimaltica
ye on netotilo, *ohuaya, ohuaya.*

Zan niquitohua, *ye ohuaya.*
zan ni Cacamatzin, *ihuiya.*
zan niquilnamiqui
in tlatohuani Nezahualpilla, *a yahue.*
Cuix on motta,
cuix om monotza
in Nezahualcoyotl, *huiya.*
huehuetitlan?

Niquimilnamiqui, *y ohuaya.*
Ac nel ah yaz?
In chalchihuitl, teocuitlatl,
mach ah ca on yaz, *huiya?*

Cuix nixiuhxhimalli, *aya,*
oc ceppa nozaloloz?
In niquizaz?
In ayatica niquimilolo, *ya?*
Tlaticpac, huehuetitlan,
niquimilnamiqui! *Ohuaya, ohuaya.*

Songs by Cacamatzin
My Friends

My friends,
listen to this:
let no one live deluded with a pretention of royalty.
The fury, the clashes,
let them be forgotten,
disappear
in due time from the earth.

Also, to me alone,
a short time ago they said,
those who were at the ball court,
they said, they murmured:
Is it possible to work mercifully?
Is it possible to act prudently?
I know only myself.
Everyone says this,
but no one speaks truly on earth.

The mist spreads,
the conch shells resound
over me and over all the earth.
Flowers rain down, they interweave, whirl about,
they come to bring joy upon the earth.

It is truly, perhaps as in His house,
our Father acts,
perhaps like quetzal plumage in springtime,
with flowers he paints,
here on the earth, the Giver of Life.
In the place where the precious drums play,
where are heard the beautiful flutes,
of the precious God, Lord of the heavens,
necklaces of red feathers
tremble over the earth.

A mist wraps round the song of the shields,
over the earth falls a rain of darts,
they darken the color of all the flowers,
there is noise of thunder in the heavens.
With shields of gold
there they dance.

I only say,
I Cacamatzin,
now alone I remember
Lord Nezahualpilli.
Perhaps they speak there,
he and Nezahualcoyotl,
in the place of the drums?
I remember them now.

Truly, who will not have to go there?
If he is jade, if he is gold,
perhaps he will not have to go there?

Am I perchance a shield of turquoise,
will I as a mosaic be embedded once more in existence?
Will I come again to the earth?
Will I be shrouded in fine mantles?
Still on earth, near the place of the drums,
I remember them.

(*Romances de los señores de Nueva España,*
Benson Latin American Library, University of Texas, Austin, fols. 5 v.–6 r.)

PART TWO

POETS OF MEXICO-TENOCHTITLAN

In the place of the colored darts,
of the painted shields,
is Tenochtitlan. . . .
There open their corollas
the flowers of the Giver of Life . . .

(*Cantares mexicanas,* National Library of Mexico, fol. 18 r.)

Head of many conquered provinces, Mexico-Tenochtitlan was a city rooted in the fulfillment of a prophecy. Its founders, according to their annals and to oral tradition, had arrived there around A.D. 1325, after a long journey they undertook in response to a promise of their tutelary god. For many years, they had lived in a northern place called Aztlan-Chicomoztoc, "Place of the Herons—At the Seven Caves." There they were servants of others, living under the authority of those who ruled the northern land.

They were called Aztecs at first, but that name pertained in reality to their ancient rulers. When their god made plain his will to free them and they undertook their journey, they changed their name. Their new appelative, Mexica, was derived from one of their god's titles, Mexihtli, which probably means "Moon's Navel." He had promised to lead them to a marvelous place, an island in the middle of a lake surrounded by fertile lands, in a region encircled by mountains covered with forests, and with transparent skies.

The god's promise became a reality, but at first it was very difficult to settle there as the place already belonged to others, the lords of Azcapotzalco. Suffering and endurance were two sine qua nons perhaps required to repay their god for the fulfillment of his promise. And one ought to recall here that, once the Mexica had settled on the island, the portentous god Huitzilopochtli enunciated another prophecy. He encouraged his people and let them forever know that "as long as the world will exist, the fame and the glory of Mexico-Tenochtitlan will not perish, will not come to an end."

What was at first a humble town, tributary to the owners of the island, the Tepanecs of Azcapotzalco, began to grow and, as if it were destiny, became increasingly powerful. Confrontation with Azcapotzalco was inevitable. Favored by their gods, the Mexica and their allies defeated their ancient rulers and, from then on, saw Huitzilopochtli's promise fulfilled beyond anything they had expected.

During the little less than 100 years before the Spanish arrival, the power and the glory of Mexico-Tenochtitlan increased at the expense of many other provinces and chiefdoms independent until then. The Mexica established the Triple Alliance with the Tezcocans and the people of Tlacopan, a town that replaced Azcapotzalco and became the head of a "puppet state." The allies conquered and made many peoples their tributaries, from the Gulf Coast to the Pacific Ocean, reaching places as far away as the modern Mexican border with Guatemala.

Conquests and commerce transformed the economy and standards of living of the Mexica and their allies. Their metropolis became a magnificent town with its Main Temple, built and rebuilt larger each time. There were also numerous palaces, schools, military headquarters, warehouses, and, of course, other temples in the various wards of the city. Mexico-Tenochtitlan was indeed the head of an impressive political organization that some authors have described as an empire.

There, in the largest metropolis of the Americas, high culture flourished in a variety of forms. The tlamatinime, "sages," transmitted the ancient wisdom in the calmecac, or centers of high learning. The calendar, the books of the years, the sacred hymns and other songs and discourses were also taught in the schools. The names of some artists, among them painters and architects, have been preserved in the ancient texts. The available testimonies also speak of the composers of songs. Some of them were born in Mexico-Tenochtitlan, such as Tochihuitzin Coyolchiuhqui; Teoxinmac; and Macuilxochitzin, a lady, daughter of the famous Tlacaelel, the adviser to several high rulers. Others came from the northern inlet of Tlatelolco. Such was the case of the unfortunate lord Moquihuitzin and the renown Captain Temilotzin. There were also composers in the allied town of Tlacopan, and in the defeated and subjugated Azcapotzalco. Those composers of songs, like King Axayacatl, who was also in love with poetry, were members of the high nobility. Totoquihuatzin and Tetlepanquetzanitzin were lords of Tlacopan, and Oquitzin was ruler of Azcapotzalco.

The songs and flowers that can be attributed to them, as well as many other compositions, anonymous creations of the priests, sages, and other people of Mexico-Tenochtitlan, give eloquent testimony to the art and wisdom that flourished in the metropolis that, in spite of the Spanish Conquest, was destined to exist forever.

Glyph of Tenochtitlan

CHAPTER VI

TOCHIHUITZIN COYOLCHIUHQUI

Poet, Son of Itzcoatl,
and Ruler of Teotlatzinco
(End Fourteenth–Middle Fifteenth Century)

It is true that the thought and symbols of flower and song flourished, as nowhere else, among the sages and poets of Tezcoco. It would be sufficient to recall the names of Nezahualcoyotl, Cuacuauhtzin, Nezahualpilli, and Caca-matzin, already known to us. Their extant poetic creations permit at least an insight into the depth of their feelings and thinking. In contrast to the spiritual leanings and philosophical reflections so frequent among the poets and sages of Tezcoco, it would seem obvious that thought and poetry in Mexico-Tenochtitlan would always revolve around the warlike themes preferred by those who considered themselves the chosen People of the Sun. This is only partly true, as shown by the Mexica Tochihuitzin Coyolchiuhqui, who left a Nahuatl version of the universal theme that envisions life as a dream.

Tochihuitzin was a contemporary of Nezahualcoyotl. According to the *Anales de Cuauhtitlan*, he was one of the several sons of Itzcoatl, the Mexica high ruler who led the hostilities against the Tepanecs of Azcapotzalco that resulted in establishing the full independence of his people, as well as the roots of their grandeur.[1] The same

Anales refer to an episode some time before the beginning of the fighting against the Tepanecs, which shows Tochihuitzin in action. It was in the year 5-Reed (1419) that Nezahualcoyotl's father, Ixtlilxochitl, was assassinated by the Tepanecs, and the life of the young Tezcocan prince was also in danger. At that time, Tochihuitzin and several of his brothers helped save Nezahualcoyotl, who was at the point of falling into the hands of his enemies, the people of Azcapotzalco.[2] It was only due to their assistance and the aid of his faithful servant Coyohua of Teopiazco that Nezahualcoyotl could find refuge with the Mexica.

The exact age of Tochihuitzin when he took part in this event is not known, but there is another fact recorded in the *Crónica mexicayotl* that helps to clarify the point. Tezozomoc mentions that Tochihuitzin married Achihuapoltzin, a daughter of the famous counselor Tlacaelel.[3] Because this probably occurred shortly after his participation in the rescue of Nezahualcoyotl, it can be assumed that in 1419 he was no more than twenty-five years old. The date of his birth can thus be placed in the late fourteenth century.

In addition to the rescue of Nezahualcoyotl, Tochihuitzin was very likely active on other occasions during the war with Azcapotzalco. At the side of his father Itzcoatl and of his father-in-law, the farsighted and powerful Tlacaelel, and also assisting his uncle, the young Motecuhzoma Ilhuicamina, Tochihuitzin contributed as a warrior to the victory that represented the beginning of the Mexica nation's greatness. According to another testimony of the *Crónica mexicayotl,* and probably as a reward for his courage, he was appointed years later as ruler of Teotlaltzinco, a town neighboring on the region of Huexotzinco on the eastern slopes of the Iztaccihuatl volcano.[4] There Tochihuitzin lived with his wife, the daughter of Tlacaelel, free to devote some time to his meditations and poetry.

Nothing more is known of his life, his actions as ruler, or the manner and date of his death, which probably took place during the second half of the fifteenth century. His nickname, Coyolchiuhqui, means "Maker of Little Bells," which could mean that he practiced this craft during his youth or, metaphorically speaking, could refer to his gifts as a composer of songs. On at least one other occasion he is mentioned, together with other well-known poets from the region of Huexotzinco, in one of the anonymous songs in the collection preserved in the National Library of Mexico.

TOCHIHUITZIN'S COMPOSITIONS

In that collection of songs there are two brief compositions attributed to Tochihuitzin. In them the "Maker of Little Bells" appears as a genuine tlamatini, a sage, deeply concerned with discovering the meaning of existence. The first of these poems conveys a comment on the concept of life as a dream. Tochihuitzin points out a parallel: We have come to earth only to dream, and our dream vanishes quickly; our being is like an herb, our heart gives forth flowers, but these also very quickly wither. In his second poem, Tochihuitzin refers with keen insight and concision to the theme of "flower and song." Sages and princes live the song and, at least in part, unveil the mystery of the flower. Tochihuitzin says he is merely a weaver of twigs. The strands of flowers fall away from him, there where the sages abide.

These two songs, the only examples of Tochihuitzin's creativity, suffice to justify his inclusion among the most celebrated cuicapicque, "composers of songs," of the pre-Hispanic Nahuatl world.

ZAN TONTEMIQUICO

In ic conitotehuac in Tochihuitzin,
In ic conitotehuac in Coyolchiuhqui:

Zan tocochitlehuaco,
zan tontemiquico,
ah nelli, ah nelli
tinemico in tlalticpac.
Xoxopan xihuitl ipan
tochihuaca.
Hualcecelia, hualitzmolini in toyollo,
xochitl in tonacayo.
Cequi cueponi,
on cuetlahuia.

In conitotehuac in Tochihuitzin;
In ic conitotehuac Coyolchiuhqui.

WE COME ONLY TO DREAM

Thus spoke Tochihuitzin,
thus spoke Coyolchiuhqui:

We only rise from sleep,
we come only to dream,
it is not true, it is not true,
that we come on earth to live.
As an herb in springtime,
so is our nature.
Our hearts give birth, make sprout,
the flowers of our flesh.
Some open their corollas,
then they become dry.

Thus spoke Tochihuitzin
thus spoke Coyolchiuhqui.

(*Cantares mexicanos*, National Library of Mexico, fol. 14 v.)

CUICATL ANYOLQUE

Cuicatl anyolque,
xochitl ancueponque,
antepilhuan;
ni zacatimaltzin, in Tochihuitzin,
ompa ye huitze
xochimecatl.

YOU HAVE LIVED THE SONG

You have lived the song,
you have unveiled the flower,
you, o princes;
I, Tochihuitzin, I am only a weaver of twigs;
the garlands of flowers
fall out there.

(*Cantares mexicanos*, National Library of Mexico, fol. 15 r.)

CHAPTER VII

AXAYACATL

Poet and Lord of Tenochtitlan

(Ca. 9-House, 1449–2-House, 1481)

It was not only in Tezcoco that some of the poets of ancient Mexico were found among the high rulers and other
prominent dignitaries. In Tenochtitlan as well, more than
one huey tlahtoani (supreme ruler) had a clear predilec-
tion for poetry. It is true that most of the songs of Mexica
provenance that have survived must be attributed to
anonymous authors, but we know at least the names
of some famous forgers of songs among the People of
the Sun.

Among those who held the rank of supreme ruler or
huey tlahtoani, the sources record that Motecuhzoma Ilhuicamina, Axayacatl, and Ahuitzotl, as well as the unfortunate Motecuhzoma II Xocoyotzin, were composers
of songs. Two particularly beautiful poems that can be attributed to Axayacatl will be considered here. The first is
a recollection of his ancestors and the second a sad song
composed after the only defeat the Mexica suffered during the days of their splendor.

The chronicler Chimalpahin recalls that Axayacatl was
the son of the Mexica prince Tezozomoctzin and a lady
from Tlacopan named Huitzilxochitzin.[1] It must be em-

Axayacatl in front of the symbolic representation of some of his conquests: Temalacan (?); Tlatelolco, with the date 5-Rain; and Ocuillan (*Códice Azcatitlan*, plate xix)

phasized that his father, Tezozomoctzin, though he never ruled in Tenochtitlan, was a descendant of Itzcoatl and had three sons who became supreme lords: Axayacatl, Tizoc, and Ahuiqtzotl. Surprisingly, as the Mexica chronicler Alvarado Tezozomoc has noted, the youngest, Axayacatl, was the first to attain this supreme honor, thanks mainly to the insistence of the powerful counselor Tlacaelel, well along in years.

The exact date of Axayacatl's birth is not known, but it can be inferred from a statement often found in the sources, as in their account of the war against the Matlatzincas in 1474, that he was "only a very young man."[2] If at the time of that war he was barely twenty-five years old, he must have been born somewhere around the year 9-House or 1449.

Axayacatl was elected huey tlahtoani (supreme ruler) of the Mexica in 1468. Thus, on the decision of Tlacaelel and with the approval of Nezahualcoyotl, the supreme

command was committed to the care of a "valiant youth"
of whom great things could be expected. His elder brothers, Tizoc and Ahuitzotl, were not of this opinion and
very promptly made their discontent public, according to
the record of Alvarado Tezozomoc: "They, the elder brothers, had no respect for Axayacatl, the youngest, and made
derogatory remarks about the conquests of the Mexica,
wherever they were, when Axayacatl led the attacks and
captured prisoners. . . . And they said, Is Axayacatl really
a man? Does he really know how to capture prisoners in
war. . . ?"[3]

But the same Mexica chronicler goes on to say: "Although Axayacatl was the youngest, he was nevertheless
a great warrior who had conquered the Huexotzinca. For
this reason they elected him first as high ruler here in
Tenochtitlan."[4]

During the thirteen years of his reign, Axayacatl, by his
accomplishments, was able to surmount the intrigues of
his brothers and confirm the opinion of Tlacaelel and Nezahualcoyotl that he was "a valiant youth." He took part
in three wars that were particularly important for the Mexica nation. The first was against the neighboring Tlatelolca, the second against the Matlatzinca of the Toluca
region, and the last against the Purepecha of Michoacan.
Although it is true that Axayacatl suffered defeat in the
last war, in all of them he acted as a strong and intelligent
captain. A brief account of these three campaigns and of
other happenings that reveal his religious concerns and
his devotion to the arts will help to delineate the spiritual side of this tlahtoani who came to occupy his place
among the distinguished poets of the People of the Sun.

The rivalry between Tenochtitlan and its twin city,
Tlatelolco, built on a neighboring islet, was of long standing. At the time Axayacatl was elected governor, Moquihuitzin, a brother-in-law of the new Mexica lord, was the
ruler of Tlatelolco. There is abundant information in the
indigenous sources about the reasons for the outbreak of

Axayacatl during the war against Tlatelolco, in which he had a fine opportunity to show his valor (*Atlas de Durán*, plate x)

the ancient quarrel between the closely related towns. Moquihuitzin found life impossible with his wife, the sister of Axayacatl. In his eyes, she had many defects, including such bad breath that any contact with her was unbearable. The result was that the Tlatelolcan lord repeatedly insulted the queen and openly turned for solace to his numerous concubines. She was obviously offended and more and more frequently took her complaints to her brother Axayacatl. To this other "aggravation" was added, as Diego Durán calls it: "Some unruly young men," sons of important people of Tenochtitlan, who struck up friendship in the marketplace with young girls from Tlatelolco and accompanied them back to their homes, "treating them with much dishonesty, violating their purity and their innocence."[5]

In the year 7-House (1473), open warfare broke out. On the advice of Tlacaelel and assisted by other captains, Axayacatl took command of the armies. The struggle was decided very quickly. Moquihuitzin, with his lieutenant Teconal, took refuge in the highest part of his city's temple. There Axayacatl caught up with them and "entering boldly . . . he killed them and dragged them out and threw them down the stairway of the temple."[6] Axayacatl's victory resulted in the incorporation of Tlatelolco as one part of Mexico-Tenochtitlan.

Shortly afterwards, around 1476, Axayacatl was to have another occasion to demonstrate his valor, which interrupted other activities in which he was greatly interested. The ancient religious doctrines, poetry, and the science of the calendar, all familiar to him since his days as a student in the calmecac (school), held his attention. Durán tells how, shortly before the war with the Matlatzinca, Axayacatl "was busy with the carving of the large and famous stone, so well carved, where were sculptured the figures of the months and years, days and weeks, so carefully that it was something to see."[7]

Besides following in detail the labor of the stonecutters who were at work on what is known today as the "Sun Stone," it is very likely that, escaping from other tasks that his duties imposed, he devoted some hours to his interest in poetry. It is very possible that at least one of his poems—the one in which he recalls his father and other illustrious ancestors—was composed at that time.

But the necessities of war, the mission of the People of the Sun, whose destiny was to extend the dominions of Huitzilopochtli and maintain with the precious liquid the life of the heavenly body on which depended the very existence of the present age, impelled Axayacatl once more to take command of his armies. To subjugate the Matlatzinca in the Valley of Toluca appeared at first an easy undertaking. Nevertheless, according to the Mexica chroniclers, the campaign was very difficult. The Matlatzinca resisted courageously. One of their captains succeeded in approaching Axayacatl, wounding him in one leg. Only the timely arrival of Mexica reinforcements determined the victory of the People of the Sun's army.

The incident of Axayacatl's wound provided the theme for the Mexica poetess Macuilxochitzin who, while recording it, at the same time emphasized Axayacatl's valor, when she said: "The flowers of the eagle remain in your hands. . . . On every side Axayacatl made conquests."

There is another anecdote of this war that testifies to

Teocalli of the holy war, right side. Aztec sculpture in stone in the Mexican National Museum of Anthropology

Axayacatl's modesty and also to his respect for the art of fine speech. When about to begin battle against the Matlatzinca, various Mexica captains asked Axayacatl to make a speech and harangue the troops. The young lord, perhaps disturbed as he faced the imminent struggle, but with an obvious appreciation for the value of the word at such a decisive moment, commissioned several older men to convey his ideas to the soldiers. According to the testimony of the chronicler who recounts this episode, "The highest ranking commanders of the army asked the King Axayacatl to make a speech to the entire army, but being a very young man, he did not want to do this himself and commissioned several elders to do it for him. And he remained beside the orator who was speaking, to give authority to the words he was saying."[8]

In the memory of the people, Axayacatl's modesty remained associated with his triumph over the Matlatzinca forces. The celebrations of the victory brought rejoicing once more to Tenochtitlan. With renewed enthusiasm, the counselor Tlacaelel, already advanced in years, now thought of undertaking another conquest that he considered important. It was necessary to conquer the people of the present-day state of Michoacan and, with the captives brought from there, consecrate the site where the Sun Stone was to be placed, the work for which Axayacatl had accepted so much responsibility.

Around 1478 Axayacatl and his allies, with an army of 24,000 men, according to the chronicles, marched westward toward the region populated by the famous Purepecha. The historian Chimalpahin (who incidentally placed this war before the one against the Matlatzinca), tells that Axayacatl, leading his men, spoke to them himself this time and said:

> Now we are approaching Michoacan,
> they have fallen on them,
> they will certainly fall, the old Mexica warriors,
> they will come to expose themselves to danger,
> will come to finish the work, the old eagles,
> the warrior,
> the experienced eagle,
> Huitznahuatl,
> the ancient nobility.[9]

The Mexica, already within enemy territory, discovered through their spies that the Michoacan army had about 40,000 men, an overpowering force. Then the unforeseen, but inevitable, happened. The Mexica "attacked the Tarascans, but the assault was so useless that, history says, they fell like flies in the water, thus all fell into the hands of the Tarascans. And so great was the massacre inflicted on them, that the Mexicans had to withdraw the people who remained, lest they be swallowed up and destroyed."[10]

This time it was a sad return to Tenochtitlan. The description left by the native chroniclers of the arrival of those who survived the defeat as well as the funeral rites and other religious ceremonies that then took place are highly dramatic: "The elders began to sing, all with their hair braided and tied, their bodies painted, token of sorrow for their captain, and like good soldiers and friends, they expressed their feelings, the wives, children, and relatives offering their tears."[11]

It is likely that Axayacatl was strengthened and consoled by the priests, the nobles, the elders, and especially by Tlacaelel. But this did not ease his deep pain, as shown in another of his poems apparently composed a short time after his return to Tenochtitlan. In the *Cantares mexicanas*, in which it is included, an even more explicit notation appears: "Lord Axayacatl had it to be sung when he was unable to conquer those of Michoacan and had to return from Tlaximaloyan, because not only many captains and warriors died but also many deserted."[12]

When composing this song in the midst of his discouragement, Axayacatl, with the same modesty he had formerly shown, asked one of the elders to assist him because he lacked confidence in his own ability as a poet. The work is entitled *Huehuehcuicatl*, "Song of the Elders." Although it bewails the defeat, it also calls on the strong warriors to take heart and remember that if they have been conquerors in the past, they must now recover their courage and triumph once more.

Axayacatl survived this disastrous event for a few years.

Ocelotl-quauhxicalli, Aztec sculpture in stone in the National Museum of Anthropology, Mexico

He still had time to experience the joys of victory as he engaged in a war against the people of Tliliuhquitepec in the region of Puebla. Also, it must have given him great satisfaction to contemplate the solemn ceremony with which he inaugurated the Sun Stone. But the tragedy of that defeat, the greatest experienced by the people of Huitzilopochtli, as well as the grumblings and intrigues that this once more aroused, mortified Axayacatl to such an extent that he never entirely recovered. Shortly afterward, around 1480, he fell seriously ill.

Feeling death near, he ordered an image to be sculptured of Motecuhzoma Ilhuicamina and another of himself on a rocky surface in the Chapultepec hill. Durán relates how the following year, 2-Cane (1481), when these were finished,

> he had himself carried to see his statue and, in the presence of the lords, he said farewell to all of them feeling himself near the end. And history says that he could not return to

Mexico alive but that he died on the road on the very stretcher in which he was carried. He died a young man. He reigned thirteen years, and before he died, Nezahualcoyotl, the lord and ruler of Tetzcuco, died.[13]

Perhaps as the only consolation in his last days, Axayacatl might have had some vague presentiment that among his various children, at least one would reach the supreme rank of huey tlahtoani. His immediate successors were his elder brothers Tizoc and Ahuitzotl, the ones who had grumbled so much against him. However, in the end not one but two of his sons did succeed him, and under even more dramatic circumstances than the defeat in Michoacan. It fell to the lot of Motecuhzoma II and Cuitlahuac, sons of Axayacatl, to look upon the last days of Mexica greatness.

THE POEMS OF AXAYACATL

The probable circumstances under which Axayacatl composed the two poems that indigenous sources attribute to him have already been mentioned. Both are poems of recollection. Perhaps to face the attacks of his older brothers who reproached him for being young, he attempted to glimpse into the past, consciously identifying himself with his ancestral lineage.

In his first poem he exclaims: "They devise it, the flowery war, in the Region of the Red Color, those who were once with us." Itzcoatl, a former great Mexica ruler who had conquered Azcapotzelco, was a great captain, but, Axayacatl comments: "You were celebrated, you expressed divine words, but you died." Young and old, all go away to "The Region-Where-in-Someway-One-Exists." The Giver of Life "makes no one durable on the earth." Also Motecuhzoma the First, Axayacatl's uncle, and the wise Nezahualcoyotl and Totoquihuatzin, Lord of Tlacopan, "left us orphans." And later, when referring to his own father, Prince Tezozomoctli, Axayacatl says again, as if speaking to his brothers Tizoc and Ahuitzotl, he also "abandoned us"; each one must find his own way out of his difficulty.

If there is nothing stable in the earth, if the lords and princes who were truly great and strong have left as orphans "the people of the village, of the cities," then there is nothing surprising in uneasiness and fear. If only the new rulers could consult those who have gone away! Faced with the mystery of the disappearance of men, the only thing left to do is to concentrate on oneself to find a path here on the earth.

The final questions expressed in this first poem of Axayacatl, while echoing those of other Nahua composers of songs, are a testimony to personal uncertainty and sadness but also to the depth of thought attained by some of the sages of ancient Mexico. "Who could teach me about this? For this I, in solitude, try to do away with my suffering."

Axayacatl's second composition is known as "Song of the Elders." After the defeat suffered by the Mexica in their attempt to conquer those of Michoacan, Axayacatl was assisted by one of the older poets in composing it. He wanted to acknowledge the Mexica failure and recall the warriors who perished there, and also adjoined a plea to the "conquerors of ancient times" to take heart.

Axayacatl makes use of the same metaphor that Nezahualpilli employs in his poem on war. The two compare it to intoxication: "They called us to become intoxicated in Michoacan, land of Camacoyahuac . . . we became drunk!"

The picture of the defeat is dramatic and is felt all the more deeply as it was the only one the Mexica experienced before the arrival of the Spaniards. "When they saw that their warriors fled before them, the gold sparkling and the banners of quetzal plumes shining green—they explained—O do not be taken prisoners! Let it not be you, make haste!" But then, coming back to himself, the great lord of Tenochtitlan cries out: "I am bold in war, I

Axayacatl. Perhaps in my old age, will these words be said by my eagle princes. . . . I am overthrown, I am scorned, I am shamed."

Axayacatl was a man whose face and heart were doubly racked with pain. In the first of his poems, he confesses uncertainty and anxiety about the mysteries of the region of the dead. Then he is distraught by the disgrace of the battle that would give his rivals, his own brothers, much to talk about. But while Axayacatl felt the bitterness of his own anguish, he always found new courage in remembering his ancestors. He exclaims: "On the mat of the eagles, on the mat of the tigers, your grandfather is exalted, Axayacatl. . . . Our darts, our weapons are still powerful, with them we brought glory to our people."

And finally, as if retreating within himself to find an answer to his problem, in a kind of scoffing skepticism, he finishes his song with these words: "For this I your grandfather, I can laugh at your women's weapons, at your women's shields. . . . Conquerors of ancient times, live once again!"

If Axayacatl, the youngest son of Prince Tezozomoc, has come down in history as a great ruler of the Mexica, he must also be included among the masters of the word who were born in Mexico-Tenochtitlan.

YCUIC AXAYACATZIN, MEXICO TLATOHUANI

Zan nican temoc y xochimiquiztli tlalpan,
aci yehua ye nican,
in tlapalla quichihuan,
tonahuac onoque, *ohuacaca yyancaca yio.*
Choquiztlehuatiuh, *ayahue,*
yece ye oncan nepan netlazalo,
ylhuicatl ytic cuicachocoa,
ica huiloan quenonamican, *ohuanca.*

Zan tonilhuizolon,
teotlatollin ticchiuh, *aya*

zan can timomiquili in itech.
In coloztetlayocotli, teicnotlamachti.
Ticchiuh, *ayyio.*
O ach anca oquitto in tlacatl?
Aya in mahmana, tlatzihui.
Ayac quiyocoyan Ipalnemoa.
Choquizilhuitl, in yehua ya yxayoilhuitl, *aya!*
Huallaocoya moyollo.
[Tehuatl a in Santa María, *ohuanca.*]
Zan nel ocpa huitze teteuctin? *a ohuaya!*
Zan niquimonilnamiqui in Itzcoatl,
notlayocol *o ohuaye* itech aci a noyol, *ayyo.*
O ach anca ciahuia,
ontlatzihui in yehuan chane,
in Ipalnemoani?
O ayac tlaquahuac quichihuan tlalticpac.
Can nelpan tonyazque?
Notlayocol, *ohuaye,* itech aci a noyol, *ayyo.*

Ye onetocoto,
ohuiloaca.
In tepilhuan, in tlatoanime, teteuctin, *aya,*
techyaicnoocauhtehuaque.
Mayan tlayocoxtli, o antepilhuan, *ayio.*
Mach oc hualquinehuaya,
mach oc hualilotihuayan
can ompa ximoa?
In cuix oc techmatiquiuh
in Moteuczomatzin, in Nezahualcoyotzin, Totoquihuatzi?
Techyiaicnocauhtehuazque, mayan.
Mayan tlayocoxti, o antepilhuan!

Can on in nemia noyollo?
In Naxayaca o za niquiyatemoa,
in techcahuaco in Tezozomoctli,
notlayocol a noconayaihtoa yan zayio.
O anca in mahcehual, atloyantepetl, *huiya.*
a inoquitquico in teteuctin,
in concauhtehuaque.
O ach acoc necehuiz?

Ach acoc huitz?
nechonmatiquiuh?
Notlayocol a noconayaihtoa yan zayio, *aya*.

SONG OF AXAYACATL, LORD OF MEXICO

Here on the earth the flowery death has descended,
it is coming near;
they devise it in the Region of Red Color,
those who are with us.
An outcry rises,
there the people are urged forward,
in the interior of heaven there are sad songs,
with them one goes to Where-In-Someway-One-Exists.

You are celebrated,
you expressed divine words,
but you died.
He who has compassion for men makes wry faces.
You have made it this way.
Perhaps no man has spoken thus?
He who perseveres becomes weary.
The Giver of Life will not invent anyone once more.
Day of weeping, day of tears!
Your heart is sad.
Will the lords have to come a second time?
Alone I remember Itzcoatl,
for him sadness enters my heart.
Was He weary then,
perhaps fatigue overcame the Master of the House,
the Giver of Life?
He makes no one durable on the earth.
Where will we have to go?
For this, sadness enters my heart.

The departure of people continues,
all go away.
The princes, the lords, the nobles,
they left us orphans.
Mourn O my lords!
Perhaps someone comes again,
perhaps someone comes back

from the region of the fleshless?
Will they come to teach us something,
Motecuhzoma, Nezahualcoyotl, Totoquihuatzin?
They left us orphans
mourn, O my lords!

Where does my heart stray?
I Axayacatl, I seek them,
Tezozomoctli abandoned us,
for this I find my way alone out of my difficulty.
Is the city what they deserve,
the lords who came to govern,
who have left them abandoned?
Will there perhaps be an end to pain?
Perhaps they will come again?
Who can teach me about this?
For this I, in solitude, try to do away with my suffering.

(*Cantares mexicanos*, National Library of Mexico, fols. 29 v.–30 r.)

HUEHUEH CUICATL

Techtlahuancanotzque
in Michhuacan, in Camacoyahuac,
tihuitzmanato ye timexica:
Tihihuintique!
Quenman inticauhque in quauhuehuetzin, yaotzin? *Yyao
ohuiya.*
Quenmach in mochiuhque in mexica,
in huehuetque xoxocomique?
Aocac quitoa in ye tiquinquequeza ilamatzitzin!
Chimalpopoca! In Axayaca! *Yioyahue.*
Ye ticauhque in amocolton Cacamaton, *yyaon, ohuiya.*
Tlahuanoyan nontlacactica in amocolton.

Mononotztoque quauhhuehuetque,
in Tlacaelel, Cahualtzin,
quilmach aconihque iachcahua,
cancauhtiquizque teuhtli Michhuacan, *yyao.*
Anozo oncan temactlanque cuecuexteca, in tlatilolca?

Noxhuihuan in Zacuatzin, in ye Tepantzin,
    Cihuacuecueltzin,

in tzontecon ica, yymelelhiquiuh ica,
on teachtitoa:
xicaquican! *cototi, cototi, cototi* . . .
Tlein yequichihua in tequihuaque?
Aocmo mictlani?,
Aoc tlamaznequi?
In oquimittaque in yaohua
imixpan hualehua,
teocuitlatl pepetzcatihuitz,
in zan quetzalpanitl ytlaxopalehua, *huiya,*
Amechana, *hui,*
ma amotzin, ya xontlazacan! *Huee.*

In maca yehuantin telpopotzitzintin,
yehua tlamacaznequi,
intla ca ye, huan yancazaoquic tiquahchocazque,
ancazaiquic tocelochocazque,
in tiquahuehuetque, *huiya,*
amechana! *hui.*
Ma amotzin, ya xon tlaccacan, *huee.*

Yiioyahue, yaonotlahueliltic,
in Axayaca,
cuix ye nohuehueyo
in innetlatoliz in noquapilhua, *huee?*
Ayn maca yehuatl, in noxhuiuh,
can namechcahuazquia.
Xochitl mantiuh, *huee*
ica momaquixtia in Huitznahuatl Yaotl, *huee.*

A, *hoo ye hee,* onontotolcatoc, nontlatlatlaztoc,
nochichichatoc, in nomocolton, in Axayaca, *huee.*
Maximotlalican, in antequihuahque, amiyahque,
maytlecax ypan anhualcholotin, anmotlatizque,
ica ahuetzi ychiquacol
yn amocolton in Axayaca, *huee.*

Ceceppa tetlaocoltehuetzquiti,
in ye quichhihua in ye mexica.
Noxhuihua, in omoxcuinque,
in nahuitica yniman ic on huehueti, *yyeyahue,*
chimalli xochitl tomac onmania, *huee.*

Auh in nelli mexica, in moxhuihuan,
cecentecpantica, ontecpantica,
in huehuetitihui *y yyoyahue.*
chimalli xochitl tomac onmania.

Quauhpetlapan,
ocelopetlapan,
onehuatica in amocol, in Axayaca.
Contlachinolpipipitztica in Itlecatzin,
mahuel yhuiquentel popocatica.
Ohuaye ayye, aic cehuiz in chimaltica,
conehca pehuitica tlacochtica,
in quixelotica yn Itlecatzin,
manel yhuiquentel popocatica, *huee.*

In oc tonnemi *huee* tamocolhua,
y patlahuac in tatlauh, in totlacoch,
ic tiquimahuiltique in tonahuac onoque, *huee.*
Tlacazo ayaxcan in huehuetihua,
tlacazo ayaxca in huehueyotl.
Can yenica ninochoquilia, namacol, yn Naxayaca,
niquilnamiqui nohuehueicnihuan,
in Cuepanahuaz, in Tecale, in Xochitlahuan, in Yehuaticac.
Ma ceme nican hualquizacan,
cecenteutli,
pan momaticotinican Chalco, *huee.*
Quecizque inquincuitihuetzi oyohualli, *yehuaya, huee,*
yequecizqui yn camilacatzoa teuhtli, *yehuaya, huee.*

Ohoehe zan amoca nihuehuetzca,
namocol,
anmocihuatlahuiz,
an mocihuachimal.
Tequihuaque *huee,* zan iuh
xinencan *huee!*

SONG OF THE ELDERS

They called us to become intoxicated
in Michoacan, land of Camacoyahuac,
we went in search of offerings, we Mexica:
we became drunk!

At what moment did we leave the old eagles, the warriors?
How the Mexica did act,
the old ones almost dead with drunkenness?
No one says we fought with old women!
Chimalpopoca! Axayacatl!
There we leave your little grandfather Cacamaton.
In the place of drunkness I heard your grandfather.

They came together, the older eagles,
Tlacaelel, Cahualtzin,
it is said they stood up to give drink to their captains,
to those who would go forth against the Lord of Michoacan.
Perhaps there the Cuexteca, the Tlatelolca surrendered?

Zacuatzin, Tepantzin, Cihuacuecueltzin,
of courageous head and heart,
they exclaim:
Listen: What do the brave do?
Are they not prepared to die?
Do they not wish to offer sacrifices?
When they saw that their warriors
fled before them,
the gold sparkling
and the banners of quetzal plumes shining green,
O, do not be taken prisoners!
Let it not be you, make haste!

Not those young warriors,
they want to sacrifice them,
if it should happen thus, we will cry like eagles,
we will roar like tigers,
we the old eagle warriors.
O do not be taken prisoners!
You, make haste!

Bold in war,
Axayacatl,
perhaps in my old age
will these words be said of my eagle princes?
Let it not be thus, my grandchildren,
I will have to leave you.

There will be an offering of flowers,
with these will be spared the Warrior of the South.

I am overthrown, I am scorned,
I am ashamed, I, your grandfather Axayacatl.
Do not rest, you strong,
may it not be, if you flee, you are destroyed,
with that falls the power
of your grandfather Axayacatl.

Again and again afflicted,
the Mexica exert themselves.
My grandchildren, those of the painted faces,
from the four sides they sound their drums,
the flower of the shields remains in your hands.
True Mexica, my grandchildren,
they remain in line, they hold firm,
sound their drums,
the flower of the shields remains in your hands.

On the mat of the eagles,
on the mat of the tigers,
your grandfather is exalted, Axayacatl.
Itlecatzin sounds conch shells in the combat,
while the quetzal plumages are obscured.
He does not rest with his shield,
there he begins with darts,
with them Itlecatzin wounds,
while the quetzal plumages are obscured.

We, your grandparents still live,
our darts, our weapons are still powerful,
with them we brought glory to our people.
Indeed now there is weariness,
certainly there is fatigue.
For this I lament, I, your grandfather Axayacatl,
I remember my old friends,
Cuepanahuaz, Tecale, Xochitlahua, Yehuaticac.
Would that they come here,
each one of those lords
who made themselves known there in Chalco.

The brave ones might come to take up the bells,
the brave ones might encircle the princes.

For this I can laugh,
I, your grandfather,
at your women's weapons,
at your women's shields.
Conquerors of ancient times,
live once again!

(*Cantares mexicanos*, National Library of Mexico, fols. 73 v.–74 v.)

CHAPTER VIII

MACUILXOCHITZIN

Poet, Daughter of Tlacaelel
(Middle Fifteenth Century)

The indigenous chroniclers speak also about several Nahua women versed in the art of poetry. Ixtlilxochitl mentions some of them, like the celebrated royal concubine, nicknamed "Lady of Tula," with whom Nezahualpilli, the ruler of Tezcoco, more than once had his pleasure. In the words of the Tezcocan chronicler: "She was so wise that she could discuss with the ruler and the wisest men in his kingdom, and was very gifted in poetry."[1] Chimalpahin, in his *Relations*, as well as the *Anales de Cuauhtitlan* also mention women who composed songs and transcribe a few fragments of their productions.

A magnificent example of the tenderness of Nahua women and their talent for poetry is found in a lengthy song in the frequently quoted *Cantares mexicanos* in the National Library of Mexico. It is the transcription of a *Cozolcuicatl,* "a cradle song," composed for the little Ahuitzotl who later was to become lord of the Mexica. It is known that this song was the work of a woman because several times she mentions herself in it: "I am a Mexican maiden . . . I, the little maid, conceived my song in the interior of the house of flowers."[2]

Nahuatl women, composers of songs (*Códice florentino*, x)

But while this poem, one of the most beautiful in the collection, can be assigned to a young girl of Anahuac who knew how to compose songs, unfortunately her name is not recorded nor is anything known about her. However, there is a poem in the same manuscript, also the creative work of a woman, whose name is known. It would be strange to refer to the "faces and hearts" of fifteen pre-Hispanic poets of Mexico without including at least one woman composer of songs. Such an omission would indicate either ignorance or prejudice. It is indeed unfortunate that no other precise references have been found in the sources that permit us to identify the authors of several compositions that undeniably were the work of talented Nahua women.

The poem that will be transcribed and commented upon here can be attributed to Macuilxochitzin, a Mexica woman of noble lineage born around 1435. She was a native of Mexico-Tenochtitlan, where she probably lived during most of the remaining years of the fifteenth century. Her father was the renowed counselor of several Mexica high rulers, Tlacaelel. The chronicler Tezozomoc provides the following information about the offspring of Tlacaelel: "The other twelve children of the aged Tlacaelel Cihuacoatl, each one had a different mother, and were engendered in various places. Here are their names. . . . These two were women, the seventh called Macuilxochitzin. Of her was born the prince Cuauhtlapaltzin."[3]

Princess Macuilxochitzin could have been called by this name because she was born on a day 5-Flower of the Mexica calendar, which is what her name means. It could also be a pet name used when her love for poetry was known, because Macuilxochitl was one of the titles by which the god-goddess of art, songs, and dance was invoked. The ancient Nahua texts, when describing the favorable or unfavorable qualities of each day, tell about the day 5-Flower and the feasts in honor of Macuilxochitl, that whoever was born on that day was destined to be a composer of songs.

Macuilxochitzin, daughter of the powerful Tlacaelel, appears to have had such a destiny. She was carefully educated from childhood and heard from the lips of her mother the ancient discourse addressed to "the little girl who is like jade, quetzal plumage, the most precious reality that come forth upon earth."[4] At that time she began to know what was to be her destiny in the world, how she was to act, and by what road one approached the gods to obtain the precarious happiness granted to mortals.

It was Macuilxochitzin's good fortune to live during the days of greatest Mexica splendor. A few years before the probable date of her birth, her uncles, the high ruler Itzcoatl and Motecuhzoma Ilhuicamina the First, who was then a captain, following the advice of her father Tlacaelel, had defeated the ancient rulers of Azcapotzalco. While Macuilxochitzin was still a young girl, her native Tenochtitlan began to be an important metropolis; to it flowed every kind of tribute as well as merchandise brought by the *pochtecas,* those merchants who went to remote regions. Presumably Macuilxochitzin received some precious jewels, fine cloth, and other gifts from her father. Like the women of her lineage, she must have known the art of weaving and embroidery and also how to prepare food and drink, which could have been a source of pleasure of Tlacaelel on more than one occasion.

Although all the people and especially the nobles respected and admired the great counselor, called "conqueror of the world" by Tezozomoc,[5] Macuilxochitzin, as shown in her poem, in addition to the respect and love she had for him as father also became interested in his activities, his triumphs and conquests, and even in the advice he gave on behalf of Tenochtitlan. It is not strange that the only poem that likely can be attributed to Macuilxochitzin is concerned with one of the most important conquests planned by Tlacaelel, her father, and carried out successfully by Lord Axayacatzin.

The Mexica, after their triumph over the Tepaneca of Azcapotzalco, began a long series of conquests, led first by Itzcoatl and later by Motecuhzoma Ilhuicamina, but always with the advice of Tlacaelel. In this way they conquered the chiefdoms of Cuitlahuac, Mizquic, Xochimilco, Culhuacan, Chalco, Tepeaca, Tecamachalco, and others, even further away in the Huexteca and in the country of the Totonaca in present-day Veracruz. In the time of Axayacatl, who was installed as high ruler in the year 3-House (1469), the old quarrels with the neighboring Tlatelolca resulted in their being forced to submit to the authority of Tenochtitlan.[6] Princess Macuilxochitzin must have known about all these conquests, not only because of her father's involvement but because she contemplated the frequent departures of warriors who returned victorious, accompanied by a great number of captives and riches, the booty of their conquests.

In the year 10-Flint (1476), the Mexica once more made ready for war. This campaign was directed against the Matlatzinca and the Otomi in the Valley of Toluca. Macuilxochitzin may even have known the words of Tlacaelel spoken to Axayacatl on that occasion. The chronicler Tezozomoc recalls that the great counselor, desirous of a complete victory, gave his advice to the supreme Mexica ruler in this form: "Now, my son, I am already very old, after my death I do not know what will happen with this affair, and therefore the authority is in your hands, that you now go against them and destroy them, so that they come under our rule and pay tribute, without any leniency."[7]

Tezozomoc and other chroniclers recorded this campaign in detail. It ended in a sweeping victory for the Mexica army but—as already noted in the chapter devoted to Axayacatl—it was not so fortunate for him personally, as he was seriously wounded in the leg by an Otomi captain named Tlilatl, a leader among his people. As the chronicler describes it,

> The hardy soldiers caught up with those of Toluca and said to them:
> Surrender, surrender, for it is your ill luck to have to pay tribute to us and be our vassals. Arriving at Tlacotepec, again there were many people on the side of those of Toluca waiting for the Mexica so as to attack them on the flank. When Axayacatl arrived with forces, and as soon as he saw them, he began to sound a tambourine which they called *yopihue-huetl*, from joy, and then with his plumage he went so fast and ran with such undaunted courage that his enemies trembled. At that moment an Otomi captain by the name of Cuetzpal [with another name, Tlilatl], a valiant warrior, was hidden under a century plant and suddenly, as Axayacatl passed, he came out and wounded him in the thigh, which made him fall on his knees.[8]

Only the timely arrival of Mexica forces saved Axayacatl from death, and in a short time assured the defeat of the enemy. Then immediately, as was customary, a messenger was sent to tell the elderly Tlacaelel the good news about this victory and, at the same time, "he was advised and knew how Axayacatl came to be wounded in the leg, that an Otomi captain had wounded him."[9]

There was a solemn welcome for Axayacatl and his men in Mexico-Tenochtitlan. Very likely much must

Woman *tlahcuilo*, artist and painter of codices (*Telleriano-Remensis*, 30)

have been said about the unpleasant side of the war and particularly about the mishap suffered by the lord of the Mexica. It is natural that Tlacaelel's relatives and friends would know not only the final outcome of the struggle but also other seemingly secondary details that the chroniclers mentioned only in passing. Macuilxochitzin, knowing all about it, composed a song in the memory of what appears to have been one of the last conquests planned by her father. In it she emphasizes the important role played by a group of Otomi women who, by their pleas to Axayacatl, saved the life of the captain who had wounded him.

THE SONG OF MACUILXOCHITZIN

Macuilxochitzin's song is included in the collection preserved in the National Library of Mexico.[10] The daughter of Tlacaelel makes her intention perfectly clear: She wants to give thanks to the supreme God of the Mexica and record for posterity the victory of her people. She says: "I raise my songs, I Macuilxochitzin, with them I gladden the Giver of Life." She confesses that she does not know if her songs would rise to the dwelling place of the Giver of Life but is consoled by thinking that at least they will be known here on earth. Recalling Lord Axayacatl, who was only to survive a short time after the conquest of the Matlatzinca, she continues, as if speaking to him: "Axayacatin, you have conquered the city of Tlacotepec! There went to make forays your flowers, your butterflies. . . . With this you have made offerings of flowers and feathers to the Giver of Life."

Macuilxochitzin then describes the preparations for war as if she had seen them with her own eyes: "Axayacatl puts the eagle shields on the arms of his men, there where the war rages, in the midst of the plain. . . . The flowers of the eagle remain in your hands, Lord Axayacatl . . . on every side Axayacatl made conquests, in Matlatzinco, in Malinalco, in Ocuilan."

Thus praising Axayacatl's deeds that brought into Mexica hands "the flowers of the eagle . . . , divine flowers," Macuilxochitzin devotes a large part of her song to recalling the role played by some women when the great Mexica chieftain was wounded: "There in Xiquipilco was Axayacatl wounded in the leg by an Otomi, his name was Tlilatl." From the chronicles it is known that, due to the prompt arrival of Mexica reinforcements, Tlilatl was taken prisoner. Macuilxochitzin depicts the Otomi turning to his women and ordering them to care for the wounded Axayacatl: "He said to them, 'Prepare a breechcloth and a cape, give these to your man.'"

When Axayacatl recovered, he had the captain Tlilatl brought to him. "And Axayacatl called out: 'Bring the Otomi who wounded me in the leg.'" The poem then comments on the well-founded fear of the Otomi, putting into his mouth words that express his great agitation: "Now truly they will kill me!" Tlilatl came fearfully, bowing low before Axayacatl and humbly offering a deerskin and a large piece of wood, which were probably rich treasures for the poor Otomis.[11] The final part of Macuilxochitzin's song shows her compassion as she says: "He was full of fear the Otomi. But then his women made supplication for him to Axayacatl." Their pleading seems to have reached the heart of the Mexica high ruler, and at least for the moment Tlilatl's life was saved.

This is the theme of the song that presumably was composed by Princess Macuilxochitzin, daughter of Tlacaelel. No other poems by this noble woman or further details of her life are known. The only positive information is that already quoted, by the chronicler Tezozomoc: "Of her was born the prince Cuauhtlapaltzin."[12] However little this may be, Macuilxochitzin confirms and exemplifies the assertion of various native chroniclers: In the pre-Hispanic Nahuatl world there were also feminine "faces and hearts" that, as in the case of the famous Lady of Tula, excelled in the art of poetry.

MACUILXOCHITZIN ICUIC

A nonpehua noncuica,
ni Macuilxochitl,
zan noconahuiltia o a in ipalnemoa,
yn maconnetotilo, *ohuaya, ohuaya!*

Quenonamican,
can o ye ichan
im a itquihua in cuicatl?
Ic zanio nican
y izca anmoxochiuh?
In ma onnetotilo, *ohuaya, ohuaya!*

Temomacehual matlatzincatl,
Itzcohuatzin:
In Axayacatzin ticmomoyahuaco
in altepetl in Tlacotepec, *a ohuaya!*
O ylacatziuh ya ommoxochiuyh,
mopapaloouh.
Ic toconahuiltia.
In matlatzincatl, in Toloca, in Tlacotepec, *a ohuaya.*

Ayaxca ocontemaca
in xochitlaihuitla
ypalnemoa, *ohuaya.*
In quauhichimalli in temac,
ye quimana, *ohuican ouihua,*
yan tlachinolli itic,
yxtlahuatl itic, *ohuaya, ohuaya.*
In neneuhqui in tocuic,
neneuhqui in toxochiuh,

can tiquaochpan,
in toconahuiltia ypalnemoa, *ohuaya, ohuaya.*
In quauhxochitl
in momac ommani,
Axayacatzin.
In teoaxochitl,
in tlachinolxochitl ic,
yzhuayotimani,
yca yhuintihua
in tonahuac onoca, *ohuaya, ohuaya.*

Topan cueponi *a*
yaoxochitl, *a,*
in Ehecatepec, in Mexico, *ye ohoye*
ye huiloya yca yhuintihua
in tonahuac onoc.

Za ye netlapalolo
in tepilhuan,
in acolihuaque,
an antepaneca, *ohuaya, ohuaya.*

In otepeuh Axayaca
nohuian,
Matlatzinco, Malinalco,
Ocuillan, Tequaloya, Xohcotitlan.
Nican ohualquizaco.
Xiquipilco oncan
oquimetzhuitec ce otomitl,
ytoca Tlilatl.

Auh yn oahcico,
quimilhui ycihuahuan:
—Xitlacencahuacan in maxtlatl, in tilmatli,
anquimacazque amoquichui.
Oquinenotzallan:
—Ma huallauh yn otomitl,
yn onechmetzhuitec!
Momauhtihtica yn otomitl,
quittoa:
—Anca ye nechmictizque!
Quihualhuica in huepantli,

in tlaxipehualli in mazatl,
ic quitlapaloco in Axaya.
Momauhtitihuitz.
Auh zan oquitlauhtique yn icihuahuan Axayaca.

SONG OF MACUILXOCHITL

I raise my songs,
I, Macuilxochitl,
with these I gladden the Giver of Life,
may the dance begin!

There Where-in-Someway-One-Exists,
to His house,
are these songs carried?
Or only here
are your flowers?
May the dance begin!

The Matlatzinca,
you well deserve these people, Lord Itzcoatl.
Axayacatzin, you have conquered
the city of Tlacotepec!
There went to make forays
your flowers, your butterflies.
With this we rejoice.
The Matlatzinca are in Toluca, in Tlacotepec.

He makes offerings
of flowers and feathers
to the Giver of Life.
He puts the eagle shields
on the arms of the men,
there where the war rages,
in the midst of the plain.
as our songs,
as our flowers,
thus you, warrior of the shaven head,
give pleasure to the Giver of Life.
The flowers of the eagle
remain in your hands,
lord Axayacatl.

With divine flowers,
with flowers of war,
is covered,
with these becomes intoxicated
he who is on our side.

Above us open
the flowers of war,
in Ehecatepec, in Mexico,
with these becomes intoxicated
he who is on our side.

They have shown themselves fearless,
the princes,
those of Acolhuacan,
you, the Tepanec.

On every side Axayacatl
made conquests,
in Matlatzinco, in Malinalco,
In Ocuillan, in Tequaloya, in Xohcotitlan.
From here he went forth.
There in Xiquipilco was Axayacatl
wounded in the leg by an Otomi,
his name was Tlilatl.

That one went in search of his women,
he said to them:
"Prepare a breechcloth and a cape,
give these to your man."
And Axayacatl called out:
"Bring the Otomi
who wounded me in the leg."
The Otomi was afraid,
he said:
"Now truly they will kill me!"
Then he brought a large piece of wood
and a deerskin,
with these he bowed before Axayacatl.
He was full of fear, the Otomi,
but then his women made supplication for him to Axayacatl.

(*Cantares mexicanos*, National Library of Mexico, fol. 53 v.)

CHAPTER IX

TEMILOTZIN OF TLATELOLCO

*Defender of Tenochtitlan and Singer of
Friendship*
(End Fifteenth Century–7-House, 1525)

Temilotzin was a famous captain. He was not only a contemporary of Prince Cuauhtemoc but also his friend and
companion, destined to play a brilliant part at that leader's side during the days of the Conquest. The indigenous
informants of Sahagún report that Temilotzin was a native of Tlatelolco and later ruler of the small town of
Tzilacatlan.

His wish to become a composer of songs was probably
born during his years as a student in the calmecac (priestly
school) of Tlatelolco, where he was able to learn the traditions, the sacred hymns, and the symbols depicted in
the ancient books. It is known that Temilotzin was an extraordinary warrior who achieved the rank of *tlacatecatl*,
or commander-of-men, and at the same time became a
singer of friendship. As a poet he states that his greatest
desire is to "make friends on the earth," but as a warrior
he has to face an unforeseen aggression by mysterious
foreigners who came from beyond the immense waters.

The memory of Temilotzin is preserved in the indigenous chronicles and also in words spoken on various occasions by his poet friends. One of these poets who sur-

vived the Conquest hailed Temilotzin as defender of the
Mexica metropolis, exclaiming:

> Exert yourself,
> give yourself over to war,
> *Tlacatecatl* Temilotzin,
> the men of Castile have come out of their boats![1]

The extant testimonies show Temilotzin especially active during the siege of Tenochtitlan. Under the most
difficult circumstances, he fulfilled the functions of his
high office as "commander of men." According to a text
in which the ideal image of a tlacatecatl is described, his
duties were to act as

> Chief of the eagles . . . whose occupation is the war which
> takes captives. Great eagle and great ocelot, eagle of the
> yellow claws and powerful wings, ferocious, emissary of
> death. . . . Trained, skillful, with watchful eyes, he arranges
> things, makes plans, carries out the war. He distributes the
> arms, orders and provides the provisions, marks out the road,
> makes inquiries about it, follows the enemy's trail. Arranges
> the war shelters, the wooden houses, the war market. He
> chooses those who guard the captives, selects the best. He
> commands those in charge of the prisoners; is disciplined,
> knows what to do, he gives orders to his people, shows them
> where the enemy will attack.[2]

From the same informants who preserved this image of
the tlacatecatl, it is known that Temilotzin honored his
high military rank while fighting against the men of Castile. During the days of the siege when the conquistadors
tried repeatedly to take possession of the Mexica capital,
Temilotzin, together with other captains and at Cuauhtemoc's side, did his best to save the city.

When the defense was withdrawn to the islet of Tlatelolco, Temilotzin, together with other warriors, went out
to meet the conquerors to cut off their advance. The indigenous record states that

> Then two eagle knights and two tiger knights stood up. . . .
> The first tiger was Temilotzin and the second Coyohuehue-

tzin himself. When the moment came to attack the men of Castile, they began to march. Together with many others they entered their boats. They rowed with all oars, his boat almost flew. . . . Then, when all were engaged in battle, the flutes sounded. Many poor people had been robbed. The Mexica warriors headed against the plunderers. When our enemies saw this, they tried to escape. Many died in the water, they were submerged, they were drowned. . . . Truly, many died there. . . . Once again I say: Many of our enemies died there. . . . The next day all was calm.[3]

Once more the final picture of the Conquest recalls, almost symbolically, the resistance of this commander-of-men: "*Tlacatecatl* Temilotzin stood guard against the enemy, but in vain. He was on guard on a wall, he was dressed like an eagle and carried a bludgeon in his hand with which he tried to prevent their advance. But seeing that it was no longer possible, he jumped into the water, by that means he escaped."[4]

Like a forewarning, a period of ominous calm preceded the fall of Tenochtitlan. Eyewitnesses recalled it: "Suddenly the fighting stopped. Everything was calm. . . . No one even spoke. Our people were falling back. The men of Castile did nothing. Only they remained in their positions. They watched us constantly."[5]

Then Cuauhtemoc and Temilotzin with other captains,

Temilotzin fighting the conquistadors during the siege of the Aztec capital (*Códice florentino*, xii)

seeing that after eighty days of siege all was lost, began to deliberate: "In what form should we submit to the men of Castile, how should it be done and what should we give as tribute."[6]

Not even for a moment did they think of flight. The various indigenous sources of the *Vision of the Vanquished* are in full agreement on this point. Temilotzin, together with other chieftains, was at Cuauhtemoc's side and shared his decision. Two extremely dramatic texts preserve the memory of these last moments: "They took Cuauhtemoc in a boat. . . . Then the people wept, saying: There goes the young prince Cuauhtemoc, there he goes to give himself into the hands of the men of Castile."[7] And then, already on the other bank: "When they came off the water, there were Coyohuehuetzin, Tepantemoctzin, Temilotzin, and Cuauhtemoctzin. They accompanied Cuahtemoctzin to where the Captain [Cortés] and Don Pedro de Alvarado and Doña Malintzin were."[8]

Temilotzin shared the fate of the vanquished Cuauhtemoc when Tenochtitlan fell, and it was also his destiny to accompany the last lord of the Mexica to the very end. In 1524, when Cortés undertook a long journey to the Hibueras in Central America to punish one of his captains who had disregarded his orders, Cuauhtemoc and other princes and warriors, among them Temilotzin, were obliged to join the expedition. At a place named Hueymolan Acalan, in the present-day state of Tabasco, Cuauhtemoc was accused of having instigated the local ruler to side with him and revolt against the Spaniards. After a summary judgment, Cortés ordered Cuauhtemoc and Tetlepanquetzanitzin—ruler of Tlacopan and also a composer of songs—to be executed, hung from a ceiba tree. From the *Anales de Tlatelolco*, it is known that Temilotzin and another noble, named Ecatzin, witnessed Cuauhtemoc's death.

The former commander-of-men and, more important, the singer of friendship who had lost his greatest friend

Priest, standard bearer. Aztec sculpture in stone in the National Museum of Anthropology, Mexico

and lord, had no desire to endure his condition as prisoner any longer. Once Cuauhtemoc was dead it was of no interest to Temilotzin to go on living.

The same *Anales*, perhaps colored by a legendary version, relate the disappearance of Temilotzin. He and the noble Ecatzin had tried to hide after Cuauhtemoc's death but were brought before Cortés and Malintzin, who were on board a ship. Malintzin questioned them chidingly. She asked: "You, Temilotzin, confess the truth. How many lords did you kill during the war?"[9] Temilotzin, who apparently had already decided how he would escape, gave little importance to the words with which he answered her: "Listen, Malintzin, it is just as Ecatzin has told you. How could I bother to count them? I fought, I wounded, I finished off many, without giving attention to it." Then, as if intending to frighten the prisoners, Malintzin said: "Now we are going to visit the great ruler, he who lives in Castile. . . . There you will perish, there you are going to die." Temilotzin, impassive, ended the conversation abruptly: "So be it, let us go there, O Malintzin."

According to the *Anales*, the ship they were on was supposedly going to Spain. In fact, it is said that it was already far from the shore. Temilotzin spoke for the last time to Ecatzin, his companion and friend: "O Ecatzin, where are we going? Where are we? Let us go to our house!" With Tenochtitlan destroyed, the ancient grandeur destroyed, Cuauhtemoc dead and all he had cherished forever lost, Temilotzin could possibly recall at that moment his own reflections on friendship: "To entwine with trembling quetzal feathers and surround with songs the community of friends . . . until all of us will have gone to the region of the dead."

What, in fact, the chronicle tells is that he decided at that moment to try an evasion. He did not know where he could escape, but in any event he could go to the Quenonamican, "Region-Where-in-Someway-One-Exists." The indigenous text offers this extraordinary picture:

Woman, much adorned, Aztec sculpture in stone in the National Museum of Anthropology, Mexico

Temilotzin would not listen nor would he be restrained. . . .
They saw how he threw himself into the water. He swam in
the water towards the Sun. Malintzin called him and said:
"Where are you going, Temilotzin? Come back, come here!"
He did not listen, he went away, he disappeared. No one
knows if he was able to reach the shore, if a serpent devoured
him, if a crocodile did away with him, or if the big fish
finished Temilotzin. . . . In this manner he did away with
himself, no one killed him.[10]

This is what is known about the life of the celebrated
"commander-of-men," Temilotzin. He has been called a
singer of friendship because one of his poems that has
survived is an affirmation of what can be meant by broth-
erhood on earth, community, and the giving of one's heart
to his friends. Like other composers of songs, Temilotzin's life appears paradoxical. The man whose destiny it
was to fight the foreigners of strange faces and witness
the death of the last ruler of the Mexica left us a most
human testimony about himself: "I, Temilotzin, have
come to earth to make friends here."

A COMMENTARY ON TEMILOTZIN'S POEM

Although it is absolutely true that all the metaphors and
forms of expression appearing in this poem can be found
in several other Nahuatl compositions, a certain original-
ity can be perceived if one considers it from two different
viewpoints. Examining its structure, one easily becomes
aware of its well-achieved unity. No deviation from the
theme of friendship occurs: The composer of songs approaches his friends; in various manners encircles them,
among other things, with his own songs. The experience
of friendship will exist until "we have gone to the region
of the dead."

The poem's final part, a variation on the same theme,
can be valued from a different perspective. Temilotzin,
well known to us as a warrior, prefers here to think of
himself as a composer of songs; he wants them to burst
forth for his friends. The supreme God has sent him to

Insignia of a *tlacatecatl,* the military rank of the poet Temilotzin (*Códice Mendoza,* lxviii)

the earth "to make friends here." But his destiny intended him to fight, as never before, against those who were to arrive from beyond the unlimited divine waters, those who at the end were to humiliate the People of the Sun. In resisting the aggression, side by side with Cuauhtemoc, his friend, taking part in all his sorrowful experiences till the moment of his death, Temilotzin demonstrated how deeply he understood the ultimate meaning of friendship.

TEMILOTZIN ICUIC

Ye ni hualla, antocnihuan in:
noconcozcazoya,
nictzinitzcamana, *aya,*
nictlauhquecholihuimolohua,
nicteocuitlaicuiya,
nicquetzalhuixtoilpiz
in icniuhyotli.
Niccuicailacatzoa cohuayotli.
In tecpan nicquixtiz,

an ya tonmochin,
quin icuac tonmochin in otiyaque ye Mictlan.
In yuh ca zan tictlanehuico, *ohuaya, ohuaya.*

Ye on ya nihualla,
ye on ninoquetza,
cuica nonpictihuiz,
cuica nonquixtihuiz,
antocnihuan.
Nechhualihua teotl,
nehua ni xochhuatzin,
nehua ni Temilotzin,
nehua ye nonteicniuhtiaco nican, *ohuaya, ohuaya.*

POEM OF TEMILOTZIN

I have come, o my friends,
with necklaces I entwine,
with plumage of the *tzinitzcan* bird I bind,
with feathers of the macaw I gird,
I paint with colors of gold,
with trembling quetzal feathers I enfold
the totality of my friends.
With songs I encircle the community.
I will bring it into the palace,
there will we all be,
until we have gone to the region of the dead.
Thus we have been loaned to one another.

Now I have come,
I am standing,
I will compose songs,
make the songs burst forth,
for you, my friends.
I am sent from God,
I have flowers,
I am Temilotzin,
I have come to make friends here.

(*Romances de los señores de Nueva España*,
Benson Latin American Library, University of Texas, Austin, fol. 2 r.)

PART THREE

POETS FROM THE REGION OF
PUEBLA-TLAXCALA

You who come from there,
from Tlaxcala,
you have come to sing
to the sound of shining drums
in the place of the kettledrums!

(*Cantares mexicanos*, National Library of Mexico, fol. 10 v.)

On the other side of the Sierra Nevada, beyond the mighty volcanoes Popocatepetl, "Smoking Mountain," and Iztaccihuatl, "White Lady," several Nahuatl chiefdoms and provinces flourished, some of them with long histories. This was the case of Cholula, where the highest pyramid in the world was built. Cholula, with its many temples and its character as a sacred city devoted to the cult of the god Quetzalcoatl, had a history so long that its ultimate roots were embedded deep in the Preclassic period, antedating the Christian era.

Other chiefdoms, such as the one made up of the four allied Tlaxcalan heads, although not having such a rich history, had managed, nevertheless, to preserve complete independence vis-à-vis the threatening power of the Mexica, lords of Mexico-Tenochtitlan and of many subject provinces. And there were several other towns that still controlled small territories in a semiindependent form of existence. Huexotzinco, Tecamachalco, and Cuauhtinchan stand out as good examples of this.

An interesting fact is that, notwithstanding the upheavals, in consequence of the Spanish Conquest, a relatively large number of indigenous testimonies concerning these chiefdoms and towns was saved from oblivion. Thus in the case of Cholula two historical books or codices exist. From the Tlaxcalan towns we have several annals, a good number of codices, and an important chronicle written in Spanish by the Mestizo Diego Muñoz Camargo. Huexotzinco, Cuauhtinchan, and Tecamachalco also gave origin to other very valuable testimonies, annals written in Nahuatl, scrolls of tributes, several codices, and other accounts in Nahuatl and Spanish. Such a documentary wealth is indicative of the cultural significance of all these centers.

Of parallel interest is the fact that in the two main sources of the Nahuatl songs and poems, *Cantares mexicanos* and *Romances*, many compositions are expressely attributed to composers of songs from the regions of Tlaxcala, Huexotzinco, and Tecamachalco. A large proportion of the songs that are transcribed with that genre of attribution cannot be assigned to any given composer. They are simply anonymous productions from Tlaxcala, Huexotzinco, or Tecamachalco. Only a few of the songs coming from one or another of these regions includes a gloss in which the name of the composer is provided. There is in particular one long production, a sort of dialogue that probably took place at the palace of Tecayehuatzin, Lord of Huexotzinco, in which the names of several participant poets are preserved, most of them members of the nobility of Tlaxcala and other provinces of what is today the territory of the state of Puebla.

Thanks to attributions like those made in the dialogue and others that accompany determined songs, we know that in the ample region beyond the mighty volcanoes, the art of song composition also flourished. Some examples of this will be offered here. They are the productions attributed to Tecayehuatzin of Huexotzinco; to Ayocuan Cuetzpaltzin, a great sage from Tecamachalco; and to the group of Tlaxcalan composers of songs, among them, Xayacamach of Tizatlan and the well-known ancient ruler Xicohtencatl, who lived during the Spanish Conquest.

Glyph of Tlaxcala

CHAPTER X

TECAYEHUATZIN OF HUEXOTZINCO

The Ruler and Sage Who Called for a Dialogue on the Meaning of Flower and Song

(Second Half Fifteenth Century–
Early Sixteenth Century)

Tecayehuatzin was outstanding among the most celebrated tlamatinime, or sages, of the Puebla-Tlaxcala region. However, his life was not primarily that of a man dedicated to poetry and meditation. Tecayehuatzin had become lord of Huexotzinco due to his lineage and by the election of his people. Various sources show him acting in this capacity around the beginning of the sixteenth century.

An insight into what Tecayehuatzin's life must have been like can be gained by recalling the position of Huexotzinco in relation to the chiefdoms of Tlaxcala, Cholula, and Mexico-Tenochtitlan. Huexotzinco enjoyed relative independence but, due to geographic location, was influenced by its Tlaxcalan neighbors and sometimes by the all-powerful Mexica. Therefore, it would be strange if Prince Tecayehuatzin could escape the oscillations and intrigues implicit in Huexotzinco's relations with Tlaxcala and Mexico.

But in spite of the anxieties connected with state affairs, Tecayehuatzin—as the poet Ayocuan Cuetzpaltzin noticed and expressed—was deeply inclined to music, and frequently "drums and tortoise shells resounded in his palace":

> There Tecayehuatzin keeps watch,
> there he plays the flute and sings,
> in his house of Huexotzinco. . . .
> There is his house,
> where the tambourine of the tigers is found,
> where songs are caught up
> in the sound of the drums.
> As if they were flowers,
> tapestries of quetzal are unfurled there,
> in the house of the paintings.[1]

Thus it would appear that Tecayehuatzin lived two different lives. He was prominent among those who sought to clarify and enrich the meaning of flower and song; but as a ruler he also learned to practice deceit and intrigue. When hard pressed, he begged aid from Motecuhzoma to save his people from the Tlaxcalans in fighting the Mexica.

Tecayehuatzin had several friends he invited to his Huexotzinco palace. However, as a ruler, he had to be concerned for his people, especially during those difficult days when there was a famine or war threatened. Thus, contrary to the words of one of his poems in which he said "the hearts of our friends are true," he had to pretend and play false, following the sinuous ways that are almost a necessity for professional politicians.

One of the chroniclers who wrote about Tecayehuatzin is the Tlaxcalan Diego Muñoz Camargo. When referring to the war with the Huexotzinca around the beginning of the sixteenth century, he says: "The Tlaxcalans laid waste the cornfields and burned the houses and palaces of the Lord Tecayehuatzin."[2]

Fray Diego de Durán in his *Historia*, Alvarado Tezozomoc in his *Crónica mexicana*, and Torquemada in his *Monarquía indiana* all mention events related to Tecayehuatzin's endeavors as ruler. Durán, telling of the

Mexica assistance received by the Huexotzinca in their fight against Tlaxcala, also mentions the change of sides that Tecayehuatzin was forced to try. Motecuhzoma soon learned of the intentions of his former ally. To be certain of what he had heard, he sent messengers to invite Tecayehuatzin to a feast in Mexico-Tenochtitlan, thus to see if he still was his old friend. Tecayehuatzin's reply to the messengers is proof of the double life forced upon this creator of poetry and initiator of intrigues. According to Durán, Tecayehuatzin "began to weep" as he replied to Motecuhzoma's messengers:

> Tell your lord that my desire is to serve him all my life because of the fine treatment which he has accorded me and my people in his city, but this fickle and unpredictable people have become friendly with those of Cholula and have asked me, under penalty of depriving me of my reign, and destroying my entire offspring, not to accept peace and friendship from you. However, in spite of this, I will send some of my nobles to be present at the celebration in my place.[3]

Perhaps Tecayehuatzin had to resort to intrigues such as this to remain alive. Very likely, he found it more pleasant to compose poems and meditate on flower and song. A dialogue, in which Tecayehuatzin played an important role, is preserved in four folios of the *Cantares mexicanos* in the National Library. Tecayehuatzin appears in it as the one who called together his friends, other sages and poets, to discern with them some of the ultimate meanings of flower and song, poetry, art, and symbolism.

THE DIALOGUE ABOUT FLOWER AND SONG

The meeting convened by Tecayehuatzin was probably held in a garden near his palace in Huexotzinco. There the various guests were seated, enjoying the place as well as the tobacco and the foaming chocolate drink that were passed around. Tecayehuatzin, according to the Nahuatl text, opens the dialogue with an invitation and a eulogy

A *tlamatini,* master of flower and song, expressing his thought (*Códice florentino* iv)

of flower and song.[4] After welcoming his friends he says
that, at least for a brief time, he has borrowed their presence: "I have brought the princes together, jades, quetzal
feathers."

It is true that in this remarkable dialogue one perceives
a recurring use of many of the well-known Nahuatl metaphors. But it is also certain that in this poetic confrontation arranged—if one gives credit to the text—by Lord
Tecayehuatzin, a further step is taken. The purpose of the
dialogue is precisely to look for the different possible
meanings of a particular metaphor. Tecayehuatzin sets
forth the theme to be discussed: "Flower and song, is this
perhaps the only truth on the earth?"

The answers of those who attended the gathering were
diverse. Some of their responses are included in the chapters of this book devoted to several of the participants, especially Ayocuan Cuetzpaltzin, Xayacamach of Tizatlan,
and Aquianhtzin of Ayapanco. The case of three more
poets, Cuauhtencoztli, Motenehuatzin, and Monencauhtzin, is different. Because little or nothing is known about
their lives, instead of dealing with them in other chapters, their expressions will be transcribed here as part of

the dialogue. They will be also commented upon in reference to Tecayehuatzin's conception of this subtle form of confrontation.

The Lord of Huexotzinco wishes to know what is the ultimate meaning and value of flower and song. His friend Ayocuan Cuetzpaltzin refers to the origins and possible endurance of poetry, art, and symbolism: To him flowers and songs are a gift of the gods, and, in the end, may be the best kind of remembrance man can possibly leave when he has to march to the region of mystery.

Aquiauhtzin, of Ayapanco, has a different view. In his opinion art and symbolism are the only possible way to invoke the supreme Giver of Life, who perhaps becomes present by way of the symbols. It could be said that we seek Him like one who, singing among the flowers, goes in quest of a friend.

One of the participants, whose name but not his life is known to us, Cuauhtencoztli, expresses his doubts about the truth and value of flower and song because he himself questions the roots that man—the composer of the songs— may have on the earth:

> I, Cuauhtencoztli, am suffering here:
> Does man have any roots?
> If not, our song will no longer be true.
> What stands and remains?
> What reaches its aim?
> Here we live, here we are,
> but we are impoverished,
> o my friends.[5]

Motenehuatzin—one of the three participants who are unknown to us—and also Tecayehuatzin reply to Cuauhtencoztli. They want to dispel what they consider to be a pessimistic attitude. Motenehuatzin declares:

> I have come here only to sing.
> What are you saying, O my friends?

> What are you discussing here?
> O princes, here is the flowery patio.[6]

Nevertheless, Motenehuatzin has to acknowledge that, even "in the midst of spring," singing is often accompanied by weeping:

> The truth is we scarcely live,
> for we are enbittered by sorrow. . . .
> Dissimilar flowers,
> dissimilar songs,
> in my house all is affliction.[7]

Tecayehuatzin's intervention, the second in the dialogue, is a kind of plea. He craves to see and hear "those who fill their flutes with laughter, those who speak with the turquoise-incrusted drums, and cause them to sound and resound." He wants to know more from those who have cultivated their fields of flowers. Prince Monencauhtzin—a third poet about whose life and deeds we are ignorant—is introduced at this point by Tecayehuatzin:

> Hear Prince Monencauhtzin,
> he opens his wings,
> as if they were golden fans,
> he hovers among the flower-decked drums.[8]

Monencauhtzin's approach to the theme of flower and song is perhaps the most simple of all: He feels he is enriched by poetry. Beyond any subtle complications, he declares he is a poet open to converse with and learn from others:

> How many have been enriched with your songs?
> You have given them much delight,
> the flowers move!
> I walk everywhere,
> I am poet.
> Fragrant, precious flowers
> have rained down,

in the flowery patio,
in the house of butterflies.[9]

The wise ruler of Tizatlan, Lord Xayacamach, enters on the scene. He claims that flower and song—the realm of the symbols—like the hallucinogenic mushrooms, are the best means to escape from boredom, sadness, and suffering. When the mushrooms are taken in the sacred ceremonies, when one thus becomes as inebriated, one sees marvelous visions, evanescent forms of multiple colors. But that world of color vanishes later as if it were a dream. Afterwards man finds himself weary, forced to again face the somber problems of daily life. This is for Xayacamach at least a part of the meaning of flower and song. He describes himself as a singer and composer of songs who collects flowers to bedeck his own little hut, and even if he has sprung up among songs, nonetheless he is to the others just a destitute friend.

When the dialogue draws to a close, Tecayehuatzin speaks for the third and last time. His heart remains open to doubt, but he is still anxious to know whether flower and song is the only way to express true words on the earth. Although the answers offered so far have been diverse, he trusts that he is able to enunciate something on which all will agree. This last part of the dialogue, in which Tecayehuatzin concludes it, is vividly expressive: At least flower and song is that which makes the poets' friendship possible. This is "the dream of a word," the path of the symbols that leads one to know that "the hearts of our friends are true."

Besides this dialogue about flower and song, few compositions attributed to Tecayehuatzin have been preserved. They all express ideas and feelings similar to those he let his friends know at the meeting they had in the garden, close to his palace in Huexotzinco. Tecayehuatzin insists, declares that his great yearning is to discover how to compose songs that could lead him to a plenitude of happiness, perhaps "in the house of springtime" or "where the Giver of Life descends."

Striving to discover the meaning of art and symbolism, Tecayehuatzin not only pondered the problem throughout his lifetime but also allowed himself to be influenced by whatever he saw or experienced. He delights in commenting on the warmth and sparkling light of the sun; he remembers the pleasure of being with his friends, the joy of having the old paintings near him, and listening to the music of the flutes. Tecayehuatzin also evokes the shouts of war, the blood as red as flowers, the tufts of quetzal feathers, and the death of Tlacahuepan, beloved son of Motecuhzoma. When the rain falls, giving new life to flowers and plants, he tries to feel at last within himself the true meaning of the songs and to come, as close as possible, to Him by Whom all live.

TLA OC TONCUICACAN

Tla oc toncuicacan,
tla oc toncuicatocan,
in xochitonalo calitec, *aya,*
antocnihuan!
Catlique?
In niquicnamiqui.
Canin quintemohua?
quen on huehuetitlan,
ya nican ah, *ohuaya, ohuaya.*
Zan nixochitlatlaoncoya,
in namocniuhtzin,
in zan chichimecatecuitli,
Tecayehuatzin.
Ac in, aoc timochin,
ticahuiltizque,
tic-huellamachtizque,
Moyocoyatzin?

Intla ca nipa, yeccan ten, Tlaxcalla,
noxoxochipoyoncuica.

Tla poyoncuica,
in Xicontencatli, in Temilotzin,
zan Cuitlizcatl tecuitli, *ohuaya, ohuaya.*
Cuauhtamiyohuachan,
oceloyohualichan,
Huexotzinco.
In oncan in itlamicohuana
in maceuhcatzin, in in Tlacahuepan.
Niman oncan on ahuiya
ixochicuapilhuan,
ixopancala itecuhhuan.
Ye ahuaya yya o yye, ohuaya, ohuaya.
Zan cacahuaxochitica,
tlapapahuitihuitze,
ye oncan in xochiahahuiya
aitec.
Yehuantzin conitquitihuitze iteocuitlachimal.
Ma tla iecacehuaz,
teoaxochicuauhcocoltica,
quetzalipantica
tonteahuiltico
xopancala itec.
O ahuaya, oaye, ohuaya, ohuaya.

Chalchiuhtetzilacatli ihcacahua, *ohuaya,*
xochiayauac quiyahuitl
on quiztoc in tlalticpac.
Zacauan cala imanca
in ixtilahuaquitequi.
Ye temohua ipiltzin.
Ayeo, ayya, ohuaya, ohuaya.

Xoxopan in ompa temoya,
in Ipalnemohuani.
In mocuicaizhuayotia
moxochiapana huehuetitlan,
momalina.
Ye motech on quiza
a ihuintixochitli,
ma xon ahuiyacan! *Ohuaya, ohuaya.*

NOW LET US SING

Now let us sing,
let us continue our songs
in the midst of the flowery light and warmth,
O my friends!
Who are they?
I go out to meet them.
Where shall I look for them?
Here indeed,
in the place of the drums,
I only invent flowery songs,
I, your friend,
I am only the Chichimec lord,
Tecayehuatzin.
Perhaps some one of us,
or probably all of us,
will give joy,
will make happy
the Inventor of Himself?

In Tlaxcala, in good season,
may my flowery dream-stirring songs be there.
May the songs that intoxicate,
those of Xicohtencatl, of Temilotzin,
of the Prince Cuitlizcatl be there.

The Tamoanchan of the eagles,
the House of Night of the tigers,
are in Huexotzinco.
There is the place of the death
of Tlacahuepan, who obtained merit with it.
There they rejoice,
the flowers which are the princes' community,
the lords, in their houses of springtime.
With flowers of the cacao tree,
He calls out and arrives quickly,
there with the flowers He is joyful
in the midst of the waters.
He arrives quickly with his shield of gold.

So with fans,
with staffs of red flowers,
with banners of quetzal feathers,
let us come to give joy
in the interior of the houses of springtime.

The kettledrums, color of jade, resound,
a shower of flowery dew
has fallen over the earth.
In the house of yellow feathers
it pours down with force.
His son has come down.

He descends there in the springtime,
the Giver of Life.
His songs make flourish,
the place of the drums is adorned with flowers,
it is interwoven.
Now they come forth from there,
the flowers that intoxicate.
O, rejoice.

(*Romances de los señores de Nueva España,*
Benson Latin American Library, University of Texas, Austin, fols. 1 r.–2 r.)

TLATOLPEHUALIZTLI

Can tyanemi a, ticuicanitl?
Ma ya hualmoquetza xochihuehuetl
quetzalticahuiconticac,
teocuitlaxochinenepaniuhticac
y ay amo aye yliamo ayehuiy, ohuaya, ohuaya
Tiquimonahuiltiz in tepilhuan,
teteucti in quauhtlo, ocelotl.

Yn tlacahce otemoc aya huehuetitlan,
ye nemi in cuicanitl,
zan quiquetzalintoma ya,
quexexeloa aya ycuic Ipalnemoa.

Quiyananquilia in coyolyantototl.
Oncuicatinemi, xochimana.
Mana ya toxocho, *ohuaya, ohuaya.*

In canon in noconcaqui ytlatol, *aya,*
tlacahzo yehuatl Ipalnemoa, quiyananquilia,
quiyananquilia in coyolyantototl,
oncuicatinemi, xochimana, *manaya.*

In chalchihuitl *ohuaye* on quetzalpihpixauhtimani,
a ym motlatol *huia,*
No yuh ye quittoa a Ayoquan, yehua yan Cuetzpal, *ohuaye,*
anqui nel in ye quimatin Ipalnemoa, *ohuaya, ohuaya.*

No iuh quichihuacon
teuctlon, timaloa
ye zan quetzalmaquiztla
matiloltica,
ya conahuiltia ycel teotl, *huia.*

Ach canon azo ceyan Ipalnemoa?
Ach canon azo tle nel in tlalticpac? *Ohuaya, ohuaya.*

Macuelachic
ma oc ixquich cahuitl,
niquinnotlanehui in chalchiuhtin,
in maquiztin, in tepilhuan.
Zan nicxochimalina in tecpillotl, *huia.*
Zan ca ica nocuic yca ya noconylacatzohua
a in huehuetitlan, a *ohuaya, ohuaya.*
Oc noncohuati nican Huexotzinco.
Y nitlahtohuani, ni Tecayehuatzin, *huiya*
chalchiuhti zan quetzalitztin,
y niquincenquixtia in tepilhuan, *aya.*
Zan nicxochimalina in tecpillotl, *huia, ohuaya, ohuaya.*

THE BEGINNING OF THE DIALOGUE

Where have you been, O composer of songs?
Make ready the flowery drum
that is wreathed with quetzal feathers,
intertwined with golden flowers.
You will delight the nobles,
the eagle warriors and the jaguar warriors.

Surely he went down to the place of the kettledrums,
surely the poet is there,

unfolding his precious songs,
offering them, one by one, to the Giver of Life.

The little-bell bird responds to Him.
It sings, it offers flowers,
it offers our flowers.
I hear its voices there,
truly it answers to the Giver of Life,
the little-bell bird responds,
it sings, it offers flowers,

Your words rain down
like jades and precious feathers!
Ayocuan Cuetzpaltzin also speaks in this way,
surely he knows the Giver of Life.

That famous lord
also comes here to speak in this way,
the lord who delights the one God,
with bracelets of quetzal feathers
and with perfumes.

Might it not be pleasing to the Giver of Life?
Might it not be the only true thing on earth?

For a brief moment,
for the time being,
I have borrowed the princes:
bracelets, precious stones,
I surround the nobles only with flowers.
I bring them together with my songs
in the place of the kettledrums.
I have called this meeting here in Huexotzinco.
I, Lord Tecayehuatzin,
have brought the princes together:
precious stones, quetzal feathers.

(*Cantares mexicanos*, National Library of Mexico, fol. 10 r.)

ITLATOL TEMICTLI

Auh tocnihuane,
tla xoconcaquican yn itlatol temictli, *ayahue,*
xoxopantla technemitia,

in teocuitlaxilotl, techonythuitia
tlauhquecholelotl, techoncozcatia.
In ticmati ye, *ohuaya ye,* ontlaneltoca
toyiollo, tocnihua! *Ohuaya, ohuaya.*

THE DREAM OF A WORD

And, O friends,
hear the dream of a word:
Each spring gives us life,
the golden ear of corn refreshes us,
the tender ear of corn becomes a necklace for us.
We know that the hearts
of our friends are true!

(*Cantares mexicanos,* National Library of Mexico, fol. 12 r.)

CHAPTER XI

AYOCUAN CUETZPALTZIN

White Eagle, of Tecamachalco

(Second Half Fifteenth Century–Early
Sixteenth Century)

Ayocuan Cuetzpaltzin was praised in several songs
as a poet and wiseman. From the region of Chalco an
anonymous composer of chants expressed the following
about him:

> There remain the interwoven flowers,
> color of the blue bird
> with shadings of the red bird:
> they are your heart, your word,
> O Prince, Chichimec Lord, Ayocuan,
> reveal yourself on earth at least for a moment! [1]

Ayocuan was from the region of Puebla. According to a
Nahuatl testimony in the *Historia Tolteca-Chichimeca*,
he was the son of the Chichimec Prince Cuetzpaltzin
the Elder, who governed the towns of Cohuayocan and
Cuauhtepec at the beginning of the fifteenth century. [2]
Another source also mentions his ruling the province of
Tecamachalco between 1420 and 1441. [3] However, in 1441
he was attacked by the people of Coatlinchan, Cholula,
Huexotzinco, and Tlaxcala and was forced to give up his
domain. [4]

The *Historia Tolteca-Chichimeca* includes an interesting entry for the year 1448 concerning Cuetzpaltzin's son, Ayocuan, who was to become a distinguished poet: "Cuetzpaltzin then took his sons Xochicozcatl, Quetzalecatl, and Ayocuan to the town of Quimixtlan to be educated."[5] That place, whose name means "The Site Shrouded in Clouds," is located northeast of the Citlaltepetl mountain, in a high region where mist and rain are frequent. Ayocuan passed his youth in close contact with nature, receiving an education from his father and teachers, who introduced him to the wisdom of the ancient beliefs and traditions.

During his adult life, Ayocuan often visited Huexotzinco and Tlaxcala, invited by Tecayehuatzin, the Lord of Huexotzinco, and his other poet friends. A commentary on one of his poems recalls that as he went along the roads of Huexotzinco and Tlaxcala, Ayocuan Cuetzpaltzin often recited out loud poems and phrases that seemed to contain the essence of his thoughts:

> Let the earth forever remain!
> Let the mountains stay!
> Thus spoke Ayocuan Cuetzpaltzin,
> in Tlaxcala, in Huexotzinco.[6]

It is not known positively whether Ayocuan, like his father, governed any towns in the Puebla-Tlaxcala region. But another anonymous song records that he became "the Chichimec lord, Ayocuan, priest [*teohua*], White Eagle," without mentioning the time or place when and where he fulfilled these functions.[7]

The *Historia Tolteca-Chichimeca* also mentions an incident that reveals another facet of the character of Ayocuan. It stated that in the year 12-Flint, or 1502, Ayocuan together with another lord named Ixcocatzin appeared before the prince Totomochtli in an effort to come to an agreement in a dispute over the ownership of some land: "Year 12-Flint. At that time Totomochtli took our land

Ayocuan, of Tecamachalco, the wise man who repeated along the roads of Tlaxcala and Huexotzinco: "Let the earth abide! Let the mountains remain standing!"

there in Tlaxcotenpan. After he had taken it, Ixcocatzin and Ayocuatzin petitioned him saying: Listen, O prince, although the property there in Tlaxocopa Zoltepec may belong to your younger brother, Tezcacohuat Quaytzin, does he perhaps only eat and drink there? Let us come to an understanding."[8]

Thus it seems that Ayocuan Cuetzpaltzin passed his life with lords and princes, conversing with poets, acting as mediator, reciting along the Huexotzincan and Tlaxcalan roads the poems in which he summed up the essence of his meditations. Although not many of his compositions have survived, what is known justifies the many eulogies accorded him. Reading them, one can only echo the wish of one who exclaimed: "Would that he come at least a moment to give you pleasure O Ayocuan, White Coyote!"[9]

AYOCUAN'S POETIC EXPRESSION

The few remaining examples of Ayocuan's poetry permit a glimpse into the heart of his thinking. As already mentioned, one of the songs composed in his honor calls him *teohua*, which means priest. Another colleague, Tecayehuatzin of Huexotzinco, stated that "certainly Ayocuan Cuetzpaltzin has come close to the Giver of Life."[10] What is known of his poetic work also reveals something of his religious sentiments.

The point of departure in Ayocuan's thinking—as was also the case with other poets of ancient Mexico—seems to have been his experience with the transitoriness of all that exists. From this experience arose a kind of awareness that led him to recognize, and finally assert, the futility of man and all his productions.

Ayocuan says, "In vain we have come, in vain we have blossomed forth on the earth." He believes in art and symbolism but because man's nature is empty, he feels obliged to accept that "our yearning spoils the beautiful flowers, the beautiful songs, and our inventiveness makes them lose their fragrance."

For him, "the earth is the region of the fleeting moment." Perhaps that is why, along the roads of Tlaxcala and Huexotzinco, he repeated: "Let the earth remain! Let the mountains stay!": But if all is insubstantial on earth, including man's creations, Ayocuan then asks himself, what can we assert about the place where, after death, they say that in some way one lives? He wants to know: "Is one happy there? Is there friendship there? Or is it only here on earth we come to know our faces?"

Seeking something that will survive beyond the "region of the fleeting moment," he recognizes the value of friendship, "a shower of precious flowers." He accepts that "in vain we have come, we have blossomed forth on the earth," but believes that at least there will remain the symbols, flowers, and songs that man has conceived and expressed. And finally, channeling his religious sentiments, he states that the best of man's destinies on earth is "to exert himself, letting his heart desire the flowers of the Giver of Life."

Ayocuan asks his poet friends if perchance any of them "have spoken with God." A result perhaps of the intervention of the one who transcribed the poem—it sounds indeed like a Christian addition—Ayocuan appears, stating that when the kettledrums, the tortoise shells, the music of the flutes, and the poems are heard, "God, our Father, comes down here." By spreading out the tapestries of quetzal in the house of paintings, "thus is venerated in the valley and on the mountain the one God." The same can be said concerning the last words attributed to him in the dialogue of flower and song: "My golden house of paintings is also Your house, one God!"

Nonetheless, the little we know about Ayocuan leads us to take as valid the assertion that he was a teohua, a priest, a "White Eagle" in search of knowledge pertaining to the gods. As in the days of his youth, when he was in Quimixtlan, that lofty place where the rains fall on the earth to rise as mist and again become clouds, Ayocuan was always in search of the heights.

MA HUEL MANIN TLALLI!

Ma huel manin tlalli!
Ma huel ica tepetl!
Quihualitoa Ayocuan, zan yehuan Cuetzpaltzin,
Tlaxcallan, Huexotzinco.
In a izquixochitl, cacahuazochitl,
ma onnemahmaco.
Ma huel mani tlalla!

LET THE EARTH FOREVER REMAIN!

Let the earth forever remain!
Let the mountains stay!
Thus spoke Ayocuan Cuetzpaltzin,
in Tlaxcala, in Huexotzinco.
Flowers of toasted maize, flowers of the chocolate tree,
may they be scattered.
Let the earth forever remain!

(*Cantares mexicanos*, National Library of Mexico, fol. 14 v.)

AYN ILHUICAC ITIC

Ayn ilhuicac itic ompa ye ya huitz
in yectli yan xochitl, yectli yan cuicatl.
Conpoloan tellel,
conpoloan totlayocol,
y tlacahzo yehuatl in chichimecatl teuctli in Tecayehuatzin.
Yca xonahuiacan! *A, ohuaya, ohuaya.*

Moquetzalizquixochintzetzeloa in icniuhyotl.
Aztacaxtlatlapantica,
ye on malinticac in quetzalxiloxochitl:
ymapan onnehnemi,
conchihchichintinemih
in teteuctin, in tepilhuan, *a ohuaya, ohuaya.*

Zan teocuitlacoyoltototl
o huel yectlin amocuic,
huel yectli in anquehua.
Anquin ye oncan y xochitl yiahualiuhcan.
Y xochitl ymapan amoncate, yn amontlahtlahtoa.
yee huaya, ohui, ohui ilili, y yao
ayyahue ho amaha ilili, ahua y yahuia.
Oh ach anca tiquechol, in Ipalnemoa?
O ach anca titlatocauh yehuan teotl? *Huiya.*
Achtotiamehuan anquitztoque tlahuizcalli,
amoncuicatinemi, *ohui, ohui, ilili* . . .
Maciuhtia o in quinequi noyollo,
zan chimalli xochitl,
in ixochiuh Ipalnemoani.

Quen conchiuaz noyollo yehua?
Onen tacico,
tonquizaco in tlalticpac, *a, ohuaya, ohuaya.*
Zan ca iuhquin onyaz
in o ompopoliuhxochitla?
An tle notleyo yez in quenmanian?
An tle nitauhca yez in tlalticpac?
Manel xochitl, manel cuicatl!
Quen conchihuaz noyollo yehua?
Onentacico,
tonquizaco in tlalticpac, *ohuaya, ohuaya.*

Man tonahuiacan, antocnihuan,
ma onnequechnahualo nican, *huiyaa.*
Xochintlalticpac, ontiyanemi.
Ye nican ayac quitlamitehuaz
in xochitl, in cuicatl,
in mani a ychan Ipalnemohuani.
y iao a ilili, i iao ayahue, aye oyohuaya.

Yn zan cuel achitzincan tlalticpac,
Oc no iuhcan quenonamican?
Cuix oc pacohua?

Icniuhtihua?
Auh yn amo zanio nican
tontiximatico in tlalticpac?
y yiao ha ilili yiao . . .

FROM WITHIN THE HEAVENS

From within the heavens they come,
the beautiful flowers, the beautiful songs,
but our yearning spoils them,
our inventiveness makes them lose their fragrance,
although not those of the Chichimec prince Tecayehuatzin.
With his, rejoice!

Friendship is a shower of precious flowers.
White tufts of heron feathers
are woven with precious red flowers,
among the branches of the trees
under which stroll and sip
the lords and nobles.

Your beautiful song
is a golden wood thrush
most beautiful, you raise it up.
You are in a field of flowers.
Among the flowery bushes you sing.
Are you perchance a precious bird of the Giver of Life?
Perchance you have spoken with God?
As soon as you saw the dawn,
you began to sing.
Would that I exert myself, that my heart desire,

the flowers of the shield,
the flowers of the Giver of Life.

What can my heart do?
In vain we have come,
we have blossomed forth on the earth.
Will I have to go alone
like the flowers that perish?
Will nothing remain of my name?
Nothing of my fame here on earth?
At least my flowers, at least my songs!
What can my heart do?
In vain we have come,
we have blossomed forth on the earth.

Let us enjoy, O friends,
here we can embrace.
We stroll now over the flowery earth.
No one here can do away
with the flowers and the songs,
they will endure in the house of the Giver of Life.

Earth is the region of the fleeting moment.
Is it also thus in the Place
Where in Some Way One Lives?

Is one happy there?
Is there friendship?
Or is it only here on earth
we come to know our faces?

(*Cantares mexicanos*, National Library of Mexico, fol. 10 r.)

HUEXOTZINCO ICUIC

Hualixtococ, hualcocoliloya
yn atl in tepetl, y Huexotzinco,
tzihuactlan, tzaqualotoc,
in tlacochahuayotoc in Huexotzinco, *ya ohuaya.*

Tetzilacatl, ayotl
cahuantoc aya amocal,
in manica Huexotzinco.
Yn oncan ontlapia in Tecayehuatzin,

quecehuatl teuctli
ontlapitza, oncuica,
zan ca ye ichan ye Huexotzinco, *ya ohuaya.*
Xontlacaquican: *yapa, papa, ilili.*
ye hualtemoya in tota Teotl.
Can ca ye ichan,
ocelocacahuehuetl comontoc, aya,
in tetzilacacuicatl,
oncahuantoc ye oncan, *ohuaya, ohuaya.*

Ach in iuhca a, *ayahue,* xochitl,
can zanitli quetzalli ia quemitl huilantoc, *ayahue,*
amoxcalitec.
Ynic onpialo tlaloyan, tepetl,
ynic onpialo yn icel teotl, *a ohuaya . . .*

Xochimitletlehuatoc
mochalchiuhcancacal.
Noteocuitlaamoxcacal,
anca ye mochan, yn icel teotl!

BESIEGED, HATED, HUEXOTZINCO WOULD BE

Besieged, hated,
the city of Huexotzinco would be
if it were surrounded by darts,
Huexotzinco encircled with sharp-pointed arrows.

The kettledrum, the tortoise shell
make echo in your house,
they are established in Huexotzinco.
There Tecayehuatzin stands guard,
the lord Quecehuatl
plays the flute there, sings,
in his house of Huexotzinco.
Listen:
God, our Father comes down here.
Here is His house,
where the tambourine of the tigers is found,
where songs hang suspended
in the sound of the kettledrums.

As if they were flowers,
there the mantles of quetzal are spread out,
in the house of paintings.
Thus is venerated in the valley and on the mountain,
thus is venerated the one God.

Like flowery and flaming darts
your precious houses rise up.
My golden house of paintings,
is also Your house, one God!

(*Cantares mexicanos*, National Library of Mexico, fol. 12 r.)

CHAPTER XII

XAYACAMACH OF TIZATLAN

A Successful Ruler Who Sings About Himself
(Second Half Fifteenth Century)

The attributes of Xayacamach as a composer of songs
were certainly valued by Tecayehuatzin, lord of Huexotzinco who, toward the end of the fifteenth century, as we
have seen, gathered with other composers of poems to
discuss the ultimate meaning of "flower and song," poetry,
and the universe of the symbols. Among those mentioned
in that remarkable dialogue, the names of Ayocuan Cuetzpaltzin, Aquiauhtzin, of Ayapanco, and Xayacamach stand
out. Their prestige as masters of the word is also acknowledged in other sources and has surpassed oblivion, as con-
firmed, among other things, by the present book.

Let us recall the information those sources give about
the life and the literary creations of Xayacamach. The
chronicles of Tlaxcala speak of two prominent men who
had the same name. The first Xayacamach was the ruler
of Tizatlan, in Tlaxcala, in the first half of the fifteenth
century.[1] He was a contemporary of Motecuhczoma Ilhuicamina. During the war of the Mexica against the Huaxteca, Xayacamach sided with the latter. The Mexica victory brought an imposition of tributes on the Huaxteca
and an ominous death to Xayacamach.

The second Xayacamach, our composer of songs, was also born in Tizatlan, around the middle of the fifteenth century. He was the son of Aztahua, who had also ruled in his hometown. Three of Aztahua's sons, Huitlaloteuctli, Xayacamach, and Xicohtencatl, were to succeed him in the government of Tizatlan. Xayacamach and Xicohtencatl attained great renown for their political wisdom and literary creations.[2]

Xayacamach was also addressed in the texts as Tlapalteuctli, a word that has a double meaning, "strong and courageous lord," and "lord of noble lineage." Thus his contemporaries probably wanted to emphasize what they considered most outstanding in his character. Although no detailed information is provided by the sources concerning his most important deeds, his reign is praised more than once in summary form. We know he died some years before 1500, as by that time his brother Xicohtencatl, who apparently was much older, was governing Tizatlan. To the latter, the gods had reserved the experience of the encounter with the men of Castile.

The Tlaxcalan chronicler Diego Muñoz Camargo describes the achievements of Xayacamach as a ruler: "He governed successfully, being a great lord. All those of Tizatlan greatly revered him. They obeyed him. When he died, he left his homeland in peace and complete order . . ."[3] His friend, the poet Tecayehuatzin, said about him:

> A beautiful song is heard,
> Xayacamach Tlapalteutzin raises it,
> these are his flowers . . .[4]

Tecayehuatzin valued Xayacamach's poetic creativity so highly that he included him among those few he chose to converse with on the meaning of "flower and song." The two poems we know of this lord of Tizatlan are actually those he pronounced in Huexotzinco, being at the home of Tecayehuatzin on that memorable occasion.

THE TWO POEMS OF XAYACAMACH

When different views had been expressed on the meaning of "flower and song" and the dialogue was coming to a standstill, Xayacamach enlivened it with words that describe his personal experience. He admits that he knows about those flowers that intoxicate the heart and make it turn asunder. Are these flowers, perchance, being compared with hallucinogenic mushrooms? The poet can be at the house of the books of paintings, but his "flowers and songs" can take him to a faraway world where he will contemplate inebriating colors of evanescent realities. This is the theme of the first part of his enlightened words.

Immediately afterward, as if he were composing a different song, he shares with the others the consciousness he has of himself as a poet. "O my friends," he says, "I have been in search of you! Here you are! Be happy, tell me your own stories; friends! Your friend has arrived!" And, humbly, as if correcting himself, he adds: "Am I perchance invited, I, who am so destitute, O friends?"

The man, about whom the Tlaxcalan chronicler was to assert later that "he successfully governed his people, being a great lord," also offered, to those taking part in the dialogue, a poetic sketch of himself. He begins with a question: "Who am I? I live as I were flying, I compose a song, I sing to the flowers. Song—butterflies, let them be born within my heart." He wants to be close to people, he who has been born among the songs. It is marvelous, he says, that songs are still being composed, even by insignificant people such as himself. But even ordinary persons can enjoy poetry: As an example, he mentions that he has put a flowery roof on the hut he has built for himself, to be noiseless and happy.

Xayacamach, who claims he was born among songs and flowers, also depicts himself tormented by some of the same questions we often find in other pre-Hispanic compositions: "Perchance, will we live again?" And, to comfort himself and his friends, he rephrases the ancient words of the sages: "With flowers the Giver of Life is invoked. We please him in this manner." He reminds us in his poetry that at the place where the drum, music, and songs are heard, there, at the house of springtime, "Your friends are waiting for you . . ."

Thus Xayacamach thought of himself and of his friends, the uniqueness of our existence on earth, the Giver of Life, and poetry, "flower and song." Now we can better understand why his name is mentioned together with those of other famous composers of songs such as Tecayehuatzin, Ayocuan, and Aquiauhtzin.

ZAN MOCH OMPA YE HUITZ

Zan moch ompa ye huitz
xochitl ycaca, *ayahue.*
Tecuecuepal xochitl,
in teyollomamalachoa ytzo, yehua, *ohuaye.*
Conmoyauhtihuitze,
contzetzelotihuitz,
in xochitla malin,
xochipoyon ayiahue.

Xochipetlatl
on ac? *ayiahue.*
Cenca ye mochan,
ye amoxcalitic,
cuica yehua on tlatoa Xayacamach,
quihuintia ye iolcacahuaxochitl, *a yio, ahuaya.*

ALL HAVE COME

All have come
from where the flowers arise.
The flowers that confuse the people,
which cause their hearts to whirl.
They have come to scatter,
to make them fall like in a rain,
garlands of flowers,
intoxicating flowers.

Who stands
on the flowery mat?
Indeed your home is here,
in the midst of the paintings.
Xayacamach speaks, sings,
inebriated with the heart of the cacao flower.

(*Cantares mexicanos*, National Library of Mexico, fol. 11 v.)

YN HUEL YECTLI ON CUICATL YCAHUACA

Yn huel yectli on cuicatl ycahuaca,
yehua conehua ye icuic Tlapalteuccitzin, *aya.*
Huel ahuia yxochiuh,
tzetzelihui xochitl,
cacahuaxochitl, *yio, ohuia.*

Antocnihuane, namechtetemohua,
cecencuemitl nictoca,
auh tzonican ancate.
Xonpahpactiacan!
xontlatlanquetztican.
Zan ye onihualacic yn namocniuh, *ohuaya.*

Yn cuix itla xochitl
can niqualcalaquia,
yn tzitziquilxochitl, mozoquilxochitl,
cuix yuhqui?
Cuix nayohui,
ninotolinia, yn antocnihuan? *Ohuaya, ohua.*

Aquin nehua?
Nipapatlantinemi, *yehuaya,*
notlalia,
nixochincuica,
cuicapapalotl, *aya*
Ma nellelquiza,
ma noyolquimati *a, ohuaye.*

Ay topan huitz *oya*
nitemoc,
in nixopanquechol,
in tlalpan nacico,

ninozozohua,
xochihuehuetitlan.
Nocuicehuallo tlalpan
on quiza, *yohuaya.*

O anqui can no ne xochiopahuia
cuicatl,
ytlan nonquiquiza,
y no zan tlatlalhuia.
Noquetzaluicolol,
Teocuitlamecatica, nic ylpia,
namocnoicniuh, *ahuaya, ahuaya.*

Zan nixotlatlapia,
namocniuhtzin *huia,*
xochintlapalyzhuatica.
Nocotzona noxochintlapixacaltzin,
ynic nonpactica,
ye cuecuentla yehuan teotl.

Ma xonahuican! *ohuaya.*
Tla oc cenca xonpacta,
xochincocozcapatzine,
tel ca yehuatl teuctli.

Cuix occepa ye tonnemiquiuh?
Yn yuh quimati moyol *hui*
zan cen tinemico, *ohuaya, ohuaya.*

Oyanihualacic xochinquahuitl,
ymapan *ayahue,*
nixochihuitzitl,
ninoyacahuilitica,
ynic nompactica huelic noten, *ohuaya.*
Yehuan teotl Ypalnemoani,
ye xochitica tontlatlauhtiloya,
ye totonpechteca,
zan timitzonahuiltia
xochihuehuetitlan.

Atempanecatl teuctli a *ohuaya, ohuaya!*
Ompialo huehuetl,
ye oncan xopancalitec mitzonchia

ye mocnihuan Yaomanatzin, Micohuantzin, yn
Ayoquauhtzin.
Ye xochitica onelcicihui in teteuctin, *ohuaya.*

A BEAUTIFUL SONG RESOUNDS

A beautiful song resounds,
Tlapalteuccitzin lifts up his song.
The flowers are precious,
the flowers sway,
the cacao flowers.

O friends, I have come seeking you,
crossing the flowery fields,
and here, at last, I have found you.
Be happy!
Tell your stories.
O friends, your friend has arrived.

Perchance have I come
to mingle less beautiful flowers,
those of the burdock and the indigo plant,
with the precious flowers?
Am I perchance invited,
I, who am so destitute, O friends?

Who am I?
Flying I live,
I compose a chant.
I sing the flowers,
butterflies of song.
Would that they leap forth from myself,
let my heart enjoy them.

From above us.
I have come down,
I, the bird of spring,
I have spread my wings on the earth,
in the place of the flower-decked drums.
My song rises over the earth,
my song bursts out.

I repeat my songs here,
I have sprung up among songs,
for songs are still made.
With golden cords
I bind my precious jar,
I, your destitute friend.

I look only at the flowers,
I, your friend,
the opening of full buds.
I have roofed my hut with colored flowers,
thus I gladden myself,
for the sowings of the God are many.

Let there be joy!
If indeed you are happy,
you, O lord [Tecayehuatzin],
adorned with collars.

Perchance will we live again?
Thus your heart knows it:
once only we come here to live.

I have reached the boughs
of the flowering tree,
I, flowery hummingbird,
I delight in the fragrance of flowers,
I sweeten my lips with them,
O Giver of Life,
you are invoked with flowers,
we abase ourselves here,
we give you delight
in the place of the flower-decked drums.

O lord Atecpanecatl!
There the drum is kept,
your friends await you there,
Yaomanatzin, Micohuantzin, Ayocuatzin.
With flowers the princes are sighing.

(*Cantares mexicanos*, National Library of Mexico, fols. 11 v.–12 r.)

CHAPTER XIII

XICOHTENCATL THE ELDER

Lord of Tizatlan, Singer of the "Flowery War"
(Ca. 11-House, 1425–4-Rabbit, 1522)

The Puebla-Tlaxcala region was fertile soil for poetry in pre-Hispanic times. There Tecayehuatzin, lord of Huexotzinco, discussed with other composers of songs the meaning of art and symbolism, "flower and song." Also called the "White Eagle," Ayocuan Cuetzpaltzin was known as the poet and sage who repeated insistently throughout the lands of Tlaxcala and Huexotzinco the words that expressed the very essence of his thought: "Let the earth remain! Let the mountains stand up!" In Tizatlan, one of the four main towns of the Tlaxcalan confederacy, Xayacamach, a prudent ruler, likewise enjoyed considerable reputation as a poet.

Tecayehuatzin and Ayocuan, natives of Huexotzinco and Tecamachalco, respectively, had colleagues and friends among the priests and nobles of Tlaxcala who were also composers of songs. They were friends in spite of their political rivalry and frequent disputes. The famous gathering that took place in the house of Tecayehuatzin is sufficient proof of this. There the Tlaxcalan poets were received joyfully with these words: "From there in Tlaxcala you have come to sing to the sound of resplendent drums, in the place of the kettledrums."[1]

A friendly relationship was particularly noticeable between the lord of Huexotzinco and certain poets from Tizatlan, in Tlaxcala, such as those who took part in the dialogue he had convoked to clarify the meaning of "flower and song." The names of these Tlaxcalan nobles and poets have come down to us: Camaxochitzin, Motenehuatzin, Xayacamach, and Xicohtencatl the Elder.

The confederacy of Tlaxcala had risen to considerable splendor in the early fifteenth century. The centers of Tepeticpac and Ocotelulco were established first, as the historian Juan de Torquemada says, by "people of importance and noble lineage."[2] Tizatlan and Quiahuiztlan came into existence some time later. Nevertheless, more abundant information is available about Tizatlan, described as a town where poetry and other forms of artistic creativity flourished. A chapter of this book has already been devoted to Xayacamach, Prince Tepolohuatl, who said that he was above all a singer and composer of songs.

One of Xayacamach's brothers, who succeeded him as ruler of Tizatlan, Xicohtencatl the Elder, is also known as a composer of songs. A son of Aztahua, he was probably born around the year 1425. Xicohtencatl's fate was to live through a century filled with important events, including the Mexica rise to power, and later, when he was already an old man, to see the arrival of strangers from across the great waters, and the subsequent destruction of the ancient way of life.

According to the Tezcocan chronicler Ixtlilxochitl, Xicohtencatl distinguished himself early as a valiant captain, allied first with the wise ruler Nezahualcoyotl. He took part in important campaigns and conquests, including one against the Huaxteca. Around the year 1455, Xicohtencatl was forced to enter into an agreement with the allied chiefdoms of the lake region—that is, Mexico-

Tenochtitlan, Tezcoco, and Tlacopan—which had very unfortunate consequences for Tlaxcala. Obliged by Nezahualcoyotl, of Tezcoco, Totoquihuatzin, of Tlacopan, Motecuhzoma and the renowed Tlacaelel, of Mexico, he had to accept the introduction of the sacred or "flowery wars." Such confrontations had to be carried systematically between the allies of the lake region and the chiefdoms of Tlaxcala, Huexotzinco, and Cholula. Ixtlilxochitl makes clear the objectives of this kind of warfare. He says they all agreed that

> a field should be marked out where regular battles would take place, and those captured and made prisoners in these wars would be sacrified to their gods. . . . In addition to this, it would be an occasion for the sons of the lords to practice so that, as famous captains, they would emerge from there; and it was understood not to exceed the limits of the field laid out for the purpose, and not to attempt to gain land or chiefdoms.[3]

The ultimate purpose of the "flowery wars" is well known, for in addition to providing training for warriors and young captains, it brought into play the political ambitions and the central beliefs within the Mexica world view. The Mexica thought of themselves as the chosen "People of Huitzilopochtli." Theirs was the mission of strengthening the life of the Sun, thus to preserve the existence of the present cosmic age. Just as the gods in a primeval time restored mankind with their own blood, so men must contribute the same precious liquid, the source of universal energy necessary for Tonatiuh, "He who continues to make the day and the warmth."

The Mexica will to power developed into a mystical, warlike world view that led them to great conquests and made them lords over large territories. Located in the middle of this ever-growing expansion, the Tlaxcalan chiefdoms became completely surrounded by people subjugated by Mexico-Tenochtitlan and its allies. This resulted in many misfortunes for Tlaxcala and caused a

Xicohtencatl, the long-lived Tlaxcalan lord, who sang of the flowery war and witnessed the greatness and the ruin of the Aztec nation (*Lienzo de Tlaxcala*, plate 1)

deep enmity that showed itself openly during the days of the Conquest.

Xicohtencatl certainly understood, better than anyone else, the ultimate significance of the unrestricted Mexica expansionism. Having been a contemporary of various high rulers of Mexico-Tenochtitlan, including Motecuhzoma Ilhuicamina, Axayacatl, Tizoc, Ahuitzotl, and Motecuhzoma the Second, it was finally his fate to make a decision when the foreigners, never before seen, arrived in 1519.

After some hesitation, the Tlaxcalan rulers, especially Xicohtencatl, of Tizatlan, and Maxixcatzin, of Ocotelolco, at last found in the men of Castile a means of confronting the Mexica. As the Tlaxcalan chronicler Diego Muñoz Camargo points out, after much deliberation and after seeing how easily the Otomi warriors of Tecoac were defeated by the Spaniards, they decided to peacefully receive and welcome the foreigners. Xicohtencatl, who at that time was nearly 100 years old, was almost blind. For this reason, "When he went out to receive Hernán Cortés, he went on the arms of two young men of his household, and in order that he should see, they raised up his eyelids which had fallen due to his age."[4]

The end of this story is well known. The Tlaxcalans became firm allies of the men of Castile. Xicohtencatl himself, as well as other princes and nobles, received baptism. Although Xicohtencatl saw the complete ruin of Mexico-Tenochtitlan before he died, he also suffered greatly because of the death of many Tlaxcalans and especially the death of his son, the young Xicohtencatl, who had strongly opposed the alliance of his people with the newly arrived foreigners.

XICOHTENCATL THE ELDER, A POET

From various sources and references, it is known that Xicohtencatl the Elder was a composer of songs, although only one from among those he may have composed is known today. This song is included in the *Cantares mexicanos* in the National Library of Mexico, inserted in a long poem, a sort of play to be sung, accompanied by music and dance, in which there are obvious allusions to Christian beliefs and persons who lived much later. Nevertheless, the portion attributed to Xicohtencatl is recognized by the ideas expressed, manifestly of pre-Hispanic origin, such as that concerning the "flowery wars." This part of the text probably comes from the years when the lord of Tlaxcala took part in those struggles that he himself had been obliged to accept.

In a language replete with symbols, Xicohtencatl evokes the wars with the people of Mexico. The Tlaxcalan captains marched to the region of the lakes. They went in search of precious water. Their shields were like vessels in which they would carry the flowery water.

In the manner of an indigenous baroque art, found at

Tlaxcallan.

The meeting of Xicohtencatl and Hernán Cortés (*Lienzo de Tlaxcala*, plate 29)

times in the chants composed in Tlaxcala, Xicohtencatl amuses himself by coining metaphors, phrases couched in the symbolism of the sacred war: "May you not go forth in vain! . . . Your precious vessel, color of obsidian, already stands upright . . . , with it we will bring the water on our shoulders, we will carry it there in Mexico, from Chapolco [Chapultepec], on the shore of the lake . . ."

In the poem he calls upon his children. He refers to Cuauhtencoztli, the Mexica captain who was also a poet. He addresses the young Xicohtencatl-Axayacatl, calling him "little son, precious creature," encouraging him to march to the place where the sacrificial waters extend.

His final words emphasize the value of war and are the key to the meaning of the poem: "The flowery war, the shield flowers, have opened their corollas. The lofty trees are standing, chosen flowers fall. . . . Water gushes forth from the precious vessel!"

It is strange and dramatic that the only remaining poem of Xicohtencatl should refer to the flowery wars that, as the years passed, became a heavy burden for Tlaxcala. If Xicohtencatl was a famous poet, as the sources insist, certainly his poems must have included other themes. However, even his description of the flowery war gives testimony to his mastery of the art of metaphor.

XICOHTENCATL ICUIC

Neh niquitoa, ni Xicohtencatl Teuctli, *aya,*
haneyatlaxiauh!
Xicana in mochimal, ah xochiacontzin!
Mohuicoltzin,
anozo ihcac motolteca itzontzotzocoltzin,
icayan tamemezque,
tazacatihui yc oncan ye Mexico,
in Chapolcopa ca atitlan, *aya.*

Annentlaxiauh,
nomache, niccahuan, *iya,* tomachuane,
anapipiltin!
Nicteca yn atl,
Quauhtencoztli in teuctli,
tlayenochtonhuian!
Tamemezque,
tazacatihui yenel!

Nequiyeontzatzia in achcauhtzin, in ye Motelchiutzin,
tocnihua!
Quilmach yeoc yohuac.
Ticanatihui tlatlamemel:
hueltetehuilotic, xiuhtehuiltic,
in quetzalitzacuecueyocatimani.
Ye ic tonaciz oncan tecomatla, *aya,*
ya anentlaxiye!

Mach nonoxicotaz ye Nanahuatl.
Nicauhhe!
Titlacatecatl, ticuitlachihuitl,
hueltoltecatic, teocuitlatica in tlacuilolli,
ye tahuicoltzin conicuiloa, Axayacatl teuctli.
Tocenmantazque,
ye ic tonaci ye chalchiuhatica.
Ontzetzelihui, pipixahui,
onneapanaltzin ye itech, *aya*.

Noxochiazazacayatzini Huanitzin,
nechyamacaco,
notlatzintihua, tlaxcalteca ye chichimeca!
Anentlaxia!

Yn tlachinolxochitl, chimalxochitl,
oncuecuepontoc.
Tlatlatzcatimani, *a*,
yacaxochitl ontzetzelihui,
anquizo yehuatl.
Ye ic contzaquaco teocuitlatlaya,
ye noconana xiuhtlacuilolli:
Yenapilolotzin icnoconmemeya,
ha nohueyohuan!

I SAY THIS

I say this, I the lord Xicohtencatl:
Do not go forth in vain!
Take up your shield, the vessel of flowery water!
Your little bowl with a handle.
Your precious vessel, color of obsidian, stands upright,
with it, we will bring the water on our shoulders,
we will carry it there in Mexico,
from Chapolco, on the shore of the lake.

Do not go forth in vain,
my nephew, my little children, my nephews,
you, children of the water!
I make the water flow,
O Lord Cuauhtencoztli,
let us all go!

We will bring the water on our shoulders,
truly we are going to carry it!

Captain Motelchiuhtzin wants to announce it,
my friends!
He says it is not yet dawn.
We take up our burden of water:
crystal clear, precious, color of turquoise,
which moves in waves.
Thus you will come there, to the place of the vessels,
do not go forth in vain!

Nanahuatl [the god] will perhaps make noise there.
My little son!
You, leader of men, you, precious creature,
a painting with gold in the Toltec manner,
paint the precious bowl, Lord Axayacatl.
We go together to partake,
we approach the precious waters.
They are falling, drops rain down,
there, close to the small canals.

He who carries my flowery water, Huanitzin,
now comes to give it to me,
O my uncles, Tlaxcalans, Chichimecs!
Do not go forth in vain!

The flowery war, the shield's flower,
have opened their corollas.
They resound,
the sweet-smelling flowers rain down,
Thus perhaps for this,
he came to conceal gold and silver;
for this I take the painted books.
O my little canal, with my vessel the water flows!
O my old ones!

(*Cantares mexicanos*, National Library of Mexico, fols. 57 v.–58 r.)

PART FOUR

POETS OF CHALCO-AMAQUEMECAN

Here is the water and the mountain,
here the altar of jade
Amaquemecan-Chalco . . .
on the edge of the woods,
close to the snow . . .
where lives the white quail . . .

(Chimalpahin, *Fourth Relation*, fol. 116 r.)

Situated on the western slopes of the two great volcanoes, Popo-catepetl and Iztaccihuatl, on the fringes of the Valley of Mexico, the chiefdoms of Chalco, Amaquemecan (today Amecameca), Tlalmanalco, Tlaltecahuacan, and a few others integrated a sociopolitical constellation in various interrelated forms.

Thanks mainly to the indigenous chronicler Chimalpahin Cuauhtlehuanitzin (1579–ca. 1660), a native of Amaquemecan, ample information is available concerning the origins and major historical events of the various groups who, at different epochs, established themselves in the region. Chimalpahin left us eight historical *Relations* and a *Diary*. To write them in Nahuatl, he spent several years of research. Besides visiting the principal sites of the region, he consulted indigenous books, some probably of pre-Hispanic origin, which were in the possession of his relatives and friends, and also took oral tradition into account. With the support of such testimonies he succeeded in preparing a comprehensive account of the past of the Chalco-Amaquemecan region. His contribution is one of the best available testimonies with which to approach the history of an area secondary in terms of power in the political and cultural setting of ancient central Mexico.

According to the sources Chimalpahin transcribes, around the tenth century A.D., invaders from the southeast conquered the Chalco-Amaquemecan region. They were known as Olmeca Xicalanca, People of the Rubberland, who originally lived near the Xicalanco area in Tabasco. Some of them had taken possession of Cholula around the ninth century A.D. Those who penetrated in Chalco-Amaquemecan were also referred as Xochteca, "People of the Flowery Region," Quiyauteca, "The Ones of the Rainy Land," and Cocolca, "Those Who Were the Great-grandfathers." Powerful and very religious people, knowers of occult things, they built a temple by a cave on top of Mount Amaqueme, close to the town of Amaquemecan. The temple was named Chalchiuhmomozco, "The Altar of Jade." A special cult was offered there to the God and Goddess of Rain. From then on, that temple became a center of religious attraction. Even now there exists a Roman Catholic sanctuary in whose interior is the ancient cave.

Other groups, of Chichimec origin but already in possession of many elements of Toltec culture, entered the region by force centuries later. A violent confrontation occurred in a year 9-House (1241), the result of which was the expulsion of the former lords of Olmeca-Xicalanca origin. The new settlers were named Tecuanipa, "Those of the Jaguar Lineage," Totolimpa-neca, "Those of That of the Turkey," Poyauhteca, "The Ones of the Place of Mist." Chronicler Chimalpahin describes himself as a descendant of the Totolimpaneca and Tecuanipa lineages.

Since the middle of the thirteen century, when the victory of these groups over the Olmeca-Xicalanca occurred, Chalco-Amaquemecan had enjoyed independence and increasing prosperity. It was not until the reign of Motecuhzoma Ilhuicamina when, in a year 5-Rabbit (1458), the "war of Chalco" began. It required almost four years for the Mexica to conquer and subjugate Chalco-Amaquemecan.

The two composers of songs whose names and deeds and also a minimal part of their work are known to us, lived in that last epoch of Mexica domination. One of them, Lord Aquiauhtzin, was born in the hamlet of Ayapanco, very close to Amaquemecan. The other, Chichicuepon, had his home in Chalco. The two were well known in local history. Their names and lives became the subject of attention of Chimalpahin and are also mentioned in other Nahuatl texts such as the *Anales de Cuauhtitlan*. The fates of these two composers of songs were to be linked forever to the destiny of their homeland, Chalco-Amaquemecan. In the case of Chichicuepon, his fate was tragic, indeed. In that of Aquiauhtzin, the ancient soothsayers most probably predicted a favorable tonalli, or destiny. The beautiful song we know by him, entitled "The Chalca Warrior Women," was to be welcomed by the high Mexica ruler and, according to Chimalpahin, helped to smooth the relations of the defeated Chalcans with their new lords of Mexico-Tenochtitlan.

Glyph of Chalco

CHAPTER XIV

CHICHICUEPON OF CHALCO

Poet and Unfortunate Litigant
(Fifteenth Century)

The chiefdom of Chalco-Amaquemecan, in the present State of Mexico, was famous in pre-Hispanic times. Its privileged geographic setting close to the volcanoes on the east, as well as the wealth it derived from the ancient lake on the west, help to explain why the area was continuously inhabited from long before the Christian era. The Olmecs, the people of the Classic period, and the Toltecs all left a mark there. Finally, as in other parts of the high plateau, the territory of Chalco-Amaquemecan was also populated by groups of immigrant Chichimecs who began to make their appearance around the twelfth century A.D.

The history of Chalco and the various other centers that flourished there such as Amaquemecan, Tlalmanalco, Xicco, Tlaltecahuacan, and many others, has been preseved principally by the chronicler Chimalpahin Cuauhtlehuanitzin. Born in Amaquemecan at the end of the sixteenth century, he wrote historic accounts and his private diary, giving as much information as he could gather about the origins and development of the main events of his people.[1]

Chimalpahin left a testimony to the pride that the people of Chalco-Amaquemecan had in everything pertaining to their ancient splendor and the beauty of the region where they were born. His words are almost an epic hymn:

> Here is the water and the mountain,
> here the altar of jade,
> Amaquemecan-Chalco,
> in the place of renown,
> a unique site,
> near the reeds,
> on the edge of the woods,
> close to the snow,
> where it is called Poyauhtlan,
> "In the Place of the Mist,"
> in the flowery courtyard,
> the courtyard of mist,
> where lives the white quail,
> where the serpent writhes
> close to the lair of the tigers,
> in Tamoanchan,
> in the place of our origin,
> where the flowers sway. . . .
> Here they came to settle down
> the Chichimec lords,
> the priests,
> the princes . . .[2]

It is also Chimalpahin who tells that the Chichimecs first established themselves in the territory of Chalco-Amaquemecan in the year 9-House, or 1241. Due to contact with the Culhuacans of Toltec descent, and also receiving the beneficial influence of some *tlailotlaque* (the returned ones) from the south who had possessed many valuable elements of high culture, Chalco reached an enviable prosperity. By the beginning of the fifteenth century, the Chalcans had developed to a point not yet attained by the Mexica. Among the rulers of Chalco famous at that time were Lord Toteoci and Prince Cuateotl.

The prosperity that the Chalcans were enjoying was soon to face an unsuspected danger, however. Around 1431, the political situation in the Valley of Mexico changed completely. The Mexica and their allies, having conquered the ancient territory of Azcapotzalco, began their unrestrained expansion. Once the Coyoacan region was conquered, the aggressive attitude of the Mexica made itself felt in Culhuacan, Cuitlahuac, Xochimilco, and Mixquic. Chalco's turn came next.

Motecuhzoma Ilhuicamina reigned in Mexico-Tenochititlan, and in 5-Rabbit (1458), according to Chimalpahin, "the war with Chalco began."[3] What happened then is not only related in detail by Chimalpahin and the Mexica chronicler Tezozomoc but is also found in various other indigenous accounts. The Chichimec chiefdom of Chalco-Amaquemecan, after a fierce resistance, finally collapsed. According to the *Anales de Cuauhtitlan*, the Chalca came under the dominion of Motecuhzoma Ilhuicamina in the year 9-Rabbit (1462).

But besides these testimonies in which the dates and the general outline of events are recalled, the war and defeat evidently made such a deep impression in Chalco that they became a subject for songs. Among the poetic records of the fall of Chalco, most of which are anonymous, there is one of particular interest. It is a poem in the style of an epic elegy composed by an important figure in the Chalcan region named Chichicuepon.

Chichicuepon was born in Tlilhuacan (Chalco) and died in the year 7-Rabbit (1486). He belonged to the ancient nobility and, like many of his compatriots, was deprived of his lands and property as result of the war. But he had seen prosperous days. In his youth, he had studied the ancient traditions and had formed his own idea as to the history of Chalco and its possible destiny, as ordained by the Giver of Life. In a poem composed by him, he contrasts the present disgrace of Chalco with its ancient

The war of Chalco (*Códice Telleriano-Remensis*, ii)

splendor, mentioning names and events associated with the lost grandeur.

Chichicuepon was more than a poet and a dispossessed noble. The defeat meant confusion. As recorded in the *Anales de Cuauhtitlan*, Chalco was governed for twenty-one years by a group of captains whose duty was to lay the foundations for the establishment of Mexica rule, mainly in matters related to the timely payment of tribute. Not until 1486, as the *Anales* state, was a local authority reestablished with the approval of the ruling Mexica: "In that year the chiefdom of Chalco-Tlacochcalco was established. Itzcahuatzin inaugurated it. At that time he set himself up as lord, but then those who had the right to the land, the Chalca who possessed the land, began to leave because he no longer considered them nobles. Only in Contlan and Tlaylotlacan they continued considering themselves as nobles."[4]

Among those who took offense at the new government imposed by the Mexica was Chichicuepon. Once the nobles were denied their rank, the result was that their lands were confiscated. Chichicuepon and some others did not accept what they considered to be insulting and unjust. Thus, they went to Mexico-Tenochtitlan to appeal their case, bringing their complaints to the ears of King Ahuitzotl himself. They said: "We are now in a wretched condition in Techinantitla. Itzcahua has taken possession of our cultivated fields. Now, like poor people, we only sweep and tend the fire."[5] Perhaps in order to calm down resentment and hold off possible unrest, Ahuitzotl listed to Chichicuepon and the others who complained. His reply was: "Take back your lands."

But the story did not finish there. Although Chichicuepon succeeded as a litigant in his first appeal, the final result was disastrous. The *Anales de Cuauhtitlan* relate how the affair ended:

> When Lord Itzcahuatzin of Chalco heard this, he was very annoyed and said: "I am going to see lord Ahuitzotzin." He came into his presence and said to him: "O Lord, you have given back the lands to those of Mihuacan, Tlilhuacan, and Tlaylotlacan. You made me lord of the lands of Chalco. What have I gained by that? In this way the rulership will be lost. Kindly look well at this. Now again they want to be considered nobles. The people of Mihuacan, Tlilhuacan, and Tlaylotlacan are rebelling."

> Lord Ahuitzotl replied, he said to him: "I have heard your words. I say this to you, I leave them in your hands. You already know about this. Beat them, hang them, all those who want to be considered nobles."

> And this Itzcahuatzin did. He killed those who wanted to be considered nobles. Everyone who called himself a noble, died.[6]

This was the sad end of Chichicuepon, who not only suffered by the downfall of Chalco but also paid with his life for his appeal to justice. But although Chichicuepon failed as a litigant, he obtained some fame as a poet. His only known composition links him forever with the memory of Chalco. It is a glorification of the ancient rulers and a sad song, recalling the misfortunes of war. Because it came from a man who knew the history of his people well, this poem, to be understood, requires some explanation.

CHICHICUEPON'S POEM

Along with other compositions from the region of Chalco, Chichicuepon's poem is preserved in the manuscript now in the National Library of Mexico. In fol. 33 r. of this collection, there is the following notation in Nahuatl: "Now give heed to the words left by lord Chichicuepon, he who fell in the struggle." And there follows his song.

The poem opens with a question concerning life after death. The ancient rulers of Chalco were jade and precious plumage. Although they have died, they continue rejoicing in the Region-Where-In-Someway-One-Lives. There they enjoy once more the warmth and light of the Giver of Life. Among the various princes mentioned, Toteoci, who built the palaces of Chalco and led the resistance during the days of war against the Mexica, occupies a prominent place. In the thought of Chichicuepon, the memory of Toteoci seems to be often present. He addresses him, saying that, although death has made him enter into the waters of mystery, he has sprung up anew as a precious willow tree.

Along with Toteoci, he remembers other famous Chalcans. Among these are Nequametzin, who acted as a diligent emmissary; Lord Cuateotl, who fought against Mexica penetration, and also Tezozomoc, a prince of Chalco (not Tezozomoc of Azcapotzalco) "whose words will not perish." The first part of the poem can thus be described as a praise of the deceased princes who are now jade and plumage in the mansion of the Giver of Life.

Then abruptly the composer of the songs puts aside his memories of former greatness to concentrate on the theme of the war Chalco was forced to fight against the conquering Mexica: "The eagle will stand before the face of the water. There will be transformation on earth, commotion in the heavens. . . . The people of Chalco are in confusion." Chichicuepon repeats emphatically that the enemy "penetrates into the interior of Amaquemecan. Chalco defends itself! No one has arrows, no one has shields." And perhaps, in the Region of the Dead, "Prince Toteoci is weeping."

At the end of the song, the trauma of the Chalca becomes manifest: "The people of Chalco are destroyed, they throb there in Almoloya." The Mexica and their allies, the Acolhuans of Tezcoco and the Tepanecs of Tlacopan, are to blame for the injustice. "Some eagles and tigers, some Mexica, Acolhuans, Tepanecs have done this to the Chalcans." In essence, Chichicuepon's poem is the remembrance of a past glory and the contemplation of a present tragedy. He could not know, when he composed this song, that his own fate would be equally tragic. He lost his life in his appeal as a litigant, but at least we know that, as a poet, he has survived death.

CHICHICUEPON ICUIC

Ac ye xoconcaqui ca itlatol
in concauhtehuac y Chichicuepon teuctli,
yaoceuhqui:

Mach oc mictlampa
y quihualittozque
ymihiyo, yntlatol in tepilhuan? *A, ohuaya, ohuaya.*

Nehhuihuixtiuh chalchiuhtli,
nehhuihuixtiuh quetzalli,
oyaximoac,
quenonamican? *A, ohuaya.*

Zan ye ontlamachotoc a in tepilhuan, in pillin:
Tlaltecatl, *aya,* in Xoquahuatzi, Tozmaquetzin, *aya,* ye
    Nequametzi.
Achinca tlacuiloa ypalnemoani.
Yn tlamacehualli ipan tonca, *aya,*
teuctli can Quateotl,
chalchiuhtlatonac.

Ma xicyocoya, xichoca,
xicelnamiqui in Toteoci teuctli,
ma ya hualaquia
in nahualapan:
itzmolinin quetzalhuexotl, y.
Ayatlami
in itlatol in Tezozomoctli,
o ayia yiohiyo ayio, ohuaye, ohuaya.

Ma xontlachia mihcan, ohuaye,
yahquin Tehconehua,
yahquin Quappolocatl, in Quauhtecolotl.
Huiya o ximohua
in toteuchuan y;
yahqui Huetzi, in Cacamatl, in Tzincacahuaca,
Ayamo ypan timochihuaz, aya,
in chichimecatl, in Toteoci teuctli,
o ayia, yio ayio, ohuaye, ohuaya.

In anchalca teuctin, ayahue,
ma xachocaca, huiya.
Tonmotlamachtian,
ypalnemoani!
Tonilhuizolohuan Atlixco,
in Toteoci teuctli, Cohuatl teuctli,
yehua mitzyollopoloa,
in Ipalnemoa,
aya ayaoaye, auhayao, ayahui.

Ticxeloan chalchiuhtli, maquiztli,
ya ticneneloa in patlahuac quetzalli,
choquiztlaya, yxayotl in pixahui, yeehuaya
zan ye onnenahuatiloc, aya,
Huitzilac teohua, o,
in Tozan, in teuctla! Ayahue.

Ca ye tommoneltocaya, ohuaye,
teohua zan Quateotl? o, ohuaya.
Zazo polihui ya moyollo?
Cauhtimaniz y quauhtli
atl yxpan.
In tlalli mocuepa, ya,

ya ilhuicatl olini, *a,*
oncan ye cahualo
chichimecatl y Tlacamazatl, *a ohuaya, ohuaya.*

Moneneloa y zan chalca,
nelihui huexotzincatl,
y zan Tlaylotlaqui,
Quiyeuhtzin teuctli
quenticalaquia yn Amaqueme.
Ytic motenantia in chalcatl, *ohuaya,*
ye Toteoci teuctla! *Ohuaya.*

Achquan tiquittoa:
i ayac ymiuh,
y ayac ychimal.
Tocoyatitlani, tocoyaihtoa in Miccalcatl.
y zan Tlailotlaqui,
Quieuhtzin teuctli,
quen ticalaquia yn Amaqueme.
Zan ye chocan teuctli nacanaya Toteoci,
Cohuatzin teuctla, *ohuaya.*
Zan ye hualicnotlamati in Temilotzin, *huiya can oya, in*
Tohtzi. *Ohuaye.*
Moxeloan chalcatl,
moneloa ye oncan Almoloya, *ayiahue,*
cequi yan quauhtli, ocelotl,
cequi ya mexicatl, acolhua, tepanecatl
o mochihua in chalca, *ohuaya.*

NOW GIVE HEED TO THE WORD

Now give heed to the word
left by Lord Chichicuepon,
he who fell in the struggle:

Perchance in the region of the dead
will be transmitted
the breath and the word of the princes?

Will throb the jades,
will still wave the quetzal plumages,

in the Region of the Fleshless,
Where-In-Someway-One-Lives?

Only there the lords, the princes are happy:
Tlaltecatl, Xoquahuatzin, Tozmaquetzin, Nequametzin.
Forever the Giver of Life shines on them.
You have deserved to be there,
Prince Cuateotl,
you who made things shine.

Ponder, weep,
recall Lord Toteoci,
there he was to enter
in the waters of mystery,
but he has sprung up as a precious willow tree.
The words of Tezozomoctli
never perish.

Consider the place of arrows
Tehconehua has gone there,
Cuappolocatl, Cuauhtecolotl have gone there.
In the place of the fleshless
are the princes;
Huetzin, Cacamatl, Tzincacahua went there.
Do not grieve for this,
O Chichimec lord, Toteoci.

You, lords of Chalco,
weep no more.
You are happy,
O Giver of Life!
In vain were you in Atlixco,
Lord Toteoci, Prince Cohuatl,
the Giver of Life
confused your heart.

You have destroyed the jade, the bangles,
you have torn apart the precious large plumage,
there is a downpour of wailing,
thus it was determined,
O priest of Huitzilac,
Prince Tozan!

Were you destroyed
O Priest Cuateotl?
Has your heart perished?
The eagle will stand
before the face of the water,
There will be transformation on earth,
commotion in the heavens,
there was abandoned
Tlacamazatl, the Chichimec.

The people of Chalco are in confusion,
those of Huexotzinco are deranged,
alone Tlailotlaqui,
Lord Quiyeuhtzin
penetrates into the interior of Amaquemecan.
The Chalca defends himself,
O Prince Toteoci!

But now you say:
no one has arrows,
no one has shields.
You plead, you say to Miccalcatl:
Alone Tlailotlaqui
Lord Quiyeuhtzin,
you penetrate into the interior of Amaquemecan.

Alone now Prince Toteoci is weeping,
Lord Cohuatzin.
Temilotzin and Tohtzin are grieved.
the people of Chalco are destroyed,
they throb there in Almoloya.
Some eagles and tigers,
some Mexicans, Acolhuans, Tepanecs
have done this to the Chalca.

(*Cantares mexicanos*, National Library of Mexico, fol. 33 r.)

CHAPTER XV

AQUIAUHTZIN OF AYAPANCO

His Song of the Warrior Women of Chalco:
An Example of Nahuatl Erotic Poetry
(Ca. 1430–ca. 1500)

Aquiauhtzin, from Ayapanco, a hamlet close to Amecameca, is a master of the word about whom historical references have been preserved, as well as two compositions that can be directly attributed to him. One is included in the text known as the "Dialogue of Flower and Song." In this work Aquiauhtzin appears concerned with the mysteries of Ipalnemohuani, the supreme Giver of Life. An extensive, and for many unexpected, erotic poem is another of his creations. Although appearing in the manuscript where it is preserved as an anonymous work, we know it must be attributed to Aquiauhtzin, thanks to evidence from the writings of the chronicler, Chimalpahin.

The latter composition is a teasing song of the delights of seduction and a sexual taunt dedicated to the great *tlahtoani*, or supreme ruler, Axayacatl, lord of the Mexica from 1469 to 1481. His predecessor, Motecuhzoma Ilhuicamina, had completed the conquest of the Chalco-Amecameca region in 1464. With the rise to power of Axayacatl, the situation of the Chalcans, while continuing to be that of a subjugated people, had become more bearable. Aquiauhtzin seeks with this song, in the guise of a subtle challenge, for a new way to increase the benevolence of Axayacatl toward the conquered nation. Here the women of Chalco are seen as precipitating a war. The poet has them challenge the lord of Tenochtitlan to a battle in which only the most highly sexually endowed could hope to win. The war is transformed into an erotic siege, with the opposing armies closing in on one another, symbolizing the sexual act with all its foreplay. This delicately pornographic song was most certainly pleasing to Axayacatl, the recipient of the challenge.

Anticipating ourselves a bit, we will add here that Aquiauhtzin was apparently quite a knowledgeable man in divine affairs. Perhaps because of this, he excelled as well in those more human attributes such as political astuteness, the pleasures of the flesh, intrigues, and wit.

Aquiauhtzin was probably born around 1430 in Ayapanco. We do not know the date of his death, but it must have occurred after 1490 because he participated around that year in a meeting of poets held by the Lord Tecayehuatzin of Huexotzinco.

In 1430, the chiefdom of Chalco-Amecameca still preserved its independence under the rule of Ayocuan, the old Chichimec ruler. Aquiauhtzin Cuauhquiyahuacatzintli—for such was his complete name—being of noble lineage, as a young boy attended the school, or calmecac, of the town where he was born. There he learned the ancient traditions of his people, the art of the noble speech, poetry, and the body of religious knowledge. Upon leaving the calmecac while still a young man, he must have become aware of the expansionist policies assumed by the Mexica after their victory over the old Tepaneca rulers of Azcapotzalco. The Mexica, led by Izcoatl, had first conquered various chiefdoms such as Cuitlahuac and Xochimilco. Indeed, they had made successful incursions into the regions of Huexotzinco and Atlixco in what today is the state of Puebla. Doubtless the zone of Chalco-Amecameca then also began to be perceived by the Mexica as fair game for their expansionist designs.

The chronicler Chimalpahin, in an expressive text from his *Third Relation*, while affirming that "Motecuhzoma Ilhuicamina and his advisor, the *cihuacoatl* ("feminine twin," i.e., close assistant) Tlacaelel, had yet to fix their teeth on Chalco,"[1] does refer to the fact that already in the year 6-Rabbit (1446), the people of Chalco and Amecameca were made to feel the demands of the Mexica obliging them to participate in the construction of the temple to Huitzilopochtli. To this extortion was added the affliction of a five-year famine from 1450 to 1455. Men and women were to sell themselves into slavery during this period.

From the year 13-House (1483), the ambition of Motecuhzoma Ilhuicamina to incorporate the chiefdom of Chalco-Amecameca into his kingdom became even more blatant. Thus, the war began in which Aquiauhtzin, the composer of songs, probably had to participate. According to several chronicles, by the year 11-Flint (1464), the Mexica had penetrated to the mountain of Amaqueme. After a long struggle, the victory of the warriors from Mexico-Tenochtitlan was consummated, fulfilling the prophecy of the sorcerer who had tersely announced that "the Chalca will be destroyed."[2] There are several accounts that tell of the flight of the 16,000 macehuales, or commoners, who had to abandon the region of Chalco-Amecameca. The much afflicted Aquiauhtzin somehow consoled himself in his dedication to poetry.

The two poems by him that we know are preserved in the manuscript of the *Cantares mexicanos* at the National Library of Mexico and can be placed in time with some precision. The erotic work was composed near the year 13-Reed (1479), or in any case very shortly before that, because in this same year, according to the chronicles of Chimalpahin, the Chalcans went for the first time to perform it in Tenochtitlan. The composition was presented before Lord Axayacatl, the successor to Motecuhzoma Ihuicamina. The second of the poems was made public for the first time by Aquiauhtzin in Huexotzinco toward 1490, when he participated there in a gathering of poets and wise men who assembled at the invitation of the noble Tecayehuatzin.

THE EROTIC SONG: THE CIRCUMSTANCES OF ITS COMPOSITION

There are two documented sources that permit us to approach this composition by Aquiauhtzin in its original version in Nahuatl as well as to analyze the circumstances in which it was formally presented. On the one hand we find, in four folios toward the end of the *Cantares mexicanos,* the Nahuatl text of this poem under the title *In Chalca Cihuacuicatl,* the "Song of the Women of Chalco," with the following annotation: "A Composition of the Chalcans. With this song they went to entertain the King Axayacatzin who had conquered them but only the little women."[3]

On the other hand, in the *Seventh Relation* of Chimalpahin, this same visit of the Chalcans to Axayacatl is mentioned in great detail and the date on which it took place is fixed in the year 13-Reed.[4] Here it is expressly stated that those who presented themselves before the ruler of Tenochtitlan came to perform the "Song of the Women of Chalco." Chimalpahin, from whose original in Nahuatl we will quote, describes the details of everything that occurred in the patio of the palace of Axayacatl, and particularly of the danger in which the Chalcans would find themselves if they failed in their purpose. The chronicler adds that the *Chalca Cihuacuicatl* was performed, and that it was the work of a noble called Aquiauhtzin Cuauhquiyahuacatzintl, "who was a composer of songs."

This dual documentation is a fortunate discovery that permits us to place one of the most beautiful and extensive poems of erotic content in Nahuatl, not only with relation to its author but also to the historical context in which it was composed and first offered to the public. Before transcribing the information we owe to Chimalpahin, let us return to something previously hinted at. When the people of Chalco went to present this song of the warrior women to Axayacatl, their intention was as much to flatter as it was to defy him. And a risky enterprise it was, going to challenge a man who, like his ancestor, Motecuhzoma, prided himself on his military prowess, guiding him on in this way to show that he was as much a man before the women who provoked him now to love and pleasure. The fact is that the Chalcans, this time with neither shields nor arrows, achieved a victory. Axayacatl, as Chimalpahin relates the affair, was extremely pleased with the song of the warrior women. What is more, "he made this song his personal property . . . when he wished to amuse himself, he would always have it sung."

Here then are the words of Chimalpahin, which set the context necessary for an understanding of Aquiauhtzin's poem:

The year 13-Reed (1479). It was also at this time that the people of Amecameca and the Chalca Tlalmanalca came to sing for the first time in Mexico. At that time they performed the song of the women of Chalco, the *Chalca Cihuacuicatl.* They came to sing for the lord Axayacatzin.
The song and the dance were begun in the patio of the palace while Axayacatl was still inside in the house of his women. But in the beginning the song was poorly performed. A noble of Tlalmanalco was playing the music very clumsily and making the great drum sound in a lazy, offbeat way until finally in desperation he leaned down over it, not knowing what else to do.
There, however, close to the place of the drums was a man called Quecholcohuatzin, a noble from Amecameca, a great singer and musician as well. When he saw that all was being lost and that the song and the dance were being ruined, he quickly placed himself next to the drums. He picked up a drum and through his effort he gave new strength to the

dance so that it would not be ruined. Thus Quecholcohuatzin made the people sing and dance. And the other noble from Tlalmanalco remained alone with his head bowed while the others continued with the song. Axayacatl, who was still inside the palace, when he heard how marvelously Quecholcohuatzin played the music and made the people dance, was surprised, and his heart filled with excitement. He quickly arose and left the house of his women and joined in the dance. As Axayacatl approached the place of the dance his feet began to follow the music, and he was overcome with joy as he heard the song and so he too began to dance and spin round and round.

When the dance was over, the Lord Axayacatl spoke, saying, "Fools, you have brought this fumbler before me, who played and directed the song. Do not let him do it again!" The people from Chalco answered him, saying, "It is as you wish, supreme lord."

And because Axayacatl had given this command, all the nobles of Chalco became terrified. They stood there looking at each other, and it is said that truly they were very frightened. Then they found out that this was the first time that this noble from Tlalmanalco had played and directed a song. And it is recorded by the ancients, the name of that individual was Cuateotzin. . . .

And these same Chalca then almost without thinking said, "Will he have him burned? Perhaps he will have him stoned, the one who has directed the music and the song! He has ruined us!" The noble Chalca said, "He has spoiled our song. What must we do? Will he have us burned right here?"

Meanwhile, the Lord Axayacatl had gone back inside his palace. He had gone there to be with the young women who were his wives. Then he ordered that Quecholcohuatzin, the one who had finally directed the dance and the song, be brought before him. Thus he spoke and demanded the messenger to the noble Chalca, saying: "Who is the man who has just finished your song, the one that has just ended your music? The lord calls him, the supreme master. We come in search of him; he will come into the palace!"

Quickly they answered, the Chalca spoke: "Here he is, for the lord to receive him." Then the noble Chalca called the young man, Quecholcohuatzin. For they feared full well that the lord Axayacatl would condemn them to death, to be burned.

And when the young musician passed by and was entering the door, the Chalca gathered, peeking in behind him, to await the word of the lord, as though it would be of fire. Then they prostrated themselves, these Chalca; they were so afraid.

But when Quecholcohuatzin drew near before Axayacatl, he quickly touched earth to his mouth, and bowing down he said: "Lord, supreme master, have pity on me, here I am your servant, a man of the people, truly we have erred before your face."

But the Lord Axayacatl had no wish to continue listening to these words. He then said to his women: "Arise my wives; come and meet this man, for he will remain by your side; here he will be your companion, as though he were a woman as well. Look on him and know that already I have proof enough, that with this, my women, your hearts will be filled with joy, because this man made me dance and sing, this Quecholcohuatzin. No one before has ever achieved such a thing, for me to come outside my house and dance. This man has done it. For this reason, he will be your companion forever. I take him now to be my singer."

Then Axayacatl ordered that a cloak and a loincloth be given him from among those that bore the personal sign of the House of Axayacatl, and another cloak and another loincloth and sandals adorned with turquoise, and a headdress with quetzal plumes, and various bundles of *cuachtlis*, or pieces of cloth of a certain value, and also cacao beans. This was the payment that was given Quecholcohuatzin. He was held in great esteem for thus having made the people dance. And Axayacatl deemed it proper to have no other sing but him, so that the song would never be ruined again by someone's clumsiness.

And the Lord Axayacatl was well pleased and continued to take delight in the "Song of the Women of Chalco," the *Chalca Cihuacuicatl*. So it was that once again he had the Chalca, all of the nobles, return, and he asked them to give him the song, and he also asked all those from Amecameca, because the song was theirs, it belonged to the *tlailotlaque*, "the men who had returned." The song was their property, the "Song of the Warrior Women of Chalco."

A noble named Aquiauhtzin Cuauhquiyahuacatzintli had composed it there, a man who was a great composer of songs. And for this song, another man also became famous, that

Lord called Ayocuatzin the Elder, a noble Chichimeca, who had governed in Itztlacozaucan Totolimpa.

Thus, Axayacatzin commanded and thus they gave him the song . . . in the year, as we had said before, of 13-Reed (1479). He made this song his personal property. He would have it sung by this man who was named before Quecholcohuatzin . . . , a man whom he held in great esteem and whom he would summon to Mexico and have him sing.

And Axayacatl left the song as inheritance to his son, the so-called Tezozomoctli Acolnahuacatl. He in turn left it to his son who was called Don Diego de Alvarado Huanitzin, who came to be the Lord of Ecatepec and who later became the governor of Mexico-Tenochtitlan. All these men had this song played and danced in their palaces in Mexico because in truth it was quite marvelous, and it was because of this that the city of Amecameca, which is seen now to be only a small village, achieved renown.[5]

The poem that, according to Chimalpahin, was the work of a "noble called Aquiauhtzin Cuauhquiyahuacatzintli, a great composer of songs," because it captured the heart of Axayacatl, came to be his property and later became the inheritance of his descendants.

In order to facilitate our appreciation of the poem, which, it must be remembered, was composed more than half a millennium ago, we must first deal briefly with its structure and with certain characteristics and elements that require some explanation.

CHARACTERISTICS OF THE EROTIC POEM

We will begin by reiterating the original intention of the poem. The previously quoted annotation that appears in the manuscript of the *Cantares mexicanos* expresses this clearly: "With this song the Chalca went to entertain the Lord Axayacatzin, who had conquered them but only the little women." Angel María Garibay, who was the first to deal with this poem, believed it to be anonymous. To him it was an example of the "mimetic production of the Nahuatl world."[6] I agree with Garibay that the text itself could have given rise to later forms of dramatic or mimetic presentations, and we now have proof, thanks to the chronicler Chimalpahin, that the poem was originally conceived to be accompanied by music and sung as a sort of challenge in the presence of the lord of Mexico-Tenochtitlan. It is indispensable to have this in mind in order to understand and evaluate its more profound meaning.

Seven sections or movements can be distinguished in the poem and are indicated in the verse arrangement. First is the invitation that a woman from Chalco makes to her companions. Using metaphors frequently found in Nahuatl, she urges her sisters to gather and cut flowers, but more precisely, only those *in atl, in tlachinolli,* of "water and fire," an evocation of war, the flowers of the shield, the flowers that appeal to men. The flower and song of combat, to take Axayacatl captive in a new way, is the important point here for the women of Chalco.

The second movement provides us with the key word that explains the meaning of the song. This time the war will become a sort of erotic siege. The challenge is caustically announced: "My friend, my little friend, you, / Lord Axayacatl, / if you are really a man, / here is where / you can fight to prove it." The woman from Chalco now deploys her weapons: "Is that all, / you don't have the strength to continue? / Get it up, make me a woman . . . / but no, not yet, do not take the flower, / you, lord, little man Axayacatl."

The intention of surrender is conveyed in the third movement of the poem: "I am trapped. . . . / Will you ruin / what I value most, / will you finish it . . . ? / here it is, make the offering to your penetrating blade . . ." Not knowing what is happening, says the poem, the mothers in Chalco must be grieving. They will have to leave the spindle and the shuttle stick. The shield must be taken up.

Once again, the challenge reappears in the fourth movement of the poem: "Make the man in you speak . . . / you still have not begun and / already you are displeased, /

little friend. / Little man . . . / your seed is pleasing to my mouth, / you taste good." Time and again the provocation is repeated: "Knead me like corn dough. . . . / Are you not an eagle, a jaguar?"

The sequence of the poem seems to lead toward teasing allusions in what we call the fifth movement. The woman of Chalco compares herself to Ayocuan, the old ruler, whose kingdom was conquered by the Mexica. If she is now able to capture Axayacatl, she will succeed in what Ayocuan was unable to achieve. Are there perhaps women like her in the allied cities of Tenochtitlan, in Acolhuacan-Tezcoco, or in Tlacopan, the land of the Tepaneca? The poor Chalca Cuauhtlatohua was conquered in war. Will the great Axayacatl be unable to seize the skirt and blouse of the little woman who has only these for her weapons? Our attention returns to Tlatelolco: There the lord of the Mexica was easily able to undo their skirts and conquer his enemies. The same thing also happened in Huexotzinco, in Tetzmelocan, and in Xaltepetlalpan, where Axayacatl took the inhabitants of Cuetlaxtlan captive.

The Mexica lord now wants to have his pleasure. It is the sixth movement in which, if the baiting continues, the fighting at last gives way to surrender: "Does your heart desire it so . . . / little by little let us tire each other, / how will you make love to me . . . ? / Let's do it this way, together."

The last section is the conclusion, and it is, up to a certain point, ambivalent. The warrior girl, who has fought this way for Chalco, now fears that she will be considered a whore, a woman of pleasure. Could anyone imagine her as already old, abandoned, and juiceless? She has come to give and receive pleasure, but with what feminine delicacy she expresses herself; only in this way has Chalco achieved victory. The metaphors frequently used in other poems here acquire different meanings: The siege, for instance, is transformed into dream and repose: "Look on my flowering painting, my breasts . . . / here are your small hands . . . / on your mat of flowers, little friend, / slowly, slowly, surrender to sleep, rest my little son / you, lord Axayacatl."

Without pretending that this brief analysis of the poem will succeed in uncovering for us this work's most profound richness and significance, it is offered rather by way of an introduction. The song of Aquiauhtzin deserves, without a doubt, much more consideration from other points of view, if we truly want to understand the flowering of eroticism in Mexico before the Conquest. I limit myself here to the presentation of a version of the poem prepared from the Nahuatl text, "The Song of the Women of Chalco."

AQUIAUHTZIN AND THE DIALOGUE OF FLOWER AND SONG

In the chapter devoted to Tecayehuatzin, or Huexotzinco, a description of this dialogue is offered. Here a recapitulation of it is presented to facilitate an appreciation of Aquiauhtzin's contribution to it. Tecayehuatzin posed the question as to whether metaphor and symbol—flower and song—were the only ways to express truth on earth. A wide variety of opinions are expressed. Among other things, the lord of Tecamachalco intimates that, for him, poems and songs were, in themselves, the only thing of lasting value that a man could hope to leave on earth. It is at this point that Aquiauhtzin begins by affirming that, more than anything, flowers and songs are a path to draw near to the Giver of Life.

For Aquiauhtzin, communicating with the Giver of Life and with humans as well is something toward which everyone should strive. It is perhaps because of this that he had chosen the women of Chalco to talk to the Lord Axayacatl. Here, in this new situation, as he advances his point of view, he refers himself to other composers of songs who were also participants in the reunion: Ayocuan, from Tecamachalco, and Xicohtencatl and Camaxo-chitzin, from Tizatlan. To the first of these, he replies that he has heard and understood him; he says of the other two that, with their poetry, they bring joy and keep the word of the gods.

Aquiauhtzin also attempts the search for the Giver of Life. He wants to bring Him joy, and thus he invokes Him in the place of the flowers and in the house of paintings. The bell-bird on the mat of the precious serpent is perhaps the answer—flower and song—that which is always awaited, the joy of the heart, realities that exist and can be understood only through metaphor and symbol. In the context of the dialogue, in the company of the other composers of songs, Aquiauhtzin thus expressed his thought.

It would be naïve to attempt to evaluate the work of Aquiauhtzin on the basis of only two poems. We can, nevertheless, affirm with these two that the chronicler Chimalpahin was right when he said that "the noble called Aquiauhtzin Cuauhquiyahuacatzintli was a great composer of songs."

His erotic poem, the "Song of the Women of Chalco," shows the subtlety of his talent. It is true that in this poem and also in the second text—the participation in the dialogue of Huexotzinco—the metaphors and modes of speech that are used appear to be the same that we find in the great body of Nahuatl verse. The greatness of Aqui-auhtzin—as of other pre-Hispanic poets—is to be found chiefly in the grasp of new poetic situations and the incisiveness with which common word metaphors are infused with new significance.

We know that "fire and water" have the connotation of war. But for Aquiauhtzin in this poem they become flowers—more precisely, the flowers that appeal to men. So begins the siege of the women of Chalco. The skirt and the blouse, as well as the spindle and the shuttle stick, in the metaphorical sense symbolize woman. In the poem of Aquiauhtzin they evoke the object of the conquest, the

conquest of anything that could stand in the way of pleasure. Finding oneself in springtime and in the house of
paintings is the frequent desire of the composers of songs.
In the second of these compositions, they become the
season and the setting for the initiation of the dialogue,
presenting the concept of friendship and the answers of
the Giver of Life in a favorable light. The precious mat,
the place of surrender to love, later becomes a place of repose on which to listen to the song of the bell-bird. We
have a last example in the theme of the spiny fruit of the
cactus—an allusion to war—which, used here as an ad-
jective for "the skirt and the blouse," becomes the sum-
mation of the erotic encounter of the woman of Chalco
with Axayacatl.

CHALCACIHUACUICATL

Toco tico tocoti, toco tico tocoti, toco tico tocoti
Xanmoquetzacan oo annicutzitzinhuan, *aye,*
tonhuian, tonhuian, tixochitemozque, *he,*
tonhuian, tonhuian, tixochitequizque.
Nican mania, nican mania
tlachinolxochitl, *oo,*
chimalli xochitl in tehicolti,
huel tematlachtli,
yaoxochitl, *ohuiya.*

Yectli yan xochitl, *yehuaya,*
manocpac xochiuh
ma ic ninapan
in noxochiuh, *aya,*
ni chalcatl
ni cihuatl, *ahuay yao ohuya.*

Nicnenequi in xochitl,
nicnenequi in cuicatl,
aytzin in totzahuayan,
in toyeyeyan, *ohueya,*

Noconehuitica icuic
in tlatohuani Axayacaton,

nic xochimalina,
nic xochilacatzohua, *a ohuaya ihuiya.*
A iuhqui in tlacuilolli yectli in cuic,
iuhquin huelic xochitl ahuiac,
a noyolquimati in tlalticpac, *ahuaya aho ohuiya.*

Tlen mach?
Ipan nicmati motlatoltzin,
neyocoltzin t'Axayacaton,
Nic xochimalina,
nicxochilacatzohua, *a ohuaya.*
Zan nictocuilehuilia
zan niquiquixhuia, *oo,*
ye tla noconahuilti
in noyecoltzin,
t'Axayacaton.
Aylilli aylililli ololo ayahue.

Xolo,
xolotzin,
ti tlatohuani t'Axayacaton, *ohuiya,*
nel toquichtli,
iz maconel titlaihtolli.
cuix nel ah oc ticuahcuauhitiuh? *ayye.*

Xoconquetza in nonexcon cenca niman,
xocontoquio.
Xic-hual, cui o xic-hual cui:
in nompaca, o xinechhualmaca,
in conetzintli, te xontlahteca tihuan.

Tonhuehuetztozque tzono, tonpaquiz,
paquiz tzono,
nic tlatlamachihuaz.
Macamo, macamo, maca no tlaximayahui,
xolotzin, ti tlatohuani, Axayacaton, *ayya,*

O zo ninicuilo,
in cuecuetzoca ye nomaton, *ayye,*
ye no cuel, ye no cuel,
tictzitziquiznequi in nochichihualtzin
achi in noyollotzin, *huiya.*

In ye ahcazomo nehuian ticmitlacalhuiz
nonecuilol *huiya,*
tzontiquitztoz;
xiuhquechol xochitica, *ohuaye,*
nihtic nimitztzonaquiz,
onca yetoz: motenchalohtzin nimitzmacochihuiz.

In quetzalizquixochitl,
in ye tlauhquechol,
cacaloxochitl, in zan moxochicuach petlapan,
tiya *onoc ye* oncan, *iyyo.*
ya aoc mohui, yao ailili.
Teocuitlapetlatl ipan tiya onoc,
quetzaloztocalco,
tlacuilolcalitic.

Iyyo aoc mohui yao ailili.
Anqui zo ye ichan ye nontlayocoya,
tinonantzin, azo huel nitzahua,
azo huel niquitia zan nen ca ni conetl tzon.
Nicihaupilli,
in ic nihtolo in noquichhua, *zan yao.*

Tetlatlahuelcauh,
teyollocococan, in tlalticpac
In quenman on nontlatlayocoya,
ninotlahuelnequi,
nonexiuhtlatilco.
Nic-hual ihtoa, cue conetl,
ma no ce nimiqui.
Toco tico tocoti, toco tico tocoti, toco tico tocoti.
Ya cue nonantzin nontlaocolmiqui,
o ye nican ye noquichuacan
a huel niquitotia in malacatl,
ahuel nocontlaza, in notzotzopaz,
noca timoquequeloa,
noconetzin, *yyao.*
Auh quennel?
Noconchihuaz,
Cuix ihuichimalli ica nemanalo
ixtlahuatl itic?

Ninomahmanantaz, *ayia oo,*
noca timoquequeloa noconetzin. *Ohuiya.*

Xolotzin,
noconetzin, titlatohuani, t'Axayacaton
zan timonencahuan,
nohuic timomahmana, *aya,*
tonmoquichitohua, *ihuaye,*
Cuix nonmati *aya,*
niquimiximati
ye moyaohuan, noconetzin?
Zan timonencahua nohuic, *ohuiya ohuiya.*
Ma te ticihuantin,
ahzo nel ah tiyecoz,
in yuhqui chahuayotl in ixochitzin,
in icuicatzin noconetzin, *yiio.*

A oquichpilli, notecuyo, titlatohuani,
t'Axayacaton,
o nozo tonpeuh,
ye no ticualani,
xolotzin,
ye noniauh in nochan noconetzin, *yao ohuiya.*
Anca zo zan nican tinechnahualan,
yectli ticchiuh ye motlatoltzin.
Iz im axcan tlahuanquetl,
mah teh titlahuanquetl,
azo no netlacamachon tochan? *yyao ohuiya.*

Cuix nozo tinechcouh, tinechnocoui, noconetzin?
cuix tlapapatlaco,
nahuihuan ye notlahuan?
Zazo tictlacanequi ye no ticualani,
xolotzin, ye noniauh in nochan,
noconetzin, *ya ohuiya.*

Ticniuhtzin, ticihuatlamacazqui,
ma xontlachia in momach moman cuicatl,
in Cohuatepec, in Cuauhtenampan.
topan moteca panohua. *aya ohuaya.*
Zo nocihuayo ninaitia,
noyollotzin mococohua. Ah quen nel noconchihuaz

ihuan noquichtiz? *o,*
Mazo oc cenca ye in cueye, ye in huipil?
In toquichhuan,
in toyocolhuan, *yyaho ohuiya.*

Xic hualquixti nonextamal,
in titlatohuani Axayacaton,
tla cen nimitzmanili,
ne oc, in noconeuh, ne oc noconeuh.
Xoconahuilti, xic tocuilehui, *ololotzin ololo, ayye.*
Ahzo ti cuauhtli, tocelotl,
in timittohua noconetzin? *Ohuiya.*
Ahzo moyaohuan
inhuic ticuecuenoti?
Meoc o noconexiuh, xocon ahuilti.

Aya tle nocue, aya tle nohuipil,
nicihuatzintli,
yehuan ya nican;
quimanaco yectli ye incuic,
nican quimanaco
chimalli xochitl.
Quen mach tontlaca,
ye ni chalcacihuatl,
n'Ayocuan? *Ohuiya.*
Niquimelehuia nocihuampohuan,
in acolhuaque,
niquimelehuia nocihuampohuan,
in tepaneca.
Quen mach tontlaca
ye ni chalcacihuatl,
n'Ayocuan? *Ohuiya.*

Ca pinauhticate ni chahuahuilo,
noconetzin, *Ihuia*
Cuix no iuh nechchihuaz
on o iuh toconchiuh in Cuauhtlatotohuaton?
Ma za zo ihuian ximocuetomacan,
ximomaxahuican antlatilolca,
in anmiyaque, *aoay ayya,*
xihuallachian nican Chalco, *ahuayya.*

Ma ninopotoni,
tinonantzin,
ma xi nexahuaco,
quen nechittaz
in noyecol?

In ixpan tonquizatiuh,
ahcazo mihicoltiz,
ye Huexotzinco Xayacamachan. *Ohuia.*
in Tetzmelocan.
Nicihuatl, ninomaoxihuia, ninocxihuia,
nocon acico ye nochcue
ye nochhuipil,
niccecentlamitaz, *aytzin, aytzin, ohuaya.*
Niquimelehui Xaltepetlapan, ye huexotzinca,
tzon in Cuetlaxtlan malin,
tzon in cuetlaxtetecuecuex.
Niccecentlamitaz, *aytzin, aytzin, ohuaya.*
In quen oc zan in tlamati?
Nechmitlania in conetl, in tlatohuani,
in Axayacaton, *cuee,*
tle on in ma ic tepal no chachahuatlalia. *Ohuaye.*
Noca titlaomepiaz
noconetzin.

Azo iuh quinequi moyollo,
ma zo ihuian,
mociahuan, *yyao, ohuiya.*
Cuix amoyollocopa, noconetzin,
ye toconcalaqui in chahuayotl,
in ic mochan. *Ahay, ayoho.*
Azo iuh quinequi moyollo,
ma zo ihuian mociahuan, *yyao ohuiya.*

Quen mach in tinechiuhnoyecoltzin? *Ayye.*
Ma ca oc ic xi mochichihuacan,
huel ah titlacatl?
Tlein tic nenelo?
Ye noyollotzin tic xochimalina,
ye motlatol, *yao ohuiya.*
Notzahuayan in mitzittoa,

in nihquitian
nimitzilnamiqui, xolotzin,
Tle in ticnenelo ye noyollotzin?

Nahuil ilama,
namonan,
nicahualilama,
ni ihcpichilama,
ipan nonchihua o nichalcotlacatl, *aha ili.*
Ni mitzahuiltico noxochinenetzin,
noxochicamapal,
nenetzin. *Yya ohuiya.*
Ye no quelehuia in tlatohuani
in Axayacaton.
Xic hualitta no xochitlacuilo,
ma tonxichualitta, no xochitlacuilolchichihualtzin. *Ohuiya.*
Macazo can on nen huetztiuh,
ye moyollotzin
t'Axayacaton?
Izca ye momatzin,
ma no matitech,
xi nech on antiuh. *Ayyaha ayo.*
Xonahuiacan.
Moxochinpetlapan
moyeyeyan, xolotzin,
ihuian xoconcochi,
xonyayamani, noconetzin,
ti tlatohuani, t'Axayaca, *yao ohuaya.*

THE SONG OF THE WOMEN OF CHALCO

You, my little sisters, get up,
let us go, let us go, we will seek flowers,
let us go, let us go, we will cut flowers.
Here they reach up, here they grow tall,
the flowers of water and fire,
the flowers of the shield, that appeal to men,
the flowers of glory;
the flowers of war.

Beautiful flowers,
flowers above,
with them, I adorn myself,
these are my flowers,
I am from Chalco,
I am a woman.

I desire, I long for flowers,
I desire, I long for songs,
I have a yearning, here in the place
we spin,
in the place our life is spent.

I sing his song,
to the lord, little Axayacatl,
I weave my song with flowers,
I put flowers around it.

A lovely song is like a painting,
like the fragrant flowers that give joy,
my heart values this on earth.

What does this mean?
Your word for me is worth this much,
you, with whom I do it, you, little Axayacatl,
I weave flowers into you,
I put flowers around you,
I lift you up to join us together,
I awaken you.
That is how I please
you with whom I do it,
you, little man, Axayacatl.

My friend,
my little friend, you,
Lord Axayacatl,
if you are really a man,
here is where you can fight to prove it.
Don't you have the strength to continue?

Do it in my warm vessel, much
light on fire.
Come, put it in, come, put it in:

It is my joy.
Come to give me that little thing,
You, let it rest.

We will have to laugh, be happy,
there will be pleasure,
I will have glory,
but no, not yet, do not hurl violently.
little friend, you, lord, little man, Axayacatl.

I, I am trapped,
my little hand slides round and round,
now come, now come.
Do you want to touch my breasts,
even my heart.

Will you ruin
what I value most,
will you finish it;
with flowers the color of the bird of fire,
I will make my womb move for you,
here it is: I make an offering to your chin.

As a precious flower of toasted corn,
as the bird with the rubber neck,
as a flower of the raven, your cloak of flowers,
on your flower-covered mat you lie.
You lie down on the precious mat,
in a house that is a cave of precious feathers,
in the mansion of the paintings. No more.

But even in your house I am sad,
you, my mother, I may no longer be able to spin.
I may not be able to weave,
it is all for nothing that I am a girl.
I am a young girl,
and they say I have a man.

There is suffering,
it is a place of despair on the earth.
So I brood sadly,
I desire evil,
I have become desperate.

I say to myself, come child,
I want to die.

O my mother, I am distressed,
here I have my man,
I can no longer make the bobbin dance,
I cannot throw the shuttle stick:
my little child,
you laugh at me.
What is left for me?
I will do it!

Perchance with a feathered shield one will be sacrificed
in the field of battle?
I will offer myself, I will offer myself,
my child, you laugh at me.

Little fiend, my little child,
you, lord, little man Axayacatl,
let yourself be my side,
offer yourself,
make the man in you speak.
Don't I know them,
have not I heard
of your enemies, my little child?
But for now, here by my side, forget.
Even though we are women,
you may gain nothing as a man.
Flowers and songs
from the woman who shares your pleasure,
my little child.

O man-child, my lord, you, great lord,
you, little man Axayacatl;
you still have not begun and
already you are displeased,
little friend. I am going home now,
my little child.
Have you bewitched me,
you have spoken lovely words.
Here, now there is drunkeness,

inebriate yourself!
Is there happiness in our house?

Have you bought me,
did you acquire me for yourself, my little child?
Perhaps you will sell me,
my pleasure, my intoxication?
Do you scorn me, are you displeased,
little friend, I am going home now,
my little child.

You, my friend, you the woman who offers herself,
see how the song endures,
in Cohuatepec, in Cuauhtenanpan.
How it reaches over us, and then is gone,
Maybe the woman in me does crazy things,
my small heart grieves. How should I make love,
to the one who is my man.
The skirts, the blouses,
the women, of our men,
of those we brought to life.

Knead me like corn dough,
you, lord, little man Axayacatl,
I will give you all of me,
I am here, my little child, I am here, my child.
Be glad, our worm rises.
Are you not an eagle, a jaguar,
do not you use these names, my little child?
Don't you play dirty tricks
on your enemies at war?
Now, in the same way, give yourself to pleasure.

My skirt and blouse are nothing,
here I am,
just a woman;
he comes to surrender his harmonious song
he comes here to surrender
the flower of his shield.
Are we not somehow the same,
I, the woman from Chalco,

I, [our former ruler] Ayocuan?
I want there to be women like me,
from afar, from Acolhuacan,
I want there to be women like me,
who are Tepaneca.
Are we not somehow the same,
I, the woman from Chalco,
I, Ayocuan?

They are ashamed I have become your mistress.
My little child,
perhaps you would treat me
like poor Cuauhtlatohua?
Slowly take off your skirts,
open your legs, you Tlatelolca,
you who shoot arrows,
look here to Chalco.

Shall I wear feathers,
my little mother,
shall I paint my face,
how should he see me,
my companion in pleasure?
Before your face we will leave openly,
perhaps they will be angry,
there in Huexotzinco, Xayacamachan,
in Tetzmelocan.

I, a woman, have rubbed my hands with,
I approach with my skirt of prickly fruit,
with my blouse of prickly fruit.
I will see them all dead.
I want the Huexotzincas in Xaltepetlapan,
the captive of Cuetlaxtlan.
the crafty Cuetlaxteca,
I will see them all dead.
How do I know this?
The boy calls me, the lord, little man
Axayacatl,
he wants to have his pleasure with me.
Because of me

you will have two to care for,
my little child.

Does your heart desire it so,
thus, little by little, let us tire each other.
Perhaps your heart is unwilling, my little child,
as you enter here, your pleasure,
your home.
Does your heart desire it so,
thus little by little, let us make each other tired.

How will you make love to me,
my companion of pleasure?
Let us do it this way, together,
are you not a man?
What is it that confuses you?
You circle my heart with flowers,
they are your word.
I will show you the place where I weave,
the place where I spin,
I will remember you, little friend.
What is it that troubles you, my heart?

I am an old whore,
I am your mother,
a lusty old woman,
old and without juice,
this is my profession, me, the woman from Chalco.
I have come to please my blooming vulva,
my little mouth.
I desire the lord,
the little man, Axayacatl.
Look on my flowering painting,
look on my flowering painting: my breasts.
Will it fall in vain,
your heart,
little man, Axayacatl?
Here are your small hands,
now take me with your hands.

Let us take pleasure.
On your mat of flowers,
in the place where you live, little friend,
slowly, slowly surrender to sleep,
rest, my little son,
you, lord Axayacatl.

(*Cantares mexicanos*, National Library of Mexico, fols. 72 r.–73 v.)

NOCONCACON CUICATL

Noconcacon cuicatl,
noconcaqui,
in tlapitza, *aya*,
Xochimecatl Ayocanteuctli,
ya ohuaye, ohuaya, ayo ohna.

Zan mitz ya nanquili,
o mitznanquili,
xochincalaitec,
in Aquiauhtzin, in tlacateuctli Ayapancatl,
ya ohuaye, ohuaya, ayo ohua.

Can tinemi, noteuh,
Ipalnemohuani?
Nimitztemohua.
In quenmanian,
in moca nitlaocoyani, ni cuicanitl, *huiya.*
Zan nimitzahuiltica,
Ye ohui, ye tantililli . . .

In zan can izquixochitl,
in quetzalizquixochitl,
pixahui ye nican,
xoppan calitec,
in tlacuilocalitec,
zan nimitzahuiltia,
ye ohui ye tantilili . . .

O anqui ye oncan Tlaxcala, *ayahue,*
chalchiuhtetzilacacuicatoque,
in huehuetitlan, *ohuaye.*
Xochin poyon poyon, *ayahue,*

Xicotencatl teuctli in Tizatlan,
in Camaxochitzin cuicatica,
mellelquiza
xochitica,
ye on chielo
itlatol *ohuaya,* icel teotl.

O anqui nohuian ye mochan,
Ipalnemohua.
Xochipetlatl ye onoca,
xochitica on tzauhtica
oncan mitztlatlauhtia in tepilhuan, *ohuaya.*

In nepapan xochicuahuitl on icac, *aya,*
huehuetitlan, ayahue.
Zan can tica, *aya,*
quetzaltica malintimani, *aya,*
yecxochitl motzetzeloa, *aya, ohuaya ohuaya.*
Zan quetzalpetlacoatl icpac,
ye nemi coyoltototl,
cuicatinemi, *ya,*
can quimanquili teuctli ya.
conahuiltican quauhtlo, ocelotl, *ohuaya, ohuaya.*

Xochitl tztzeliuhtoc in,
ma on netotilo, antocnihuan,
huehuetitlan!

I HAVE HEARD A SONG

From afar I have heard a song
I listen to it,
the King Ayocuan
plays his flute, a garland of flowers.

Now he answers you,
now he responds,
from deep within the flowers,
Aquiahtzin, lord of Ayapanco.

Where do you live, my God,
Giver of Life?
I look for you.

Sometimes I, the poet,
am sad because of you,
even though I try to bring you joy.

Here where the flowers of toasted maize
rain down,
the precious white flowers,
in the midst of spring,
in the house of paintings,
I only wish to bring you joy.

O, you who from afar, from Tlaxcala
have come to sing,
to the sound of
the brilliant timbrels,
in the place of the drums,
the fragrant flowers,
the Lord Xicohtencatl of Tizatlan,
Camazochitzin, happy
with flowers and songs,
keep the word of God.

Your house is everywhere,
O, Giver of Life.
Upon the precious mat,
woven with flowers,
upon this, the princes invoke you.

The many different trees, rise up flowering
in the place of the drums.
You are there:
enmeshed with fine plumes,
the lovely flowers are scattered.
On the mat of the precious serpent,
the bird of bells comes ringing,
he comes singing,
only the lord answers him,
bringing joy to the eagles and jaguars.

Now the flowers have rained down,
begin the dance, O friends together,
in the place of the drums!

(*Cantares mexicanos*, National Library of Mexico, fol. 10 r.)

A LAST WORD

The indigenous sources have revealed us something of the lives and creations of these fifteen poets. Some flowery volutes—the scroll glyphs representing the speech and song in the books of paintings—have come together with the faces and hearts of these composers of chants.

Nahuatl poetry, still produced in some contemporary Mexican rural communities, has to be included among the great spiritual creations of those whose ancestral home is in the Americas. One of the ancient poets clearly foresaw it:

> One by one I bring together
> your songs.
> I am linking the jades,
> with them I make a bracelet
> of everlasting gold.
>
> Bedeck yourself with them;
> they are your wealth
> in the region of flowers,
> they are your wealth
> on the earth.

Macehual, common man. Aztec sculpture in stone in the National Museum of Anthropology, Mexico

Detail of the votive stone of Tizoc. Aztec sculpture in the National Museum of Anthropology, Mexico

Musicians and poets (*Códice florentino*, ix)

NOTES

INTRODUCTION

1. See James C. Langley, *Symbolic Notation of Teotihuacan: Elements of Writing in a Mesoamerican Culture of the Classic Period* (London: B.A.R. International Series, 1986), pp. 125–132; and Thomas S. Barthel, *"Deciphering Teotihuacan Writing,"* Indiana 11 (Berlin, 1987): 9–18.

2. Sahagún, *Historia general*, vol. 1, p. 105.

3. *Códice matritense*, vol. 8, fol. 192r.

4. Tezozomoc, *Crónica maxicayotl*, p. 6.

5. *Códice florentino*, vol. 3, book 3, fol. 39r.

6. *Cantares mexicanos*, fol. 14 v.

7. "Leyenda de los soles (Legend of the Suns)," in *Códice chimalpopoca*. translated by P. F. Velázquez (Mexico: National University, 1975).

8. *Códice chimalpopoca*, p. 119.

9. "Historia de los Mexicanos por sus pinturas," in *Nueva colección de documentos para la historia de México*, ed. Joaquín García Icazbalceta, 2 vols. (Mexico, 1886–1892), vol. 3, pp. 231–286.

10. Mercedes de la Garza, "Análisis comparativo de la *Historia de los Mexicanos por su pinturas* y la "Leyenda de los soles," *Estudios de Cultura Náhuatl* (Mexico: National University, 1983), vol. 16, pp. 123–134.

11. *Códice vaticano a*, with a commentary by Ferdinand Anders (Graz, Austria: Akademische Druk und Verlaganstalt, 1972).

12. References to these works are listed in the bibliography.

13. References to these works are listed in the bibliography.

14. Zurita, *Breve y sumaria relación*, pp. 112–113.

15. See the descriptive catalog of the stelae with inscriptions from Monte Albán, Oaxaca, by Roberto García Moll *et al.*, *Monumentos escultóricos de Monte Albán* (München: Verlag C. H. Beck, 1986).

16. On Maya writing, see Linda Schele and Mary Ellen Müller, *The Blood of the Kings: Dynasty and Ritual in Maya Art* (Fort Worth: Fort Worth Art Museu, 1986). On Mixtec writings, see Mary Elizabeth Smith, *Picture Writing from Southern Mexico, Mixtec Place Signs and Maps* (Norman: University of Oklahoma Press, 1973). On Nahua writing, see Charles E. Dibble, "Writing in Central Mexico," *Handbook of Middle American Indians* (Austin: University of Texas Press, 1971), vol. 10, pp. 322–332.

17. *Códice florentino*, vol. 3, book 3, fol. 39r.

18. There are several collections of *Huehuehtlahtolli*. The two most ample are that collected by Andrés de Olmos and published in 1600 by Fray Juan Baptista, *Huehuehtlahtolli: Testimonios de la antigua palabra*, facsimile reproduction with an introduction by Miguel León-Portilla, translated by L. Silva Galeana (Mexico: Comisión del V. Centenario, 1988); and the collection included by Sahagún in the *Códice florentino*, vol. 2, book 6.

19. See the collection of "Modern Huehuehtlahtolli," published by Miguel León-Portilla, in "Yancuic Tlahtolli: Palabra Nueva," *Estudios de cultural nahuatl* (Mexico: National University, 1986), vol. 18, pp. 143–169.

20. Jack Goody, *The Domestication of the Savage Mind*, (Cambridge: Cambridge University Press, 1977).

21. Walter Ong, *Orality and Literacy* (London and New York: Methuen, 1982).

22. Eric A. Havelock, *The Muse Learns to Write: Reflections on Orality and Literacy from Antiquity to the Present* (New Haven: Harvard University Press, 1986).

23. The problem of intercultural contamination, commenting on Goody's work, is discussed by Havelock, *The Muse Learns to Write*, p. 44.

24. See Jorge Klor de Alva, "Sahagún and the Birth of Modern Ethnography," in *The Work of Bernardino de Sahagún*, ed. J. Klor de Alva *et al.* (Albany: State University of New York at Albany, 1988), pp. 45–47.

25. See Louise M. Burkhardt, *The Slippery Earth: Nahua Christian Moral Dialogue in Sixteenth Century Mexico* (Tucson: University of Arizona Press, 1989), p. 5.

26. See *Anales de Tlatelolco*, or *Anales de la nación mexicana*.

27. The *Anales de Cuauhtitlan* are included in *Códice chimalpopoca*.

28. The *Romances de los señores de Nueva España* will be described in the following pages of this book.

29. See *Codice matritense*, vol. 8, fol. 118 r.

30. *Coloquios y doctrina cristiana*, the Dialogues of 1524, ed.

and trans. Miguel León-Portilla (Mexico: National University, 1986), pp. 140–141.

31. See Frances Karttunen and James Lockhart, "The Huehuehtlahtolli Bancroft Manuscript: The Missing Pages," *Estudios de cultura nahuatl* (Mexico: National University, 1986), vol. 18, p. 175.

32. The Twenty Sacred Hymns are included in *Códice matritense*, vol. 6, fols. 274 r.–281 v.

33. *Códice florentino*, vol. 1, book 2, fol 137 r.

34. See Eduard Seler, "Die religiösen Gesange der alten Mexicaner," *Gesammelte Abhandlungen zur Amerikanischen Sprach und Altertumskunde*, 5 vols. (Berlin: Verlag A. Ascher und Co., 1902–1923), vol. 2, pp. 959–1107; and Angel María Garibay K., *Veinte himnos sacros de los nahuas* (Mexico: National University, 1958).

35. *Codice matritense*, vol. 8, fols. 191 r.–194 r.

36. Ibid.

37. *Historia Tolteca-Chichimeca*, p. 33.

38. See Alfonso Caso, *Reyes y reinos de la Mixteca*, 2 vols. (Mexico: Fondo de Cultura Económica, 1977).

39. *Anales de Tlatelolco*, fols. 20, 25, 33.

40. *Anales de Cuauhtitlan*, pp. 1, 5, 8–11, and 29–64.

41. See the partial edition of *Cantares* by Angel MaríGaribay K. in *Poesía nahuatl*, 2 vols. (Mexico: National University, 1965–1968).

42. Sahagún, *Psalmodia christiana*, prologue.

43. *Códice florentino*, vol. 1.

44. Garibay K. *Poesía nahuatl*, vol. 2, p. 38.

45. Karl A. Novotny, "Die Notation des Tono in den aztekischen Cantares," *Baessler Archiv* (Neue Folge, 1956), vol. 2, pp. 186–198.

46. In the only available edition and Spanish translation of the *Romances*, its editor included *Pomar's Geographical Relation: Angel María Garibay K., Poesía Nahuatl, Romances de los señores de la Nueva España* (Mexico: National University, 1964).

47. Durán, *Historia de las Indias*, vol. 2, p. 233.

48. Such a song is in the *Anales de Tlatelolco*, fol. 20, and the *Anales de Cuauhtitlan*, fols. 16–17.

49. See *Proceso criminal del Santo Oficio de la Inquisición y del fiscal en su nombre contra don Carlos, indio principal de Tezcoco* (Mexico: Archivo General de la Nación, 1910).

50. *Cantares mexicanos: Songs of the Aztecs*, translated from the Nahuatl with an introduction and commentary by John Bierhorst, (Stanford: Stanford University Press, 1985).

51. *A Nahuatl-English Dictionary*, p. 15.

52. *Cantares mexicanos*, Bierhorst, p. 5.

53. One reads in the *Códice florentino*, for example, the following words addressed "to him who had died": "For you are gone to the abode of the dead, to the place of descent . . . and to the place of no outlets and no openings. For no more may you return your way back . . ." (book 3, appendix 1).

54. *Cantares mexicanos,* Bierhorst, p. 18.
55. Karen Dakin, review of *Cantares mexicanos: Songs of the Aztecs, American Anthropologist,* vol. 84, no. 4 (December 1986): 1015. Bierhorst's interpretation has been the subject of numerous adverse critical appraisals, in particular that of James Lockhart, in "Care, Ingenuity and Irresponsibility: The Bierhorst Edition of *Cantares mexicanos,*" *Reviews in Anthropology,* vol. 16 (1991): 119–132.
56. Concerning the concept of "Sun" as a cosmic age and the indigenous conveyors of these traditions, see León-Portilla, *Aztec Thought and Culture,* pp. 37–57.
57. Far from denying the religious and mystical connotations of human sacrifice, one has to recognize, with Alfonso Caso and the many who have followed him, that "the Aztec, like anyone who believes himself to have a mission, was more eager to carry it out if, in so doing, the conquest of other peoples was brought about . . ." Alfonso Caso, "El águila y el nopal," *Memorias de la Academia Mexicana de la Historia,* vol. 5, no. 2 (1946): 103.
58. Many of the so-called Mesoamerican pyramids, not only in the central plateau but in other areas as well, exhibit structural elements and symbols described here that make of them a plastic representation of the celestial universe as conceived by the priests and sages.
59. See León-Portilla, *Aztec Thought and Culture,* pp. 80–103.
60. *Códice matritense,* vol. 1, fol. 260 r.
61. Fernando de Alva Ixtlilxochitl, *Obras históricas,* 2 vols. (Mexico: Universidad Nacional Autónoma de México, 1975–1977), vol. 1, p. 527.
62. See the chapter in this book devoted to Lord Tecayehuatzin of Huexotzinco.

CHAPTER I

1. *Cantares mexicanos,* fol. 33 r.
2. Alva Ixtlilxochitl, *Obras históricas,* vol. 1, p. 136.
3. Ibid., vol. 1, p. 137.
4. Ibid., vol. 1, p. 117.
5. Ibid., vol. 2, p. 73.
6. *Romances de los señores,* fol. 7 r.
7. *Códice maltritense,* fol. 129 r.
8. *Códice matritense,* fol. 180 v.

CHAPTER II

1. *Romances de los señores,* fol. 18 v.
2. Ibid., fol. 34 r.
3. José María Vigil, *Nezahualcóyotl, el rey poeta* (Mexico: Biblioteca Mínima Mexicana, Ediciones de Andrea, 1957) deserves special mention.
4. José Granados y Gálvez, *Tardes americanas* (Mexico, 1778), p. 90.
5. Alva Ixtlilxochitl, *Obras históricas,* vol. 2, p. 82.
6. See León-Portilla, *Aztec Thought and Culture.*

7. Domingo de San Antón Muñon Chimalpahin Cuauhtlehuanitzin, *Seventh Relation*, fol. 162 v.

8. Chapter 6 of this book is devoted to Tochihuitzin Coyolchiuhqui.

9. *Anales de Cuauhtitlan*, p. 34.

10. Ibid.

11. Alva Ixtlilxochitl, *Obras históricas*, vol. 2, pp. 173–181. *Codex Quinatzin*, an indigenous manuscript of Tezcocan origin, includes a pictorial representation of the palaces of Nezahualcoyotl. See *Anales de Museo Nacional de Arqueología*, epoch 1, vol. 2 (Mexico, 1885), pp. 345–346.

12. Alva Ixtlilxochitl, *Obras históricas*, vol. 1, pp. 236–239, and vol. 2, pp. 187–193.

13. Ibid., vol. 1, p. 227.

14. Ibid., vol. 2, p. 242.

15. Ibid., vol. 2, pp. 243–244.

16. Ibid., vol. 2, pp. 244–245.

17. *Cantares mexicanos*, fol. 17 r.

18. *Romances de los señores*, fol. 35 r.–36 r.

19. *Cantares mexicanos*, fol. 17 v.

20. Ibid., fol. 70 r.

21. *Romances de los señores*, fol. 19 v.

22. *Cantares mexicanos*, fol. 16 v.

23. *Romances de los señores*, fol. 35 r.

24. *Cantares mexicanos*, fol. 13 v.

25. *Romances de los señores*, fols. 19 v.–20 r.

26. Ibid., fols. 4 v.–5 v.

CHAPTER III

1. Alva Ixtlilxochitl, *Obras históricas*, vol. 2, pp. 167 and 176–178.

2. See chapter 2 of this book, note 11.

3. *Tira de Tepechpan*.

4. Alva Ixtlilxochitl, *Obras históricas*, vol. 2, p. 214. There is an interesting study by Angel María Garibay K. concerning the life and work of Cuacuauhtzin: "Cuacuauhtzin, romántico nahuatl," in *Estudios de Cultura Nahuatl* (Mexico, 1965), vol. 5, pp. 9–18.

5. Alva Ixtlilxochitl, *Obras históricas*, vol. 2, p. 217.

6. *Cantares mexicanos*, fol. 25 r.

7. Alva Ixtlilxochitl, *Obras históricas*, vol. 2, pp. 213–214.

8. Ibid., pp. 214–215.

9. Ibid.

10. *Tira de Tepechpan*, p. 90.

CHAPTER IV

1. Torquemada, *Monarquía indiana*, vol. 1, p. 188.

2. Ibid.

3. Alva Ixtlilxochitl, *Obras históricas*, vol. 2, p. 328.

4. Torquemada, *Monarquía indiana*, vol. 1, p. 216.

5. Alva Ixtlilxochitl, *Obras históricas*, vol. 2, pp. 241–242.
6. Ibid., vol., 2, pp. 285–286.
7. Ibid., vol. 2, p. 268.
8. Ibid., vol. 2, p. 294.
9. *Huehuehtlahtolli A*, manuscript no. PM 4068 J.83, Bancroft Library, University of California, Berkeley, fol. 124 v.
10. Ibid.
11. Alva Ixtlilxochitl, *Obras históricas*, vol. 2, p. 294.
12. Ibid., vol. 2, pp. 299–300.
13. Torquemada, *Monarquía indiana*, vol. 1, p. 189.
14. Ibid., vol. 2, p. 188.
15. Ibid., vol. 2, p. 194.
16. Ibid., vol. 1, pp. 194–195.
17. Alva Ixtlilxochitl, *Obras históricas*, vol. 2, p. 310.
18. Ibid., vol. 1, p. 331.

CHAPTER V

1. Alva Ixtlilxochitl, *Obras históricas*, vol. 2, p. 330.
2. Ibid., vol. 2, p. 329.
3. See the English version, León-Portilla, ed., *The Broken Spears*, pp. 32–36.
4. Bernal Díaz del Castillo, *Historia verdadera de la Conquista de la Nueva España*, introduction and notes by Joaquín Ramírez Cabañas, 2 vols. (Mexico: Editorial Porrúa, 1955), vol. 1, p. 259.
5. See *Proceso de residencia contra Pedro de Alvarado*, published by Ignacio López Rayón and José Fernando Ramírez (Mexico, 1847).
6. León-Portilla, *The Broken Spears*, pp. 74–75.
7. *Romances de los señores*, fol. 5 v.
8. León-Portilla, *The Broken Spears*, pp. 74–75.
9. Ibid.
10. Ibid.

CHAPTER VI

1. *Anales de Cuauhtitlan*, fol. 36.
2. Ibid.
3. Tezozomoc, *Crónica mexicayotl*, p. 127.
4. Ibid.

CHAPTER VII

1. Chimalpahin Cuauhtlehuanitzin, *Seventh Relation*, fol. 165.
2. Durán, *Historia de las Indias*, vol. 1, p. 275.
3. Tezozomoc, *Crónica mexicayotl*, pp. 115–116.
4. Ibid.
5. Durán, *Historia de las Indias*, vol. 1, p. 256.
6. Ibid., vol. 1, p. 269.
7. Ibid., vol. 1, p. 272.
8. Durán, *Historia de las Indias*, vol. 1, p. 275.

9. Chimalpahin Cuauhtlehuanitzin, *Fourth Relation*, fol. 101 r.

10. Durán, *Historia de las Indias*, vol. 1, p. 291.

11. Tezozomoc, *Crónica mexicana*, p. 233.

12. *Cantares mexicanos*, fol. 73 v.

13. Durán, *Historia de las Indias*, vol. 1, p. 302.

CHAPTER VIII

1. Alva Ixtlilxochitl, *Obras históricas*, vol. 2, p. 268.

2. *Cantares mexicanos*, fol. 39 v.

3. Tezozomoc, *Crónica mexicayotl*, p. 128.

4. *Códice florentino*, book 6, chapter 17, fol. 74 v.

5. Tezozomoc, *Crónica mexicayotl*, p. 121.

6. See chapter 7 of this book, where more information is provided concerning the war against Tlatelolco.

7. Tezozomoc, *Crónica mexicana*, p. 205.

8. Ibid., p. 208.

9. Ibid., p. 210.

10. The reasons for attributing this poem to Macuilxochitzin are as follows: (1) The second line of the poem gives the name of the person who conceived it, Macuilxochitl. (2) This name was common among the Nahuas, for both men and women, and a search in the principal sources (Chimalpahin, Ixtlilxochitl, Tezozomoc, *Annals de Cuauhtitlan*, *Annals of Tlatelolco*, *Informantes de Sahagún*, *Ms. de Cantares*, and others) has helped to identify various persons of the same name. However, because the person who composed the poem had to be of Mexica origin and a contemporary of Axayacatl (as inferred from the text itself) and because we have found no other person who fulfills these conditions, we conclude that it must have been the Princess Macuilxochitzin, daughter of Tlacaelel. (3) The fact that the poem gives detailed information about the war planned by Tlacaelel, concerning which Tezozomoc says, "they sent a messenger to advise him and tell him about it," shows that the song very probably was conceived by someone closely connected with the great counselor of the Mexica rulers. (4) Finally, the part of the poem devoted to the brave action of the Otomi women who begged for the life of the Matlatzinca chief appears to indicate that it was a woman attempting to show the important role women can play in a very serious situation.

11. As a confirmation of what has been said about the very few possessions and resources of the Otomi, one can quote the words of the Matlatzinca lord Chimalteuctli to Axayacatl after the Mexica victory. Axayacatl had gone to Toluca to recover his strength, and it was there that Chimalteuctli, lord of the Matlatzinca, came and said, "Mexica lords, leave off your pride and your bravery, for now we are your vassals paying tribute. Look, lords, how in this land the people have nothing but maize, kidney beans, sage and candlewood to burn at night, and there is the flower of the chestnut tree, and rushes. This, my lord, is what grows and is cultivated in this your village, and nothing more."

12. Tezozomoc, *Crónica mexicayotl*, p. 128.

CHAPTER IX

1. *Cantares mexicanos,* fol. 54 v.
2. *Códice matritense,* vol. 8, fol. 115 v.
3. *Códice florentino,* book 12, chapter 38, fol. 75 r.
4. Ibid.
5. Ibid.
6. Ibid., chapter 39, fol. 80 v.
7. Ibid.
8. *Annales de Tlatelolco,* fol. 35.
9. Ibid., fol. 10.
10. Ibid.

CHAPTER X

1. *Cantares mexicanos,* fol. II V.
2. Muñoz Camargo, *Historia de Tlaxcala,* p. 127.
3. Durán, *História de las Indias,* vol. 1, p. 477.
4. *Cantares mexicanos,* fol. 9 v.
5. Ibid., fol. 10 v.
6. Ibid., fol. 11 r.
7. Ibid.
8. Ibid., fol. 11 r.
9. Ibid., fol. 11 v.

CHAPTER XI

1. *Cantares mexicanos,* fol. 35 v.
2. *Historia Tolteca-Chichimeca,* fol. 32. See Luis Reyes García and Lina Odena Güemes, ed., *Historia Tolteca-Chichimeca,* facsimile reproduction with paleography and Spanish translation of the Nahuatl texts (Mexico: Instituto Nacional de Antropología e Historia, 1976).
3. *Annals of Tecamachalco,* in *Documentos para la historia de Mexico,* ed. Antonio Peñafiel (Mexico, 1903), p. 3.
4. *Historia Tolteca-Chichimeca,* fol. 44.
5. Ibid.
6. *Cantares mexicanos,* fol. 14 v.
7. Ibid., fol. 34 v.
8. *Historia Tolteca-Chichimeca,* fol. 52.
9. *Cantares mexicanos,* fol. 31 v.
10. See the complete text in chapter 14 of this book.

CHAPTER XII

1. Muñoz Camargo, *História de Tlaxcala,* p. 95.
2. The figure of Xihcotencatl and of his extant poetic work are discussed in chapter 13 of this book.
3. Muñoz Camargo, *História de Tlaxcala,* p. 96.
4. *Cantares mexicanos,* fol. 11 r.

CHAPTER XIII

1. *Cantares mexicanos,* fol. 10 v.
2. Torquemada, *Monarquía indiana,* vol. 1, p. 274.
3. Alva Ixtlilxochitl, *Obras históricas,* vol. 2, p. 203.
4. Torquemada, *Monarquía indiana,* vol. 1, p. 275.

CHAPTER XIV

1. The chronicler Chimalpahin, whose complete name was Domingo de San Anton Muñon Chimalpahin Quauhtlehuanitzin, was born in old Amaquemecan, today Amecameca (present State of Mexico), during the night of May 26, 1579. As he stated in his journal (written in Nahuatl), he was a descendant of the ancient nobility of Chalco. At about fifteen years of age he went to the City of Mexico and entered the monastery of San Antonio Abad, where he learned to read and write.
    He succeeded in persuading his superiors to allow him to read classic works, among them some books of history. In addition, during his frequent visits to Amecameca and other villages, he became acquainted with the traditions and some extant indigenous codices. Thus he was conversant with two types of history—the European and the indigenous. He died around the year 1660.
    Chimalpahin's most important works are the *Eight Relations,* known under the general title *Diferentes histórias originales,* the *Memorial breve acerca de la fundación de Culhuacán,* the *Crónica mexicana,* and his *Journal,* all of which are in Nahuatl.
2. Chimalpahin, *Fourth Relation,* fol. 116 r.
3. Chimalpahin, *Third Relation,* fol. 98 r.
4. *Anales de Cuauhtitlan,* fol. 53.
5. Ibid.
6. Ibid.

CHAPTER XV

1. Chimalpahin, *Third Relation,* fol. 95 v.
2. Chimalpahin, ibid., fol. 99 r.
3. *Cantares mexicanos,* f. 72 r.
4. Chimalpahin, *Seventh Relation,* fol. 174 v.
5. Ibid., fols. 174 v.–176 r.
6. Angel María Garibay K., *Poesía náhuatl,* (Mexico: Universidad Nacional Autónoma de México, 1968), vol. 3, pp. 52–53 and 55–63.

BIBLIOGRAPHY

SOURCES

Alva Ixtlilxochitl, Fernando de. *Obras históricas*, 2 vols. Mexico, 1891–1892. *Anales de Cuauhtitlan.* Manuscript in the Nahuatl language from Central Mexico. A copy of the sixteenth-century original is in the Archive of the National Museum of Anthropology, Mexico City. Editions and translations: *Códice Chimalpopoca.* Study and translation into Spanish by Primo F. Velazquez, 2d ed. Mexico: National University of Mexico Press, 1975. *Die Geschichte der Königreiche von Culhuacan und Mexico.* Introduction and translation into German by Walter Lehmann, 2d ed. Stuttgart, 1976.

Anales de Tlatelolco (Anales de la Nación Mexicana). Mexican manuscript number 22, National Library, Paris. Facsimile reproduction in *Corpus Codicum Americanorum Medii Aevi,* vol. 2, edited by Ernst Mengin, Copenhagen, 1945. *Anales de Tlatelolco,* edited and translated into German by Ernst Mengin, *Baessler Archiv,* vols. 1–2, Berlin, 1939–1940. *Anales de Tlatelolco y Códice de Tlatelolco,* translated into Spanish by H. Berlin. Mexico, Editorial Robredo, 1948 and 1980.

Cantares mexicanos (Collection of Mexican Songs). A sixteenth-century manuscript in Nahuatl, preserved in the National Library, Mexico. *Colección de cantares mexicanos.* A facsimile reproduction. Edited by Antonio Peñafiel. Mexico, 1904. *Alt-aztekische Gesänge nach einer in der Biblioteca Nacional von Mexico aufbewahrten Handschrift,* Edited by Leonhard Schultz Jena. Stuttgart, 1957. *Poesía nahuatl,* vols. 2 and 3. With an introduction, paleography, and translation into Spanish by Angel María Garibay K. Mexico: Universidad Nacional, 1965–1967. Numerous compositions taken from this manuscript, translated into English, are included in Miguel León-Portilla. *Pre-Columbian Literatures of Mexico*. Norman: University of Oklahoma Press, 1968, and several reprints.

Chimalpahin Cuauhtlehuanitzin, Domingo. *Eight Relations*. Facsimile reproduction by Ernst Mengin, 3 vols. *Corpus Codicum Americanorum Medii Aevi*. Copenhagen, 1949–1952.

Codex Borbonicus. A sixteenth-century Aztec book of calendrical and religious content preserved at the Library of the French Chamber of Deputies (Palais Bourbon). Codex Borbonicus. Commentary by Karl Anton Nowotny. Graz: Akademische Druck-und Verlaganstalt, 1974.

Codex Borgia. A pre-Columbian Nahuatl book of calendrical and religious content, preserved at the Vatican Library. Códice Borgia, facsimile edition and commentaries by Eduard Seler, 3 vols. Mexico: Fondo de Cultura, Económica, 1963. *Codex Borgia*, commentary by Karl Anton Nowotny. Graz: Akademische Druck-und Verlaganstalt, 1976.

Códice en cruz. Facsimile reproduction and commentary by Charles E. Dibble, 2 vols. Salt Lake City: University of Utah Press, 1981.

Códice florentino [*Florentine Codex*]. A sixteenth-century manuscript in 3 vols., containing the Nahuatl text of the native informants of Friar Bernardino de Sahagún, in twelve books. It includes a Spanish free translation of the Nahuatl testimonies and numerous drawings in which European influence is evident. The original manuscript is preserved at the Laurentian Library, Florence, Italy. Francisco del Paso y Troncoso, *Códice florentino* (illustrations only). Madrid, 1905. *Florentine Codex*. Edited and translated into English by Arthur J. O. Anderson and Charles E. Dibble, 12 vols., Santa Fe, N.M.: School of American Research and the University of Utah, 1950–1982. Facsimile reproduction in 3 vols., published by the Archivo General. Mexico, 1979.

Codex mexicanus. Edited by Ernst Mengin. Paris: Societé des Americanistes, 1952.

Códice Aubin (or of 1576), *Historia de la nación mexicana*. Facsimile reproduction with a translation into Spanish by Charles E. Dibble. Madrid, 1963.

Códice Azcatitlan. With a commentary by R. H. Barlow. Paris, 1945.

Códice Ramirez. Mexico: Editorial Leyenda, 1944.

Códice Xolotl. Facsimile reproduction, 2d ed. Commentary by Charles E. Dibble, 2 vols. Mexico: National University, 1980.

Códices matritenses, Sixteenth-century transcriptions of texts in Nahuatl of sages and elders, native informants of Friar Bernardino de Sahagún. The first part (*Memorials*) preserved at the Library of the Royal Palace, Madrid; the second part at the Library of the Spanish Royal Academy of History. Francisco del Paso y Troncoso, editor, *Codices matritenses. Historia general de las cosas de Nueva España*.

Edited by Francisco del Paso y Troncoso. Facsimile reproduction, 3 vols. Madrid, 1906–1907. *Einige Kapitel aus dem Geschichtwerk des P. Sahagún, aus dem Aztekischen überstz von* . . . . Edited by Eduard Seler. Stuttgart, 1927. *Ritos, Sacerdotes y Atavíos de los dioses*, Texts of the informants of Sahagún 1 (*Códices matritenses*). Edited by Miguel León-Portilla. Mexico: Universidad Nacional, 1958 and 1969. *Veinte himnos sacros de los Nahuas, textos de los informantes de Sahagún* 2 (*Códices matritenses*), edited by Angel María Garibay K. Mexico: Universidad Nacional, 1958.

Durán, Diego. *Historia de las Indias de Nueva España y Islas de Tierra Firme*. 2 vols. Edited by José Fernando Ramírez. Mexico, 1867–1880.

Florentine Codex. See *Códice florentino*.

Historia Tolteca-Chichimeca. A manuscript in Nahuatl preserved at the National Library in Paris. (Mexican manuscript number 46–58.) Facsimile in *Corpus Codicum Americanorum Medii Aevi*, vol. 1. Edited by Ernst Mengin. Copenhagen, 1942. The paleography and a German translation in *Die mexicanische Bilderhandschrift Historia Tolteca-Chichimeca*. Baessler Archiv, vols. 1–2. Berlin, 1937–1938. A new facsimile reproduction, paleography, and Spanish translation is by Luis Reyes García and Lina Odena Güemes. Mexico: Instituto Nacional de Antropología e Historia, 1976.

Huehuetlatolli [The Ancient Word]. There are several collections of the *Huehuetlatolli*, preserved in the National Library of Mexico; The Bancroft Library, Paris; the National Library, Madrid, to which the texts that form Book 6 of the *Florentine Codex* have to be added. Friar Juan Bautista. *Huehuetlatolli, Pláticas de los viejos*. Mexico, 1600. Angel María Garibay K. "*Huehuetlatolli*, Documento A." *Tlalocan* (a magazine on the native cultures and languages of Mexico), vol. 1, number 1 (1943–1944), pp. 31–33 and 81–107. The paleography and translation into Spanish of other *Huehuetlatolli* have been included in vols. 10–13 of *Estudios de cultura nahuatl*. Mexico: National University, 1972–1978.

Leyenda de los soles. Edited by Francisco del Paso y Troncoso. Florence, 1903. In *Códice Chimalpopoca*, trans. P. F. Velázquez, Mexico, National University, 1975.

Mapa Quinatzin. Facsimile with a commentary by J. M. A. Aubin. *Anales del Museo Nacional de Arqueología, Historia y Etnología*, 1st epoch, vol. 2. Mexico, 1885.

Mapa Tlotzin. Facsimile with a commentary by J. M. A. Aubin. *Anales del Museo Nacional de Arqueología, Historia y Etnología*, 1st époch, vol. 2. Mexico, 1885.

Motolinía, Friar Toribio de Benavente. *Memoriales*. Paris, 1903.

Motolinía, Friar Toribio de Benavente. *Historia de los indios de la Nueva España*. Edited by Chávez Hayhoe. Mexico, 1941.

Muñoz Camargo, Diego. *Historia de Tlaxcala*. Edited by Alfredo Chavero. Mexico, 1892.

Pomar, Juan Bautista. *Relación de Texcoco*. Nueva Colección de Documentos para la Historia de Mexico. Mexico: J. García Icazbalceta, 1891.

Romances de los señores de Nueva España. A manuscript in Nahuatl preserved in The Nettie Lee Benson Latin American Collection, Library of the University of Texas, Austin. *Poesia nahuatl* 1, introduction, paleography, and translation into Spanish by Angel María Garibay K. Mexico: National University, 1963. Several compositions from this manuscript have been translated into English in Miguel León-Portilla. *Pre-Columbian Literatures of Mexico.* Norman: University of Oklahoma Press, 1968, and several reprints.

Sahagún, Friar Bernardino de. *Historia general de las cosas de Nueva España.* Edited by A. M. Garibay, 4 vols. Mexico: Editorial Porrúa, 1956.

―――. *Psalmodia christiana y sermonarios de los santos en lengua mexicana.* Mexico: Casa de Pedro Ocharte, 1583.

Tezozomoc, Fernando Alvarado. *Crónica mexicana.* Edited by José María Vigil. Mexico: Editorial Leyenda, 1944.

―――. *Crónica mexicayotl.* Paleography and Spanish translation by Adrián León. Mexico: Imprenta Universitaria, 1975.

Tira de Tepechpan (Colonial codex). Edited by Xavier Noguez. 2 vols. Mexico: Enciclopedia del Estado de Mexico, 1978.

Torquemada, Friar Juan de. *Los 21 libros rituales y monarquía indiana.* 7 vols. New edition prepared by Miguel León-Portilla. Mexico: Universidad Nacional de Mexico, 1975–1983.

Zurita, Alonso de. *Breve y sumaria relación de los señores de la Nueva España.* Nueva Colección de Documentos para la Historia de Mexico, edited by J. García Icazbalceta. Mexico, 1891. Reprint. Mexico: National University, 1972.

STUDIES RELATED TO THE POETS AND THEIR COMPOSITIONS

Brinton, Daniel G. *Ancient Nahuatl Poetry.* Philadelphia, 1887.

Brinton, Daniel G. *Rig Veda Americanus.* Philadelphia, 1890.

Campos, Rubén M. *La producción literaria de los aztecas.* Mexico, 1936.

Cline, Howard F., ed. "Guide to Ethnohistorical Sources," *Handbook of Middle American Indians,* vols. 12–14. Austin: University of Texas Press, 1972–1974.

Edmonson, Munro S., ed. *Sixteenth Century Mexico: The Work of Sahagún.* School of American Research. Albuquerque: University of New Mexico Press, 1974.

Eschmann, Anncharlott. *Das Religiose Geschichtsbild der Azteken.* Edited by Gerdt Kutscher in collaboration with Jürgen Golte, Anneliese Mönnich, and Heins-Jürgen Pinnow. Berlin: Iberoamericanisches Institut, 1976.

Garibay K., Angel María. *Historia de la literatura nahuatl.* Mexico City: Editorial Porrúa, Mexico, 1953–1954.

León-Portilla, Miguel. *Aztec Thought and Culture: A Study of the Ancient Nahuatl Mind.* Norman: University of Oklahoma Press, 1963, and several reprints.

———. *The Broken Spears: Aztec Account of the Conquest of Mexico.* Boston: Beacon Press, 1966.

———. *Pre-Columbian Literatures of Mexico.* Norman: University of Oklahoma Press, 1968, and several reprints.

Seler, Eduard. *Gesammelte Abhandlungen zur Amerikanischen Sprachund Altertumskunde.* 5 vols. Berlin: Ascher und Co. (and) Behrend und Co., 1902–1923.

———. Einige Kapitel aus dem Geschichteswerk des P. Sahagún. Aus dem Aztekischen übersetzt von Eduard Seler (Herausgebeben von C. Seler-Sachs in Gemenschaft mit Prof. Dr. Walter Lehmann). Stuttgart, 1927.

Van Zantwijk, Rudolf, A. M. "Aztec Hymns as the Expressions of the Mexican philosophy of Life." In *Internationales Archiv für Etnographie,* vol. 48, number 1 (Leiden, 1957): 67–118.

Vigil, José María. *Nezahualcóyotl, el rey poeta.* Mexico: Ediciones de Andrea, 1957.

INDEX